THE SINO-SOVIET
TERRITORIAL DISPUTE

The Sino-Soviet Territorial Dispute

by

TAI SUNG AN

THE WESTMINSTER PRESS

Philadelphia

BOOK DESIGN BY
DOROTHY ALDEN SMITH

Published by The Westminster Press®
Philadelphia, Pennsylvania

PRINTED IN THE UNITED STATES OF AMERICA

Library of Congress Cataloging in Publication Data

An, Tai-sung, 1931–
    The Sino-Soviet territorial dispute.

    Includes bibliographical references.
    1. China—Boundaries—Russia. 2. Russia—Boundaries—China.
I. Title.
DS740.5.R8A65   327.47′051   72–10380
ISBN 0–664–20955–6

To the late Yoon Jung An

Contents

Acknowledgments

First of all, a debt of special thanks is due to my wife, Sihn-ja, for her devoted understanding and constant encouragement given to me while I was preparing for this book. I am also indebted to Professor Glen G. Alexandrin, of Villanova University, and William C. Stallings, Jr., of the University of Pennsylvania, for translation into English of the Russian and the French texts of old international treaties for the document section of the book. Thanks is also due to the Office of the Geographer of the United States Department of State for permission to reprint materials from a State Department publication entitled International Boundary Study No. 64, *China-USSR Boundary*.

Full responsibility for any possible errors of fact or interpretation rests, needless to say, with the author alone.

TAI SUNG AN

Chestertown, Maryland

Introduction

The Sino-Soviet boundary falls into two major sections—the Central (i.e., western) Asian and the Far Eastern (Manchurian-Siberian). Between the sectors lies the Mongolian People's Republic, or Outer Mongolia, a nominally independent country once under Chinese tutelage but at present strongly pro-Soviet. Outer Mongolia shares a 2,500-mile frontier with Communist China and a 1,800-mile frontier with the Soviet Union. The Central Asian sector of the boundary extends from the Altai Mountains in the north westward 1,850 miles to the rugged Pamir Mountains in the south, and the Far Eastern sector extends eastward from the uplands of Transbaikalia 2,300 miles to the icy Sea of Japan southwest of Vladivostok. For a detailed geographical-physical study of the Sino-Soviet boundary, see *Document 1* at the back of this book.[1]

The 4,150-mile Sino-Soviet boundary, which has been the scene of chronic friction since the seventeenth century, is today the longest two-nation border and one of the most explosive international boundaries in the world.

The Sino-Soviet conflict, which began as an ideological dispute in 1960, has degenerated into a nationalistic clash based on territorial issues. The still-current Sino-Soviet territorial dispute came into the open on March 8, 1963, when the Chinese Communists publicly raised the issue of their historical claims to Soviet territory.[2] Their territorial claims against the Soviet Union were based on the premise that Imperial Russia "grabbed" about 600,000 square miles of the land in Siberia and Central Asia from a weak Manchu China by "unbridled aggression" in the nineteenth century under "unequal" treaties.[3] They asserted that border questions with the Soviet Union were "outstanding issues" which, when conditions were ripe, should be settled peacefully through negotiations. Pending a settlement, they were prepared to maintain the *status quo*.[4]

Communist China subsequently demanded of Moscow a public admission that the treaties under which Czarist Russia appropriated large areas of China were "unequal" and unfair.[5] While doing this, Peking called for both review and rectification of the entire length of the Sino-Soviet boundary line. Although it was prepared to take the old "unequal" treaties as a basis for negotiations, Peking insisted that a new, "equal" treaty be concluded to replace the old, "unequal" ones.[6]

The Soviet Union has usually responded to Communist China's territorial demand with hawkish outrage and denounced it as "merely the Hitler-type raving of the Mao clique" in Peking.[7] At the same time, Moscow warned Peking that "very dangerous consequences could arise from any attempt to recarve the map of the world." [8]

For the past ten years the Kremlin leaders have consistently denied that the old boundary treaties between Manchu China and Czarist Russia were "unequal." They have refused to recognize that a dispute exists along the entire Sino-Soviet frontier, asserting that it has been legally and historically fixed. But they have said that they are ready to settle minor "disputable" border issues by negotiation.[9]

Because of their fundamentally irreconcilable positions on the territorial issue, Moscow and Peking signaled a rupture in their 1964 boundary discussions only a month after the negotiations began.

Thousands of border incidents have taken place since 1963 as relations between the Chinese and the Soviets have been marked by a rapid upward spiral of bitterness and hostility. In September 1963, for example, Peking publicly accused Moscow of "large-scale [anti-Chinese] subversive activities" in Sinkiang.[10] The Soviets, in turn, charged the Chinese Communists with having "systematically" violated the Soviet border in Central Asia about 5,000 times in 1962 alone.[11]

The intensification of the territorial dispute between the two Communist giants after 1963 was accompanied by reports of reinforcement of Soviet and Chinese armed forces along the Sino-Soviet frontier: the Soviets had 400,000 troops, and the Chinese, 550,000, at the time of the bloody armed skirmishes on a disputed island in the Ussuri River in March 1969.[12] About 40 percent of the troops on each side of the frontier were reportedly concentrated along its most easterly—and most heavily settled—stretch.[13] In 1968, Soviet medium-range surface-to-surface missiles were believed to have been deployed in the eastern part of Outer Mongolia (at Choibalsan) and near the Mongolian-Chinese border (at Bor Nor), thus threatening all of Manchuria, northern and central China, and the Chinese nuclear center in Sinkiang (at Lop Nor).[14]

In 1969, three years after the advent of Mao Tse-tung's radical Cultural Revolution, the duration and the intensity of Sino-Soviet border clashes rose sharply. Long-simmering Sino-Soviet enmity exploded on March 2, 1969, in a brief but bloody battle over a disputed, obscure island in the icebound Ussuri River, called Damansky by the Russians and Chenpao ("Treasure") by the Chinese. Each side claims the island for its own. Situated in the Ussuri River, which forms the boundary between Manchuria and the Soviet Maritime Province, the island is no more than desolate frozen marsh in winter. But as a symbol of the antagonism between Moscow and Peking, it took on added importance when the savage border clash in the Ussuri River pushed the prospect of major war between the two neighboring powers into the realm of possibility.

There was no way to ascertain which side started the March 2, 1969, armed incident, since each maintained that the other was responsible.[15] The rival versions varied sharply, and the truth may bear little resemblance to either version. Both Moscow and Peking agreed, however, that for several hours the violence along the Ussuri was as close to war as the two Communist giants had come in the long succession of border incidents and shoot-outs since their ideological split in 1960. At least the equivalent of a battalion of troops was engaged on each side, and armor, artillery, mortars, and heavy machine guns were employed before the battle was over. Each side claimed that it had beaten off the attacker. The Soviets claimed that thirty-one of their border guards were killed and fourteen wounded. Communist China did not release casualty figures, reporting simply that it had lost "many."

Immediately, the Soviet Union and Communist China exchanged sharp protest notes.[16] In the weeks following, a wave of anti-Soviet demonstrations swept over China. These in turn set off counterdemonstrations in Moscow.

Just as the demonstrations began to subside, the Chinese and the Soviets clashed again on March 14 and 15, 1969, in the same area. This time the fighting lasted about twelve hours. A number of troops were killed on each side.

Sino-Soviet border clashes continued to take place thereafter. During the summer of 1969 a series of new armed clashes, some of them comparable to those of March on the Ussuri River frontier, broke out on the Ussuri and Amur rivers,[17] and on the Sinkiang border. As expected, each side charged the other with intrusions, provocations, and attacks.[18]

The border skirmishes of March 1969 were, in point of fact, the most violent and bloody in a series of incidents dating back to 1963. But more significant was the sharp reaction displayed by Moscow and Peking to them. Earlier border skirmishes had been played down by both sides. The intriguing question was why both sides gave these particular border incidents the special treatment of harsh official protests, thereby triggering a much more violent propaganda duel.

The Soviet Union and Communist China had been quick to turn the March 1969 border clashes to propaganda purposes. While Peking's vicious anti-Soviet slander had precedents, the violence of Moscow's anti-Chinese posture exceeded anything seen during the last decade.

The main theme in Communist China's anti-Soviet propaganda following the March 1969 border skirmishes was, and still is, that the Kremlin leaders, whom the Chinese Communists contemptuously call the "Soviet revisionist renegade clique" and "social imperialists," [19] are direct successors to the Romanov czars ("the new czars"), who repeatedly nibbled at China's "sacred soil." [20] The Maoist press blamed the Russians for having colonized Outer Mongolia, which Mao had claimed was "Chinese soil," [21] and for "vainly" striving to grab other Chinese territory that the czars had not occupied. It also added that the Soviet invasion of Czechoslovakia in 1968 and its efforts to establish a "sphere of influence" in Eastern Europe were "an attempt to set up a colonial empire of the czarist type" spanning Europe, Asia, Africa, and Latin America.

The Soviet press, reaching for new expletives to describe Mao Tse-tung, declared that the aging supreme leader had stained himself with human blood. The invective, which ran alongside ringing praise for Russian soldiers involved in the March 1969 armed clashes, also portrayed Mao as a killer and obliquely compared him with Hitler. On March 23, 1969, the Soviet army newspaper *Krasnaya Zvezda* ("Red Star"), in obvious reference to Peking's claims to Soviet-held territory in the Far East, said:

Once upon a time a certain Adolf Hitler marked Moscow and the Urals also as his own territory on his map. He marked them—and rotted away—and the earth is glad of this.[22]

It also said that Mao was "simply a traitor to the sacred cause of Communism. The reddest of the red is not red at all but painted with human blood." [23]

Furthermore, the Soviet Union opened a classic atrocity

campaign, complete with grisly photographs and charges that the Chinese border guards were raised to a high pitch of bloodthirstiness by large doses of vodka before trapping Soviet soldiers in an ambush.[24] The Soviet press described in unusually full detail that some of the Soviet soldiers died atrociously—gunned down point-blank or bayoneted while lying wounded. On March 19, 1969, Soviet poet Yevgeny Yevtushenko identified today's China with the Mongol hordes that overran Russia almost a millennium ago.[25]

In the spring and summer of 1969, in short, the Kremlin leaders and the Soviet press were bombarding their citizens with horror propaganda of the goriest sort, fully comparable to Soviet anti-Nazi propaganda at the height of the Second World War. Moscow was apparently attempting to create a sense of another "Yellow Peril" in the minds of the Soviet people.

Along with this mutual exercise in propaganda overkill, there was also an escalation in the threats and counterthreats that Moscow and Peking hurled at each other. In a Chinese-language broadcast beamed over Moscow's "Radio Peace and Progress" in March 1969, for example, the Soviets unabashedly rattled their nuclear saber. The broadcast said:

> The world knows that the main weapons of the Soviet army are its rockets. Their destructive range is virtually unlimited. They are capable of carrying nuclear warheads many times more powerful than all the explosives ever used in past wars put together. They can hit their targets with pinpoint accuracy. . . . What can Mao summon to counter the reply of the Soviet armed forces to a military adventure against the Soviet Union? Does he have rockets capable of carrying nuclear warheads? As we know, the Chinese armed forces have no such weapons.[26]

In the summer of 1969 tensions rose to the point where the Soviet Union hinted that it might even launch a preemptive nuclear strike against Communist China's nuclear installations in Sinkiang unless Peking agreed to negotiations aimed at settling the border dispute peacefully.[27]

Apparently undaunted by these Soviet attempts at nuclear blackmail, Mao himself reportedly convened an emergency meeting in Peking in March 1969, and, according to one account, he bluntly informed his subordinates: "If the Russians dare use nuclear missiles, we will do the same." [28] In August 1969, Peking said that the Soviet Union had publicly "raved wildly about launching an unexpected surprise attack just as Hitler boasted of blitzkrieg in his day. . . . If the Soviet revisionist renegade clique is bent on following the old road of aggression taken by Hitler and the Japanese Fascists, then like them it will come to a despicable end." [29]

Since March 1969, China and the Soviet Union have substantially increased their military strength—armored formations, rocket troops, missiles, nuclear weapons, and air power —along their border as well as along the 2,500-mile frontier between China and Outer Mongolia, whose border the Soviets pledged to protect. The best current estimate is that China and the Soviet Union have a combined total of about two million troops deployed.[30] Chinese and Soviet border troops are now undoubtedly on combat alert. At the same time, each side has insisted that the other is preparing a "war of aggression" or nuclear blackmail.[31]

The Soviets have emplaced nuclear-armed missiles along their Siberian frontier, inside Outer Mongolia, and presumably adjacent to China's Sinkiang Province. The Soviet military forces are apparently well deployed for either a swift blow against Communist China or defense and quick reaction to attack rather than for the defensive operations of a lengthy land war. For this purpose, the Soviet army in 1969 systematically started to defoliate the vegetation along some five hundred miles of the Ussuri River frontier in an effort to provide itself with an open field of fire.[32]

Chinese military deployments farther back from the frontiers do not indicate preparations for a quick strike against the Soviet Union, but, on the contrary, conform to the pattern of the classic Maoist strategy of a protracted war in which the enemy position is weakened by time and space. Advocates of a Maoist "people's war" envisage the feasibility of a protracted, "broken-back" war, in which the invading enemy forces would not be met head on but would be sucked in, enveloped, and smashed by mobile military contingents and the entire population, which would be armed under the concept "everyone a soldier." [33] It must be noted, however, that Communist China is now also actively developing its own nuclear defense against possible Soviet attack.

In 1969, internal propaganda on both sides increasingly assumed a preparation-for-action stage. In other words, the two Communist powers made efforts to condition their people to the possibility of a major military confrontation with their former ally.

For the first time in the spring of 1969, the Soviet military deployments along the Sino-Soviet frontier were discussed publicly in terms of possible confrontation with Communist China. In August 1969, *Pravda* followed up with an even more grave and blunt warning that war with Peking was a real possibility and that, if it ever came, it would inevitably be nuclear.[34] Moscow has been intensifying civil defense training in schools and factories near the borders, against the possibility of mass incursions by the Chinese,[35] and, in addition, tightening control over its border zones. In the Soviet Central Asian republics and the Far East there were public appeals for vigilance and patriotic pledges by military forces to defend the frontiers.

Massive preparations in Communist China for the possibility of war with the Soviet Union have apparently gained momentum since March 1969.[36] Increased army and militia training, stockpiling of strategic metals, storing of food, transfer of factories from vulnerable urban areas,[37] evacuation of population (especially children) to the countryside, construction of air-raid shelters and tunnels,[38] psychological conditioning about the invincibility of Mao's "people's war" strategy—these and other measures have been taken. Communist China's fiery rhetoric, moreover, has been even more frenzied than its action; the Chinese people are constantly being warned to prepare for "a big war or a small war, a conventional war or a nuclear war, a war at an early date or at any other time." To be sure, the prepare-against-war campaign also serves Mao's domestic interest: to restore order and unity behind his leadership in the wake of the disruptive Cultural Revolution.

A hint of the seriousness of Chinese Communist apprehensions about the possibility of war with the Soviet Union is given by recent well-informed reports of both the Indian Foreign Ministry and the French Air Force magazine, *Forces Aériennes Françaises,* that the Chinese Communist leaders are now moving their nuclear installations in Sinkiang to a "safe place" in northern Tibet, leaving behind some false installations to fool Soviet and American spy satellites.[39]

For much of 1969, the threat of a major conflict hovered over the 4,150-mile border between Moscow and Peking. But a temporary thaw in Sino-Soviet relations developed in the wake of the surprise meeting of Soviet Premier Aleksei Kosygin and Chinese Premier Chou En-lai at the Peking airport on September 11, 1969, that eventually led to the start of high-level border talks between the two countries on October 20, 1969. There have since been no fresh border incidents. Neither have the sinister words "preemptive nuclear strike" been heard from Moscow. But each side has kept up the steady exchange of hostile polemical blasts against the other.

The current Sino-Soviet border negotiations, which have been held intermittently since October 1969, appear to have been deadlocked.[40] The continuing viciousness of the invective flying between Moscow and Peking suggests that the current border talks are once again on the verge of collapse, as happened in 1964, or that both sides have apparently abandoned all hope of resolving their differences at the boundary discussions in Peking. If a negotiated settlement on the territorial dispute is ruled out, what will come next in Sino-Soviet relations?

The inevitable result must be that conditions along the Sino-Soviet boundary will continue to be tense and explosive, with the possibility that new shooting incidents may recur with all the dangers of possible escalation—even up to the nuclear level—which that would imply. Today the Sino-Soviet conflict has deepened to the point that the two Communist giants are opposed in practically every sphere of party and government affairs.

In this vein, the following important questions are raised. What is the historical basis for the Sino-Soviet territorial dispute? How and why did the border dispute come into the open in March 1963? How have the two countries reacted to their border conflict in the past ten years? Were the bloody armed clashes in March 1969 simply a series of accidental incidents, such as two border patrols happening upon each other in an icy no-man's-land? Or were these clashes carefully and deliberately provoked by both sides for domestic and external purposes? What factors were responsible for inducing the Soviet Union and Communist China to reopen their border talks in October 1969? What are the issues at stake in their current boundary negotiations? Why have the two countries failed to make any progress in their current border discussions? Is there a genuine danger that the Sino-Soviet territorial dispute might escalate into full-scale hostilities in the wake of the long-deadlocked border talks in Peking? To put it another way, is war between Moscow and Peking inevitable? If war breaks out between China and the Soviet Union, what will be its course and its consequences? If such a war is not inevitable, what will be the likely development of the Sino-Soviet boundary conflict in the foreseeable future? Are the current Chinese Communist gestures toward improved diplomatic relations with the United States, exemplified by President Nixon's recent trip to Communist China, related partly to Peking's attempts to reduce the military threat posed by the Soviet Union along their common boundary?

The following chapters will attempt to answer all the questions raised above by examining in closer detail, and in historical depth, the Sino-Soviet territorial dispute. The main objective of this book is to put the territorial issue into proper perspective.

CHAPTER 1

The Historical Background of the Sino-Soviet Territorial Dispute

In the past three hundred years emperors, czars, dynasties, political leaders, and ideologies have come and gone, but the dispute between the Chinese and the Russians over their common boundary continues. The Chinese-Russian border troubles date back to the seventeenth century when Czarist Russia began to expand across Siberia to the Pacific and southward into Central Asia at the expense of China's weak Manchu Dynasty. At least a portion of the territory acquired by Czarist Russia during the period of its imperialistic expansion (the seventeenth, eighteenth, and nineteenth centuries) belonged—for longer or shorter periods—to the Chinese Empire. "From a historical point of view," as C. P. Fitzgerald correctly points out, "the Chinese have several just grievances, at least in terms of prior claims and occupation." [1]

Communist China's present grievance is that during the eighteenth and nineteenth centuries, the Russians took every advantage of the weakness of the Manchu Dynasty to force the Middle Kingdom to sign a series of "unequal" treaties. These treaties recognized what Communist China calls Czarist Russia's "illegal" or "imperialistic" seizure of a large chunk of Chinese territory in Siberia and Central Asia. The Chinese Communists assert that if the Soviet Union were a genuine

Communist state dedicated and faithful to Marxism-Leninism, it would now wish to make amends for the past "criminal policy" of the czarist regime in China by restoring to a brother Communist state what had been taken away from it in the shameful days of imperialistic expansionism. When the current Sino-Soviet territorial dispute was aired publicly on March 8, 1963, Communist China attacked the continuing validity of three so-called "unequal" treaties, i.e., the treaties of Aigun (1858), Peking (1860), and St. Petersburg (1881), which have defined the most important sections of the present Sino-Soviet boundary in the Asian heartland for almost a century.[2] How did what the Chinese call "imperialistic land-grabbing" by Czarist Russia begin and develop in the distant past?

By 1411 the Chinese Empire under the Ming Dynasty (1368–1644) had extended itself from Heilungkiang to the mouth of the Amur River. The area the empire controlled in the northeast extended as far as the coast north of the Tumen River and the Kurile Islands. In the north, a considerable portion of Siberia above the Amur lay within the frontier of China, and on the west the Great Khingan Range served as a boundary. Of course, there was at that time no well-defined formal frontier or border agreement.

With an agricultural economy based upon irrigated rice culture, the early Chinese Empire found that the steppes and deserts of Inner (Central) Asia, the grasslands of Inner Mongolia, the desert waste of Outer Mongolia, and the Manchurian forest lands were ill-suited to Chinese settlement. These outlying areas of the old Middle Kingdom were inhabited by numerous and fragmented non-Han tribes or ethnic groups. The old Chinese Empire faced periodic threats from these non-Han tribes along the settled frontier. To maintain order and peace, it often became necessary for the Chinese kingdom to launch a military expedition into its outlying territories. For example, as many as 95,000 soldiers were maintained in the northeast during the early part of the Ming Dynasty.[3] Furthermore, political and military control of these outlying areas was essential to protect and preserve key centers of Chinese power located in the fertile Hwang and Yangtze basins of northern China—the cradle of Chinese civilization.

The Ming Dynasty had overextended itself, and in later years it began to be plagued by serious internal unrest and attacks by outsiders. By the latter part of the sixteenth century it lost much of its hold on Manchuria and was compelled to retreat to within the Great Wall. In 1644, the Manchus overthrew the Ming Dynasty and established the new Ch'ing (or Manchu) Dynasty, a dynasty that was to last until the beginning of the twentieth century.

After conquering China, the Manchus restored the old large colonial empire and carried its suzerainty far beyond its previous extent. During the early years of the Manchu Dynasty, Tibet, Sinkiang (Turkestan), Mongolia (both Inner and Outer), and Manchuria were added to the Chinese Empire and owed allegiance to the Manchu emperors as suzerains. In the early eighteenth century, the western frontier of Manchu China extended to Lake Balkhash and northward to the west of Lake Zaisan to include Tannu Tuva, and the northwestern frontier extended to the Stanovoy and Yablonovoy mountains north of the Amur River.

The ascendancy of the Manchus to power in China coincided with Czarist Russia's three-hundred-year *Drang nach Osten*—southeastward expansion into Siberia and Central Asia. Beginning in the 1640's, Czarist Russia was attracted by the wealth that the natural environment of Siberia offered in the form of furs, minerals, timber, and the like. Moreover, Siberia and Central Asia offered an appealing outlet for the czarist ambition to build empires, which was frustrated and blocked in Europe by the major powers. Recurring frictions and conflicts were soon to develop between the two empires in the borderlands, which were sparsely populated by minority nationalities neither ethnically Slavic nor Han Chinese. The Russian push was relentless, and the Russians moved with troops and traders, but with few real settlers.

On July 15, 1643, one year before the Manchus entered Peking, a Russian expedition led by Vasilei Poyarkov left Yakutsk[4] in northern Siberia in search of a fertile valley rumored to be somewhere to the south. After traveling down the Aldan River, Poyarkov crossed the Stanovoy Mountains to the sources of the Zeya River. This river led him to the Amur River. He and his men, after numerous bloody encounters with the native tribes of this territory under the suzerainty of the Manchus, reached the mouth of the Amur River in 1645; and in June of the following year they returned to Yakutsk.[5]

Poyarkov was the first Russian to explore the Amur. Many of the tribes that he had encountered, including the Tungus and Daurien tribes, were already paying tribute to the Manchus. Only toward the mouth of the river did he find tribes that had not yet come under their influence.[6] It was not until 1652, however, that the Manchus met the Russians in an attempt to put a stop to their forays into the Amur region.

In 1649, another expedition, under Erofei Khabarov, had left Yakutsk and traveled, this time to the southwest, down to the Olekma River to a point not far from one of the headwaters of a tributary of the Amur River. Khabarov descended the Amur; and in the autumn of 1650, he met and defeated a force of Daurien natives at the village of Albasin. After building a small fort there, he continued downstream to the mouth of the Ussuri River. At this location (the present-day city of Khabarovsk), early in 1652, the Russians were attacked by some 2,000 Manchus—the first major battle between Russian and Chinese forces in Siberia. Khabarov lost only 10 men in this engagement, while 676 Manchus were slain. Recognizing that he would soon be facing much larger forces, he retraced his steps up the river.[7]

In 1654, Onuphrius Stepanov, advancing down the Amur and taking possession of settlements that had first been founded by Khabarov, met and defeated a large army of Manchus and Daurien natives at the mouth of the Sungari River. Stepanov remained in control of much of the Amur valley for the next four years. Part of this success was due to the fact that the Chinese were deeply engrossed in internal problems at home.

Finally, the native tribes, having given up hope of receiving further Manchu aid, gathered a force of some 10,000 men and attacked the Russians. Stepanov and all his 500 men, except those who deserted him, were slain. This was 1658; there was no further Russian movement into the Amur region for another ten years.[8]

In 1669, a Polish criminal, Nikophor Romanov Tchernigofskii, with a group of sixty-nine men, returned to the Amur valley and reestablished the fort of Albasin. Shortly afterward he was reinforced by other men, and in 1671 a Russian administrator was sent from Nerchinsk[9] to take command. In 1672, Tchernigofskii was pardoned, and he and his men were rewarded for their efforts.[10] By 1681, Tchernigofskii and his expedition reached as far as the Ussuri River and part of the Sungari up to the mountains.[11]

By 1683 the rate of Russian expedition into the Amur basin progressed so fast that the Manchus were roused into action. Chinese troops were sent to Manchuria in large numbers and fortresses were built at Tsitsihar. By 1685 most of the Russian settlements in the lower Amur valley had been destroyed; in June of that year, 15,000 troops advanced on Albasin from Tsitsihar. The Russians, their Cossack troops numbering only 430 men, were easily defeated and the survivors who escaped fled to Nerchinsk.

Two hundred Cossacks returned to the ruins of Albasin in October 1685. They were attacked by the Manchus in July 1686, and fighting lasted until the Chinese were forced to retreat before the following winter set in. Early in the next year they attacked again. The Russians were so depleted in number that their resistance could not have lasted long. They were saved, however, when the governments of Russia and China agreed to negotiate a peace. In September 1688, the Chinese forces returned to Aigun and Mergen.[12]

The Manchu (under Prince Songgotu) and Russian (under Fyodor Golovin) delegations met at Nerchinsk in 1689. The Russians proposed that the border be established along the Amur River. The Chinese, on the other hand, wanted the boundary to be at Lake Baikal or even at the Lena River, to which they had laid claim since it had once been in the possession of Genghis Khan. The Chinese finally agreed, however, to make the border somewhere near Nerchinsk, but the Russians still found this unacceptable.

When the Russians pushed for more concessions, the Chinese, close to the height of their power, sent their 15,000 troops to surround the city. Faced with the possibility of a siege, the Russians could do little more than accept Chinese terms.[13]

On August 27, 1689, the Treaty of Nerchinsk between Czarist Russia and the Manchu Kingdom was signed (see *Document 2*). The treaty was significant in two respects: first, it was the first international agreement ever made by a Chinese emperor with a European power on the basis of formal sovereign equality,[14] and, secondly, a common frontier between China and Russia was formally established for the first time in Chinese history.[15]

Under the terms of the Treaty of Nerchinsk, it was agreed that the boundary between Czarist Russia and Manchu China would extend from the Argun River in the west, continuing along the Amur to the south of the Kerbechi (present-day Shilka), thence along the Kerbechi northward to the Stanovoy Mountains. The boundary then progressed eastward along the Stanovoy Mountains to the mouth of the Bay of Ud, on the Sea of Okhotsk. (See *Map.*) The entire Amur-Ussuri basin was to belong to Manchu China, while northeastern Siberia was ceded to Czarist Russia. The Russians were prevented from navigating the Amur River. In the most easterly part of Siberia (the Ud valley region), where the Stanovoy Mountains turn north near the Sea of Okhotsk, the boundary line was never precisely defined.[16] In all, approximately 93,000 square miles of territory was ceded to Czarist Russia by China.

For a century and a half after the Nerchinsk Treaty was signed, the Manchu Dynasty attained the height of its power. Yet its authorities paid little attention to the defense of the Amur frontier. The Russian push through Asia to the Pacific was diverted from its normal or logical course along the broad Amur-Ussuri basin far north to the Bering Strait (1648) across the Aleutians into Alaska (1741) and ultimately into California (ca. 1812).

The Chinese-Russian border along the Amur basin remained unchanged for close to 170 years until finally, in 1858, it was revised. The Argun River settlement, however, presently remains in effect.

In the first quarter of the eighteenth century, the Manchus were afraid that the Russians were conspiring with the Turguts and the Kalmuks in Mongolia to join forces against China. Actually, the Russians at this time were only interested in extending their commercial and economic interests in the Manchu domain. For different reasons, therefore, both China and Russia sought to come to an agreement concerning their common border, which extended across northern Mongolia as far as the Argun.[17]

Preliminary negotiations lasted for two years, from 1723 to 1725. In 1726 much of the frontier between the Sea of Okhotsk and the regions near Mongolia were mapped by a team of Russian surveyors under Peter Skobeltsyn. Although the maps they made had many errors and a large number of omissions, the Russians now had in their possession a generalized cartographic coverage of most of their northern frontier as well as part of Manchuria. This map gave them an advantage over the Chinese in establishing the border.

The Chinese and Russian empires signed the Bur Treaty on August 20, 1727,[18] and then exchanged two boundary protocols superseding it, one on October 12 at Abagatuy[19] and the other on October 27 on the Bur River.[20] (See *Documents 3* and *4*.) Also on October 27, 1727, Czarist Russia and Manchu China signed the Treaty of Kiakhta.[21] (See *Document 5*.) The two protocols and the Treaty of Kiakhta defined a large section of the border, most of which is now the boundary between the Soviet Union and Outer Mongolia (see *Map*). The boundary west of the Bay of Ud remained undefined as in the Treaty of Nerchinsk of 1689 and in the Russo-Chinese Agreement in Peking on April 1, 1727.[22] There still existed exceedingly little geographic knowledge of this area.

The two agreements of October 27, 1727, defined the new Chinese-Russian boundary west of the Argun, including the short portion of the Manchurian border just north of where lies the twentieth-century town of Manchouli,[23] and designated the Sayan Mountains, south and west, as the dividing boundary line between the two empires. Thus Northern, or Outer, Mongolia (including Tannu Tuva, or Uriankhai[24]—see *Map*), as well as the lands to the south, or Inner Mongolia, was clearly recognized as part of the Manchu domain.[25] China recognized Russian sovereignty over the southeastern region of Lake Baikal, in which the towns of Transbaikalai, Udinsk, Seleninsk, and Nerchinsk were located. The new boundary west of the Argun was finally established by the Treaty of Kiakhta. This boundary left the Argun in a general northwest direction, meeting the present-day boundary between Inner Mongolia and Outer Mongolia after approximately seventy miles.

Through the two agreements of 1727, in short, Manchu China lost to Czarist Russia nearly 40,000 square miles, between the Upper Irtysh and the Sayan Mountains, as well as south and southwest of Lake Baikal. The delimitation remained valid in the main for over a century and a quarter.[26]

Under the Manchu Dynasty, from the end of the eighteenth century on, the Chinese Empire began to decline sharply and perilously. Following the Opium War (1840–1842), which verified Manchu weakness and decay, China was troubled by internal disorders and foreign invasions. As the "scramble for China" opened in the mid-nineteenth century, Czarist Russia regained its appetite for territory in China's backyard and gradually repenetrated the Amur valley in violation of the Treaty of Nerchinsk of 1689.

In 1847, Czar Nicholas I decided to promote a policy that would stimulate the development of far-eastern Russia. In that same year he made Nikolai Muraveyev governor-general of Eastern Siberia. Muraveyev's conviction was that Russia's future lay in the East. He was asked by the Naval Ministry to investigate the possibilities of establishing an ice-free port on the Sea of Okhotsk. The following year he sent Captain Nevelskoi to explore the coast of Siberia as far south as the mouth of the Amur.[27] Muraveyev learned from Nevelskoi that Sakhalin was not a peninsula, as was previously thought, but an island. This meant that the Amur was accessible to seagoing vessels from the south as well as from the north.

Nevelskoi explored the mouth of the Amur. The reports so inspired Muraveyev that the governor-general pressed the Russian government for further authority to investigate the region and to station troops there. His request was granted, and in June 1850 Nevelskoi established a settlement on the coast slightly north of the river. Unfortunately, this site was found to be icebound, and it soon had to be abandoned. Nevelskoi, on his own initiative and without any instructions, took six men and sailed up the Amur for a short distance. Here he built a post to which he gave the name Nikolaevsk. It was a clear-cut violation of the Treaty of Nerchinsk of 1689.

Although there were many Russians who thought that this action would bring on hostilities with the Chinese, Czar Nicholas agreed that the post should be maintained. In the late spring of 1852, an expedition was sent up the Amur; and in the following years, much of Sakhalin and the Siberian coast opposite this island were explored.[28] By the end of 1853 Nevelskoi and his expedition occupied the most important harbors in the Gulf of Tartary and established posts in Sakhalin.

In the face of rapidly increasing Russian expansionism in the Amur frontier in the 1860's, the Manchu Dynasty reversed its traditional policy of forbidding Chinese settlement (colonization) in the outlying (i.e., beyond Mukden) territory of Manchuria and gave its official blessing to the Sinification of the sparsely populated border regions in Manchuria and the

Amur basin to counter Russian territorial encroachment.[29] To carry on a systematic program of Chinese colonization, the Manchu emperors sent military forces to these areas, gave the troops land to till, and made them into farmers. Unfortunately, the Manchu policy of fortifying northeastern Manchurian borderlands, as Peter S. H. Tang accurately states, "came almost half a century too late." [30]

In 1854 the Crimean War broke out. Muraveyev, afraid of an Anglo-French naval attack on the coast of eastern Siberia, convinced the czar of the necessity of accomplishing the Russian objective of acquiring the Amur-Ussuri territory with troops. On May 14 of the same year, he personally led his first expedition down the Amur. His expedition was composed of a steamer and seventy-five barges and rafts. Two weeks later he and his men passed the Chinese-fortified town of Aigun, but their advance was not challenged. On June 14 the Muraveyev expedition arrived in Mariinsk.[31]

In the latter part of August 1854, an Anglo-French fleet attacked the Russian base at Petropavlovsk on Kamchatka, but they were beaten off with the loss of some three hundred men. Realizing that in all likelihood they would be attacked again in the following year, Muraveyev ordered the remote base abandoned. English war vessels became extremely active in Siberian waters throughout the summer of 1855, but their lack of knowledge of the Siberian coastal region hindered them from coming in contact with the small Russian naval force. Only a few small skirmishes were actually fought.

In May 1855, Muraveyev's second expedition down the Amur started with 104 large boats. He took with him some 9,000 people (including women), 300 horses, 300 cattle, and a good supply of war goods. On the way down the river, they met four junks with Chinese officials who were on their way to the Gorbiza, a tributary of the Shilka, to delimit the frontier and erect boundary posts. Muraveyev wanted them to return to Aigun, but he let them pass in order to preserve harmonious Chinese-Russian relations. The settlers reached Mariinsk on

June 13, 1855; shortly afterward they founded five towns. Irkut-skoe, Borgorodskoe, Mikhailofskoe, and Novo Nikalofskoe were located on the right bank of the Amur, while Serghiefskoe was built on the left bank.[32]

When the Crimean War ended in 1856, a third expedition had already been organized for transfer to the lower Amur. Although hostilities had ceased, this expedition was sent on. Some 110 boats carrying over 1,600 soldiers reached Aigun on May 21, 1856. Their leader, General Korsakov, informed the Chinese that settlers were coming down the river that summer and that garrisons were to be set up on the left bank of the Amur. The Manchus made no attempt to stop this movement, and in the following months four posts were built. Kumarski, with twenty-four men, was established opposite the mouth of the Kumara River. Ust-Zeiski, at the mouth of the Zeya River, had fifty men, and Khinganski was built at the beginning of the Little Khingan Range. In May of the following year, Kor-sakov established the town of Ust-Zeiski (Blagoveshchensk)[33] on the site of the Ust-Zeiski post. Somewhat later he founded Khabarovsk on the right (east) bank of the Amur at the mouth of the Ussuri. Then, even farther downstream and close to the sea, he established the town of Sofyevsk.[34]

By the end of 1856, by and large, the Russians were already entrenched along the entire course of the Amur, with many strategically located posts along the river. Czarist Russia had already been trying to obtain China's official recognition of its *de facto* military occupation of the Amur. The Manchus, how-ever, never seemed particularly anxious to do so. Neither did they ever seem inclined to push their own claims to the Amur region by trying to expel Russians with force. The truth was that they were in no position to do much about the Russian invasion. In 1857 they were beset with internal disturbances, i.e., the Taiping Rebellion (1850–1864); and there was every possibility that the British and the French—who were carving out spheres of influence in China—would conclude their ven-tures by dictating terms of peace. At the same time, the Russians had on the frontiers of Manchuria and Mongolia some 16,000 infantrymen, 5,000 cavalrymen, 1,000 artillerymen with forty pieces, and an additional reserve of 1,000 men who were stationed at Irkutsk and Yeniseisk.[35] Unable to resist, the Manchus were compelled to negotiate and to recognize the conquest that the Russians had achieved.

In 1858 the Chinese agreed to negotiate the Amur question. Faced with troubles at home, they desired to settle the dispute at Aigun rather than at Peking. At Peking any renunciation of territory would have meant a loss of prestige and face by the government in the eyes of its own subjects and of foreign enemies.

On May 16/28, 1858,* the Treaty of Aigun was signed by Czarist Russia and China (see *Document 7*).[36] The Russians took advantage of the Manchu involvement in struggling with the Taiping and Nienfei (1853–1868) rebels as well as with British and French forces, and imposed on the hapless Chinese government this treaty, which is now being contested by Communist China.

The Treaty of Aigun established a new Chinese-Russian boundary along the course of the Amur as far east as the mouth of the Ussuri, the Amur's principal tributary (see *Map*). That is to say, Manchu China ceded to Czarist Russia the northern part of the Amur River valley (185,000 square miles), an area that had been denied to the Russians by the Treaty of Nerchinsk of 1689. Navigation on the Amur, Sungari, and Ussuri was restricted to Russian and Chinese vessels. Although the chief Russian negotiator, Muraveyev, had originally desired the border to run along the course of the Ussuri to its source and then to Korea, this land (150,000 square miles) was placed under the joint administration (or ownership) of the two

---

* For all double dates recording treaty-making events between Russia and China referred to in this chapter, the first date is that of the old Julian calendar, which Russia used until 1918. The second date is that of the Gregorian calendar, now in general use. Chinese dates have been transcribed into corresponding dates in the Gregorian calendar.

empires and was to remain so until a boundary was permanently fixed. As a concession to the Manchus, a very small enclave on the north bank of the Amur between the Zeya River and the village of Holdoldzin was allowed to remain in perpetuity under Chinese jurisdiction. This concession was, however, short-lived. During the Boxer Rebellion of 1900 Czarist Russia expelled all of the Han Chinese inhabitants of this enclave and annexed it to Soviet territory.[37]

In the beginning of 1859, Muraveyev's attention was directed to the Ussuri territory and he ordered that Cossack stations be built along the banks of the Ussuri and its tributary, the Sungacha. A survey corps was then sent up the river to explore the area and to determine the frontier. That same year there were some minor skirmishes between the Russians and the Chinese along the Ussuri, and not long afterward the Russians were forced out of their advanced posts on the Sungacha. This situation remained tense until early in 1860 when the Manchus became completely preoccupied with the threat of the British and French invasion of China. The Russians took advantage of this situation and joined in the grab by forcing another territorial settlement on the Manchus—the Treaty of Peking of 1860 (see *Document 9*).

Imperial China's consent to the Treaty of Peking was obtained by the Russian envoy, General Ignatiev, as a reward for his key role as the "honest broker" at the time of the British and French occupation of Peking in October 1860.

The Treaty of Peking of November 2/14, 1860, nullified both the Treaty of Nerchinsk of 1689 and the Treaty of Kiakhta of 1727. The Peking treaty defined the new Chinese-Russian border west of the Amur River. However, it did not change the boundary line north of Manchouli, and it established the better-defined Russian-Mongolian border in the west, continuing from the last boundary sign that had been erected under the Treaty of Kiakhta.

Under the terms of the Treaty of Peking, 133,000 square miles of territory east of the Ussuri,[38] which had been left under the joint Chinese-Russian jurisdiction by the Aigun treaty of 1858, were ceded to Russia. The new boundary between the two countries was to follow the Ussuri south to and along its tributary, the Sungacha, thence across Lake Hinkai (Lake Khanka) southward to the Korean frontier, and on the Tumen River 20 *versts,* or 13.2 miles, above its mouth. The frontier was marked on a map with twenty specific points (shown by Russian letters and Chinese phonetic equivalents).[39] A mixed border commission was to be appointed by the Chinese and Russian governments to survey and map the frontier from Lake Hinkai to the Tumen River (and this was done on June 16/28, 1861—see *Document 10*). Combined with the Treaty of Aigun of 1858, the Treaty of Peking established the basic boundary in existence today between Manchuria and the Soviet Far East (see *Map*).

During the 1860's Russian expansionism was not confined to the Amur and Ussuri territories but took a southwesterly direction toward Chinese Turkestan (Sinkiang)—a sparsely populated land of towering, snowcapped peaks and arid deserts that historically often served as a critical political, military, commercial, and cultural link between China, South Asia, and Europe.

Historically, Central Asia and Chinese Turkestan had formed a single territory. As early as 102 B.C. the Middle Kingdom claimed control over all of this area. The Chinese Empire under powerful emperors received tribute from the areas that are today Kazakhstan and Soviet Central Asia. But Chinese Turkestan was never an integral part of the Chinese people and their Middle Kingdom; it remained a frontier area.

The Mongols ruled Sinkiang and most of Inner Asia during the thirteenth century. After the collapse of the Yüan (or Mongol) Dynasty in China during the mid-fourteenth century, the area was dominated by petty tribes (e.g., the Kalmuks and the Monguls). The Ming Dynasty (1368–1644)—which overthrew the power of the Mongols in China—won tribute from them, but was unable to establish military control over them.

The Manchus, who had become the ruling dynasty in China in the middle of the seventeenth century, invaded Chinese Turkestan and established a military garrison there during the eighteenth century. In 1759, a new administrative province was created: Dzungaria and the Tarim basin (Kashgaria) were united and called Sinkiang, "the new dominion." But Sinkiang had no long-established Chinese settler population, because the Chinese did not consider it an attractive place to live. In the decades that followed Manchu military occupation, Chinese control of Sinkiang was exercised through the local Moslem chieftains and headmen, who acted as vassals of the Manchu emperors.

Meanwhile, by 1855 Czarist Russia's southern boundary in Central Asia had advanced to a line reaching from the central Caspian to Lake Aral to a point south of Alma-Ata, before turning sharply northward. The Chinese military occupation of Sinkiang coincided with the start of the Russian southward expansion into Central Asia from the earlier line of Siberian penetration. There was at this time no formal (legally defined) frontier separating Sinkiang from Russian-occupied territory in Central Asia, the first attempt to establish one being made in the Treaty of Peking of 1860.

The Treaty of Peking, which defined the Ussuri River boundary in the Far East, also created a Chinese-Russian boundary in Sinkiang for the first time (see *Document 9*). It stated that the boundary between the two empires in Central Asia should be based on the then-existing line of permanent pasture pickets, which the Chinese had established to limit the use of pastures by the nomadic Kazakhs. During the 1850's, the Chinese had displayed their territorial claims to a vast, ill-defined area in Central Asia both by a system of permanent pickets, or boundary markers, near cities, and by a wide-ranging system of temporary or movable pickets enclosing a much larger territory. China now consented to conclude a boundary agreement based upon a limited area defined by permanent pickets, giving Czarist Russia a quitclaim to a large portion of the Ili region of Chinese Turkestan (350,000 square miles), over which, however, the Chinese had held little more than regulatory control.[40] Article III of the Peking Treaty vaguely delimited the Chinese-Russian boundary from Chabindabaga (Shaban-Dabeg) southward along the mountains south of Issyk Kul (Ala Tau) to the limits of the State of Kokand. A detailed delimitation of this western boundary remained for a mixed border commission to arrange.

Four years later, representatives of the two empires met at Tarbagatai. Through the Tarbagatai Protocol, they specifically drew the Chinese-Russian boundary in Central Asia along the line of Chinese permanent pickets, as agreed upon at Peking in 1860 (see *Document 11*). The Tarbagatai Protocol of September 25/October 7, 1864, delimited the new Chinese-Russian boundary in Central Asia from Shaban-Dabeg (in what is now Mongolia) southward to Lake Zaisan, thence to the mountains situated to the south of Lake Issyk Kul and along these mountains as far as approximately 40°15′ North and 74°40′ East, the limits of Kokand.

The Tarbagatai Protocol, which was hastily concluded because of a Moslem revolt in Sinkiang, had left many vague or unsettled points. To complete the unfinished business of the Tarbagatai Protocol, representatives of Manchu China and Czarist Russia met in 1870 and signed a new boundary agreement, called the Russian-Chinese Boundary Treaty of Uliassutai. This treaty completed the demarcation of the boundary line in the Kobdo, Uliassutai and Tarbagatai regions of Mongolia and Sinkiang.[41] When the boundary stakes were set up around Tarbagatai, Russia encroached farther (another score of miles) into China, cutting the main thoroughfare between Tarbagatai and Altai.[42]

In 1864, a series of Moslem revolts (the Dungan Rebellion —the movement to separate Moslem Sinkiang from the Chinese Empire)[43] occurred in the whole area of Sinkiang against the oppressive Chinese military rule, and succeeded in throwing off the Manchu yoke. In the same year Yakub Beg, who was the leader of one of these revolts, took control of the entire Moslem revolt and set up an independent Moslem state centered on Kashgar (or Kashgaria)—covering nearly all of the Tarim basin.[44] In the thirteen years before a Chinese imperial army destroyed his kingdom,[45] Yakub Beg got a trade treaty from Czarist Russia, arms and other support from the British, who desired to create a buffer state between the Russian position in Central Asia and their empire in India, and the title of "Commander of the Faithful" from the Sultan of Turkey.

Czarist Russia took advantage of these chaotic conditions in Sinkiang and, coveting the fertile Central Asian lands, began to exploit local Moslem insurrections against Chinese rule. In May 1864, Russian troops occupied Tashkent, and by the fall of that year they occupied Chimkent. Samarkand was seized in 1868, and in 1875 Khiva became a Russian protectorate.[46]

In 1871, when Yakub Beg was struggling against the Chinese, Russian troops occupied the fertile upper Ili River valley in Sinkiang.[47] They did so on the pretext of maintaining law and order, and they attempted to extend czarist influence beyond the valley. Russia promised to return the Ili area as soon as Manchu China was able to govern it effectively. This magnanimous offer was undoubtedly made in the belief that the Chinese would never regain control of Sinkiang.

After the Taiping Rebellion in the east was crushed, the Manchus turned against the revolting Moslems in the west by sending a powerful military expedition to Sinkiang to reconquer the area. In 1874 the Chinese army, under Commander Tso Tsung-t'an, reconquered Hami, in 1876 Urumchi and Mansa, and in 1877 the Tarim basin (Aksu, Yarkand, Kashgar, and Khotan).[48] By 1878 the Moslem rebellion against the Chinese Empire was virtually crushed. The Manchus reestablished firm administrative control over Sinkiang in the same year.

After the Dungan Rebellion was crushed, the Chinese reclaimed the Ili River valley, but the Russians were evasive and refused to leave. The Chinese were not strong enough to force

the evacuation of Russian troops. Therefore, the Chinese envoy, Ch'ung-hou, and Russian Prince Gorchakov signed a new
Chinese-Russian agreement, the Treaty of Livadia, at the
czar's Crimean residence at Livadia in September 1879 to end
a decade of Russian occupation of the Ili region in Sinkiang.[49]

By the Treaty of Livadia, China agreed to cede to Russia
about 30 percent of the Ili territory (the western part of the
Ili region, including Muzart Pass and the Tekes River valley),
along with the passage of Kashgar and Yarkand, and to grant
Russians important trading privileges.[50] In return, Russia
promised to withdraw from the rest of the Ili area. This transfer of most of the strategic area between Dzungaria and the
Tien Shan to Russian sovereignty cost Sinkiang a substantial
section of its most fertile valley. Manchu China also allowed
Russia to establish consulates at Kiayukuan, Kobdo, Uliassutai,
Hami, Turfan, Urumchi, and Guchen, in addition to those
already allowed at Ili, Tarbagatai, Kashgar, and Urga.[51]

The Treaty of Livadia aroused such a storm of anger and
protest among the Chinese that the Manchu court in Peking
refused to ratify the treaty.[52] Ch'ung-hou, the Chinese envoy
who had negotiated the treaty, was thrown into prison and
sentenced to be decapitated. This forced new negotiations between the two empires. With the tacit support of European
powers (Great Britain and France), which were unfriendly to
Czarist Russia's territorial expansionism in Central Asia, the
Manchus negotiated a revised treaty. After further negotiations, Ch'ung-hou was pardoned, and another Russian-Chinese
treaty, the Treaty of St. Petersburg (or Ili), was signed on
February 12/14, 1881 (see *Document 12*).[53]

Under the terms of the Treaty of St. Petersburg, Czarist
Russia was to evacuate almost the whole of the Ili region, and
the Tekes River valley and the strategic Muzart Pass were
returned to China (see *Map*). The Khorgos River line became
the dividing line across the Ili River line.[54] Only a small area
of Sinkiang—the Lake Zaisan territory eastward along the
Chernyy Irtysh (15,000 square miles)—was ceded to Russia. In

turn, China agreed to pay Czarist Russia nine million rubles "occupation costs." In addition, a very small area west of the Holkuts River was ceded to Russia, for the purpose of settling "voluntary emigrants" from Chinese Sinkiang, that is, those non-Chinese inhabitants of the Chinese territory who preferred to live under Russian rule. The boundary lines east of Lake Zaisan and west of Kashgar, as determined by the Tarbagatai Protocol of 1864, were to be redemarcated. Russian trade privileges in Sinkiang for the most part were kept intact.

The Treaty of St. Petersburg was not sufficiently detailed and comprehensive in determining the Chinese-Russian boundary in Sinkiang, however. For this reason additional demarcation protocols were signed between the two countries during the period from 1882 to 1893 to complete the boundary "to the limits of Kokand"—the protocol signed at Ili in August 1882; the protocol signed at Goulimtou in October 1882; the protocol signed at Kashgar in November 1882; the protocol signed at Tarbagatai in September 1883; the protocol signed at Novi-Margelan in May 1884; the protocol signed at Kashgar in May 1885; and the protocol signed at Tarbagatai in December 1893.[55] Each protocol covered a specific portion of the boundary in detail. In short, the Treaty of St. Petersburg and these additional boundary protocols delimited (in part) the boundary between Russian Turkestan and Chinese Sinkiang as far south as Kizil Jik Dawan (pass) located at approximately 38°40′ North and 73°50′ East (see *Map*), and China lost about 15,000 square miles of territory to Russia.[56]

The Pamir mountain area was never covered by the Treaty of St. Petersburg and additional boundary protocols. On March 11, 1895, Russia and Great Britain simply agreed on borders in that remote area of Sinkiang, apparently without consultation with China. The British wanted to stop the Russian advance into Central Asia in order to secure the northwest frontier of India against Czarist Russia. The narrow Wakhan Corridor was created as an Afghan buffer zone between Russian Turkestan and British India, through the Anglo-Russian agreement of March 11, 1895, concerning the sphere of influence of the two European powers in the Pamir region (see *Map*). According to this Anglo-Russian agreement, the Chinese-Russian boundary in the Pamirs extended southward from Kizil Jik Dawan (the limits of Kokand) to (peak) Povalo Shveikovski along the main ranges that form the water divides in the region (see *Map*).[57] That is to say, Povalo Shveikovski became the Russian-Chinese-Afghan tripoint in the Pamirs. Manchu China refused to recognize the boundary defined by the Anglo-Russian agreement of 1895.[58]

Despite the withdrawal of Russian military forces from Sinkiang after the Treaty of St. Petersburg, Russian expansionist interest in the area did not abate for a long period after 1881. In spite of China's success in subduing the Moslem revolts in the 1870's, its control over Sinkiang remained perilously weak in the decades that followed, although Sinkiang had been made a regular province of the Chinese Empire in 1884. In the first half of the twentieth century, China never quite lost Sinkiang to the Russians, but it never eliminated Russian influence in the area either. The Chinese-Russian boundary in Sinkiang has remained unchanged.

During the late nineteenth century Czarist Russia launched a bold drive on Manchuria (and Korea) for political, military, and economic influence there in competition with Japan. In 1896 the Russians extracted from the weak and faltering Chinese Empire a defensive alliance against Japan[59] and the right to build the Chinese Eastern Railway in Manchuria as a shortcut link between European Russia and the Soviet Maritime Province (Vladivostok);[60] in 1898 they obtained another railroad concession to extend the Chinese Eastern Railway into southern Manchuria;[61] they obtained a territorial lease on the warm water port of Dairen, the naval base of Port Arthur, and the Liaotung Peninsula[62]—the very area denied to Japan by the Russian-led Western intervention as one of its most significant prizes for winning the war against China three years earlier.

Needless to say, the principal objective of the above two railways was to spread Russia's political, economic, and military influence in Manchuria. Only Russia's defeat by Japan in 1905 reversed this advance and caused the Russian sphere of influence to recede to the northern part of Manchuria. By the Treaty of Portsmouth of September 5, 1905, Russia was compelled to cede to Japan the southern half of Sakhalin Island, its territorial lease of the Liaotung Peninsula, the South Manchurian Railway, the great naval and industrial complex of Port Arthur and Dairen, and, above all, its predominant influence in Manchuria.[63]

The defeat of Czarist Russia in 1905 did not end, but temporarily halted, its expansionist ambition toward the east. Just several years after that serious setback, the Russians again conceived their imperialistic plans in China and in China's sphere of influence. The next Russian chance came in 1911 when the Manchu Dynasty fell and the new Republic came into being in China.

On November 18/December 1, 1911, when Manchu China collapsed in the throes of revolution, the Mongols, who had suffered some two hundred years of Manchu domination, declared their independence, with the Living Buddha of Urga (i.e., the city now called Ulan Bator) as a ruler (*bogdo khan*) of Outer Mongolia, and asked for support and protection from Russia. It may be noted that czarist agents had played an active role in promoting the Mongolian independence movement.[64] Taking advantage of the chaotic domestic disorders in China, Czarist Russia sent arms to the Mongols[65] and the Russo-Mongolian treaty of October 21/November 3, 1912, recognized the "autonomy" of Outer Mongolia.[66] The 1912 agreement, which granted the Russians special trading privileges and the right to station troops in the Mongolian country, for all practical purposes created a *de facto* Russian protectorate in Outer Mongolia. This agreement was followed by the secret military agreement of 1913 between the two countries.[67]

In 1911 Czarist Russia seized Uriankhai, which until then

had been administratively part of western Outer Mongolia under the suzerainty of the Manchu Dynasty. In 1914 it was made a Russian protectorate. In 1921 the Soviet Union under the Bolshevik regime proclaimed it an "independent" Tuvinian People's Republic and changed the name of Uriankhai into Tannu Tuva. On October 13, 1944, the area was quietly annexed by the Soviet Union as part of its territory—an autonomous region of the Russian Soviet Federated Socialist Republic.[68]

Russian interference in Outer Mongolia soon brought protests from the new (1911) Chinese Republic. At one point Russia and China were very close to war. A series of negotiations, however, helped to avert the immediate threat of hostilities; and on October 23/November 5, 1913, an accord was reached.[69] Through this agreement, the Russians admitted Chinese suzerainty over Outer Mongolia, while extracting from China the recognition of the autonomy of Outer Mongolia. This was later formulated in the tripartite Russo-Chinese-Mongolian treaty of June 1915 at Kiakhta.[70]

On December 7/20, 1911, China and Russia signed the Treaty of Tsitsihar because of a long series of border disputes which occurred along the Chinese-Russian frontier that ran northwest from the Argun River. This border had been determined by the Treaty of Kiakhta of 1727 and had been reaffirmed by the Treaty of Peking of 1860.[71] However, the Russians demanded that it be delimited again. The Chinese were in no position to refuse them because of the chaotic period of the Manchu collapse and the 1911 republican revolution.

The Treaty of Tsitsihar of 1911 redelimited the boundary from Mongolia to the Mutnol Protok ("muddy stream") and then to the Argun (see *Document 13*). This segment of the boundary stemmed from the 1727 Kiakhta agreement, which placed pillars on certain specified points. By taking advantage of the internal anarchy in China, Czarist Russia renegotiated the boundary by either moving the original pillars (nos. 58 to 63) or by constructing new ones. The Tsitsihar frontier generally encroached about five miles into China along a six-mile front. In addition, differing channels of the Argun were utilized by Russia for additional forays of up to fifty miles into China.[72]

With respect to the boundary east of Mongolia, the Tsitsihar agreement of 1911 redefined the boundary between Mongolia and the Argun, ceding approximately 375 square miles to Russia.[73] China has since maintained that the agreement was void because of lack of ratification.[74]

Debilitated by the strains of the First World War, Czarist Russia collapsed in 1917—only six years after the end of the Manchu Dynasty in China. But neither Russian interest in the Chinese borderlands nor Russian encroachment on Chinese territorial sovereignty lessened with the ascendancy to power of the Soviet Bolsheviks in 1917. Like "old wine in a new bottle," the revolutionary Soviet Union proved to be just as expansionist and predatory as imperial Russia had been in its time. While the Bolshevik leaders initially made a great point of condemning czarist imperialism in the Far East, they were no less inclined to preserve whatever they could of Russian influence and privileges there.

In one heady moment early in the Bolshevik reign—July 25, 1919, to be precise—the Deputy Commissar for Foreign Affairs, L. M. Karakhan, issued a declaration repudiating the "unequal" treaties and renouncing all Soviet claims to territories "ravenously" taken away from China by the czars and the Russian "bourgeoisie." [75] The declaration said in part:

> We are marching to free the people from the yoke of military force, of foreign money, which is crushing the life and the people of the East, and principally of the people of China. . . . The Soviet Government has renounced all the conquests made by the Czarist Government which took away from China Manchuria and other territories. The population of these territories shall decide for themselves to which country they would like to belong.

The Karakhan Declaration clearly gave the Chinese the impression that the Soviet regime was willing to give up many territorial gains made by Czarist Russia in Manchuria and

THE SINO-SOVIET BOUNDARY

1   Boundary defined by Treaty of Nerchinsk, 1689
2   Boundary defined by Treaty of Kiakhta, 1727
3   Boundary defined by Treaty of Aigun, 1858
3a Territory ceded to Russia in 1858
4   Boundary defined by Treaty of Peking, 1860
4a Territory ceded to Russia in 1860
5   Tannu Tuva (or Uriankhai)
6a Borders marked by Treaty of St. Petersburg, 1881
6b Ceded to Russia by China in 1881
6c Evacuated by Russia in 1881 (Occupied 1871-1881)

6d Yielded to Russia by China in 1881 resettlement of voluntary emigrants
7   Kizil Jik Dawan
8   Wakhan Corridor
9   1840 Chinese border
10 "East Turkestan Republic" (1945-194 proclaimed by anti-Chinese Moslem insurgents with Soviet support

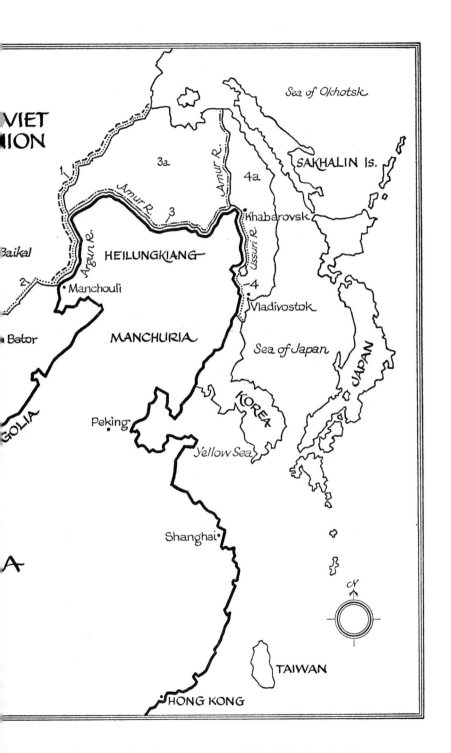

other areas in Asia.[76] Such an impression was reechoed and strengthened on September 27, 1920, when the Soviet government issued the Karakhan Manifesto to the Chinese government in Peking.[77] The manifesto declared:

The Government of the Russian Socialist Soviet Republics declares null and void all treaties concluded with China by the former Government of Russia, renounces all seizures of Chinese territory and all Russian concessions in China, and restores to China, without compensation and forever, all that had been predatorily seized from her by the Czar's Government and the Russian bourgeoisie.

In the subsequent diplomatic negotiations with the Chinese, however, the Soviet regime had hasty second thoughts and backed away from their generous 1919 and 1920 pledges, taking advantage of political chaos in China. That is to say, the "forever" in the 1920 Karakhan Manifesto did not last long, and the Soviets clung to territories seized by the czars as well as Russia's share in the Chinese Eastern Railway in Manchuria.

Even before negotiations with the Chinese, the Soviet leaders were already busy and active in trying to establish a Communist satellite in Outer Mongolia, over which China recovered its theoretical sovereignty in 1915.

The First World War and the revolutions of 1917 completely absorbed the attention of Russian diplomacy. With the political power of Russia in Outer Mongolia virtually destroyed by the fall of the czarist regime, the Chinese (under General Hsu Shu-tseng) in 1919 reestablished their control over the Mongolian country and canceled Mongolian autonomy.

Outer Mongolia was the scene of bloody fighting during the Russian civil war.[78] In 1921, the last remnants of the White Russian Army under Baron Roman Nikolaus von Ungern-Sternberg invaded Outer Mongolia and seized the capital of Urga. This action was utilized by the Soviets as an excuse to enter the country. In July 1921, the Soviet Red Army invaded Outer Mongolia, expelled the White Russian forces, and recognized Mongolian independence.[79] In the same year the Soviet Union also annexed Tannu Tuva, making it Soviet territory by force.[80] In 1924 pro-Communist revolution established the Mongolian People's Republic, which soon became the first Soviet satellite. The name of the Mongolian capital of Urga was changed to Ulan Bator, meaning Red Hero. Formally, however, the Soviet Union continued to pay lip service to the legality of Chinese control over Outer Mongolia. At the beginning of 1925 Soviet troops were withdrawn from the country.

Events in Outer Mongolia, however, did not divert the Soviet leaders from their concern with developments in China, and from 1921 on they made every effort to preserve and even increase their influence there. During the early 1920's the new Republic of China was deeply divided. There was the Peking government (North), ruled by reactionary warlords, and the revolutionary Kuomintang (Nationalist) regime in Canton (South), led by Sun Yat-sen. Manchuria was in the hands of Marshal and Warlord Chang Tso-lin. The Soviet Union decided to deal with these governments and leaders separately in traditional divide-and-rule fashion. It was not until 1928 that Chiang Kai-shek, successor to Sun Yat-sen, succeeded in unifying China under one government through his Northern Expedition.

On January 26, 1923, Sun Yat-sen and a Soviet agent, Adolf Joffe, signed the Sun-Joffe Declaration, through which the Soviet Union promised to lend support and advice to the Kuomintang, as a unique national party, in its efforts to attain national unification and independence—not a Communist revolution.[81] It should be remembered that two years before this declaration was signed, i.e., in July 1921, the Soviet Bolsheviks, with the Comintern acting as a midwife, had organized and supported the Chinese Communist movement.[82] Despite the Sun-Joffe Declaration, the Soviets insisted on their right to keep troops in Outer Mongolia and extracted from Sun the acceptance of the *status quo* in that country in exchange for the withdrawal of their demand for Outer Mongolia's independence.

A new agreement was signed between the Soviet Union and the Peking government on May 31, 1924. This agreement declared null and void all previous Chinese agreements with Czarist Russia, at least on paper, and established normal diplomatic relations between the two governments.[83] The Soviet Union surrendered its extraterritoriality in China, but the Chinese government agreed to joint Sino-Soviet operation of the Chinese Eastern Railway in Manchuria. The Soviets formally recognized Outer Mongolia as "a component of the Chinese Republic" under Chinese sovereignty, while the Chinese acknowledged Moscow's *de facto* dominance there. Moreover, the Soviet Union committed itself to withdraw all of its armed forces from Outer Mongolia as soon as measures had been taken that would ensure the establishment of the safety of the frontiers. Finally, a new delimitation of the Sino-Soviet boundary was agreed upon, but it was never implemented. As will be seen later in this chapter, Chinese sovereignty over Outer Mongolia remained in shadowy title until it was finally abolished in 1945.

On September 20, 1924, the Soviet Union and Marshal Chang Tso-lin, military governor of Manchuria, signed the Mukden agreement. This reiterated the substance of the May 31, 1924, agreement between the Soviets and the Peking government.[84] On March 15, 1925, the Chinese government in Peking ratified the Mukden agreement as a supplement to its 1924 pact with Moscow.[85] Later developments may be summarized as follows: In 1935, four years after the Japanese occupied Manchuria and established the puppet state of Manchukuo in September 1931, the Soviet Union sold the Chinese Eastern Railway to Manchukuo and thus liquidated its vulnerable position in Manchuria to avoid a confrontation with Japan. During the 1930's the Soviet and Japanese troops were occasionally engaged in localized armed clashes along the Soviet-Manchurian and Manchurian-Mongolian frontiers.

Post-1917 Russian expansion into Chinese territories was also evident in Sinkiang, which, between 1912 and 1949, fell under a succession of locally powerful Chinese warlords independent of the central Chinese government.[86] Although the Soviets, after the Bolshevik Revolution of 1917, repenetrated Sinkiang largely for political and economic gain, the Sino-Soviet boundary in the area has remained unchanged.

The Soviet Union's influence in Sinkiang grew steadily and reached its height in the 1930's, during which China's Nationalist government was distracted by the invading Japanese in the east and also preoccupied with the civil war with the Chinese Communists. The Chinese General Sheng Shih-ts'ai, who became Sinkiang's governor (warlord) in 1933, was forced to lean heavily upon the Soviet Union for financial loans, arms, technical aid, and—more than once—direct military assistance to attain several objectives: (a) exclusion of Japanese influence from the area; (b) buildup of his own personal empire; and (c) suppression of anti-Chinese Moslem rebellions. For example, when there was a series of bitter and bloody Moslem revolts in Sinkiang during the 1930's as a result of Chinese misrule, Sheng had to ask for Soviet troops to help crush the uprisings, and the Soviet Red Army twice entered the region, in 1934 and 1937, to help him. This aid grew out of the Soviets' own fear of Moslem nationalism in Soviet Central Asia.

In return for Soviet assistance, Stalin extracted from Sheng extensive political and economic concessions in Sinkiang and particularly in the Ili valley, thus placing the province under an informal Sino-Soviet condominium.[87] In short, during the period from 1932 to 1942, when Mao Tse-tung and his Chinese Communists were engaged in their life-and-death struggle against the Chinese Nationalists, Sinkiang under Sheng was a *de facto* or disguised satellite of the Soviet Union, although nominally under the Republic of China. During the same period Sheng also maintained temporary good relations with Mao and his Chinese Communist Party. In 1939 Mao sent his younger brother, Mao Tse-min, to Sinkiang to establish a Chinese Communist beachhead there. But when Sheng wanted to join the Chinese Communist Party, Stalin vetoed his membership application and arranged to have him enrolled in the Soviet Communist Party.

Sheng broke with Moscow in 1942, when the Soviet Union was concentrating on the war against Nazi Germany in Europe. He decided to cooperate with the Chinese Nationalist government,[88] probably because he feared that the Soviets would be defeated by the Germans. In the same year Sheng also decided to turn against the Chinese Communists. As a result, Mao Tse-tung's brother, who was in Sinkiang under the alias Chou Ping, was executed with some one hundred other Chinese Communists.

But Sinkiang was immediately wracked by Moscow-supported, anti-Chinese, Moslem uprisings and rebellions. In January 1945, the Moslem rebels established the short-lived "East Turkestan Republic" in Ili and controlled the northwestern portion of Sinkiang (see *Map*) until the Chinese Communist troops occupied all of the province, disarmed the Moslem insurgents, purged their leaders, and ended overt Soviet interference in the region.

Even on the eve of the complete Chinese Communist take-over of mainland China, Stalin made a last-minute attempt to deny Sinkiang to Mao Tse-tung, who had, since 1927, played an increasingly independent role in the Stalin-dominated world Communist movement. In the summer of 1949, when Mao Tse-tung's Red Army was rapidly advancing toward Sinkiang after the capture of Peking, the Soviet consul general in Urumchi approached General Tao Shih-yueh, Chinese Nationalist commander in Sinkiang, and urged him to declare Sinkiang independent in the same way that the Outer Mongolians had declared their independence in 1921. The Soviet Union would then extend immediate diplomatic recognition to the new state and also direct the Chinese Communist forces, already in neighboring Kansu Province, to halt their advance into Sinkiang. Later on, after Mao's victory, Sinkiang would be incorporated into the Soviet Union as an autonomous republic.

The Nationalist Chinese failed to respond to the Soviet

proposal favorably, so Stalin's Machiavellian plot received a bitter setback. The victory of the Chinese Communists in 1949 put an end to dominant Soviet influence in Sinkiang.

The Sinkiang episode exemplified the fact that Stalin, through the end of the Second World War, gave high priority to Soviet national interest even at the expense of the comradely Chinese Communist cause. As far as he was concerned, in other words, the Chinese, both Nationalist and Communist, were simply pawns to be played in accordance with the best strategic and other interests of Mother Russia. That disposition was especially well reflected in the bargain that he struck with Churchill and Roosevelt at Yalta concerning the re-creation of the traditional Russian sphere of influence in China's borderlands.

In February 1945, Stalin, Churchill, and Roosevelt met at Yalta. Japan had yet to surrender. As an inducement to sway the Soviets to join the final stages of the Second World War against Japan, the United States was willing to promise the Russians a generous portion of the spoils that victory would bring. In return for this participation, in a secret Yalta agreement dated February 11, 1945, Stalin succeeded in obtaining the following terms: (a) a guarantee of the status quo (independence) of Outer Mongolia; (b) the outright cession of the southern half of Sakhalin and the Kurile Islands to the Soviet Union; and (c) the restoration to the Kremlin of its former rights in Manchuria before the Russo-Japanese War of 1904–1905, with specific safeguarding of the "preeminent interests" of the Soviet Union in the internationalized free port of Dairen, in a naval base (leased) at Port Arthur, and in joint Sino-Soviet control and operation of the Chinese Eastern Railway and the South Manchurian Railway.[89] Nationalist China, however, was to retain full sovereignty in Manchuria.

Nationalist China later confirmed the Yalta stipulations on Outer Mongolia and Manchuria through the Soviet-Chinese Treaty of Friendship and Alliance of August 14, 1945.[90] As far as the issue of Outer Mongolia was concerned, this agreement recognized the independence and territorial integrity of the country if a plebiscite should "confirm the desire." The plebiscite was held on October 20, 1945; it confirmed the desire.[91] On January 5, 1946, Nationalist China officially recognized the independence of the Mongolian People's Republic, and the Soviet Union signed a new treaty of military alliance with that country.[92]

The Soviet troops occupied Manchuria in August 1945 and withdrew from there in May 1946.[93] During this occupation period, Stalin's occupation forces were engaged in the predatory stripping of Manchurian industries.[94] The Soviet Union aided the Chinese Communists by permitting Mao's Eighth Route Army to gain strategic footholds in Manchuria and also by turning over to them captured Japanese military equipment and supplies.[95] But Stalin also maintained "correct" diplomatic relations with Chiang Kai-shek's Nationalist regime, even giving it some assistance.[96] That is to say, the characteristic of Stalin's China policy immediately after the end of the Second World War was the cynical double-dealing tactic of simultaneously aiding the two antagonists in the Chinese Civil War in different ways. This, as Raymond L. Garthoff correctly observes, "may be explained by Stalin's uncertainty as to the outcome of the Civil War." [97] But it can also be said plausibly that he wanted to fish in troubled Chinese waters by keeping China divided and weak. By the time the Soviet troops withdrew from Manchuria in May 1946, the Chinese Nationalists held nominal control over the area—but the Chinese Communists effectively controlled the northeastern two thirds of the region.

Without active Soviet support, the Chinese Communists emerged victorious in mainland China in 1949, and the Soviet Union was willing to establish new friendly relations with the People's Republic of China, which came into being at Peking on October 1, 1949. It was the victory of the Chinese Communists under the leadership of Mao Tse-tung, and nothing else, that stopped the Soviet Union's expansion into the Chinese borderlands. However, as will be shown in the next chapter, Stalin's greedy interests in these areas did not immediately cease with the establishment of Communist rule in mainland China; they were stopped completely only through Communist China's forceful territorial consolidation and accompanying strong countermeasures against them. Between 1949 and 1954 the two brotherly Communist giants were secretly engaged in a tug-of-war for the domination of Manchuria and Sinkiang.

CHAPTER 2

The Sino-Soviet Territorial Dispute Before the Ussuri Border Clashes of March 1969

Immediately after the Chinese Communists came to power in 1949, Peking's foreign policy with the Soviet Union as well as the Communist bloc can be described as "leaning to one side." Communist China allied itself with Moscow through the Sino-Soviet alliance treaty of 1950. At the same time, the Chinese Communists collaborated with the Soviets in a workably friendly fashion over a broad range of affairs and refrained from making public expression of disagreements on territorial questions. But even in this new relationship the Chinese Communists provided evidence that the Peking regime, like the Kuomintang government that preceded it, harbored resentment over a frontier shaped a century ago by the czarist advance into territories in Central Asia and eastern Siberia that historically lay within the empire of the Middle Kingdom.

One of the most basic trends in twentieth-century Chinese history has been the urge to complete the unification of China by reasserting China's control over its "lost territories." This urge appears to have certainly endured even under the Chinese Communist regime. A corollary to this is the persistent desire for more secure frontiers, for national security, for additional national resources, and for greater international influence as a major power center in Asia.

The motivation to unite and consolidate territories comes partly from modern Chinese nationalism, which has been and still is, as A. Doak Barnett puts it, "one of the strongest and most fundamental forces shaping the course of events in modern China." [1] It must be emphasized that nationalism is one of the driving forces behind Communist China's domestic and international actions. Modern Chinese nationalism is a product of such objective and historical causes as the national indignation at China's miseries at the hands of predatory foreign imperialists in the nineteenth and twentieth centuries. Not surprisingly, Mao Tse-tung proclaimed in September 1949: "Our nation will never be insulted again. We have already stood up." [2]

The desire to unify territories also derives partly from China's long history with its impressive imperial tradition, a cultural heritage that has bred within the Chinese people, both Nationalist and Communist, a deep sense of cultural superiority and a chauvinistic belief in China's natural supremacy in Asia.

Sun Yat-sen, the father of the Chinese Republic, regarded Siam, Burma, Nepal, Tibet, Vietnam, the Himalayas, the Amur and Ussuri river basins, and the northern Ili region as historically "having belonged" to China.[3] When he spoke of China in the *San Min Chu I* ("The Three Principles of the People"), he really thought of a Great China, which included all the territories of the old Chinese Empire. He said in his lecture on nationalism:

What about the place nearest to us—Hong Kong—or a little farther away Burma, Bhutan, Nepal or such places which formerly belonged to China. China has no sufficient strength at present to recover her lost territories. . . . Because of the loss of our nationalism, our ancient morality and civilization have not been able to manifest themselves. The cosmopolitanism [that] Europeans are talking about today is really a principle supported by force without justice. . . . Our culture had already advanced two thousand years beyond yours [i.e., Western culture]: we are willing to wait for you to progress and catch up with us, but we cannot recede and let you pull us down.[4]

Sun's successors, both Nationalist and Communist, although they violently disagree about questions of politics and ideology, have shared his view of China's "manifest destiny" to recover its "lost territories."

Chiang Kai-shek has also seen China's rightful territory as extending beyond the present Chinese border in the Asian heartland.[5] During the period of the Nationalist regime under Chiang, China's "lost territories" were listed as follows:

TABLE I

CHINA'S "LOST TERRITORIES" [6]

Date	Area, in square kilometers	Location	New Ownership
1689	240,000	North side Khingan Mountains	Russia
1727	100,000	Lower Selenga valley	Russia
1842	83	Hong Kong	England
1858	480,000	North of Heilungkiang	Russia
1858	8	Kowloon	England
1860	344,000	East of Ussuri River	Russia
1864	900,000	North of Lake Balkhash	Russia
1879	2,386	Liuchiu Islands	Japan
1882–1883	21,000	Lower Ili valley	Russia
1883	20,000	Irtysh valley east of Lake Zaisan	Russia
1884	9,000	Upper Koksol valley	Russia
1885–1889	738,000	Annam and all Indochina	France
1886	574,000	Burma	England
1890	7,550	Sikkim	England
1894	122,400	West of the upper Salween	England
1894	91,300	West of the upper Yangtze	England
1894	100,000	Upper Burma, Savage Mts.	England
1895	220,334	Korea	Japan
1895	35,845	Taiwan	Japan
1895	127	Pescadores	Japan
1897	760	The edge of Burma	England
1897	2,300	The edge of Burma	England
Total	4,009,093		

Mao Tse-tung, the supreme leader of Communist China, and his Communist colleagues are still influenced, consciously or subconsciously, by some powerful cultural forces from China's ancient past. Mao himself has never considered his Communist regime divorced from the past history of the Middle Kingdom. He said:

Our nation has a history of several thousand years, a history which has its own characteristics and is full of treasures. . . . The China of today has developed from the China in history; as we are believers in the Marxist approach to history, we must not cut off our whole historical past. We must make a summing-up from Confucius down to Sun Yat-sen and inherit this precious legacy. This will help much in directing the great movement of today.[7]

In 1936 Mao Tse-tung upheld Sun's nationalistic idea when he said to Edgar Snow:

It is the immediate task of China to regain all our lost territories. . . . We do not, however, include Korea, formerly a Chinese colony, but when we have reestablished the independence of the lost territories of China, and if the Koreans wish to break away from the chains of Japanese imperialism, we will extend them our enthusiastic help in their struggle for independence. The same thing applies for Formosa. . . . The Outer Mongolian Republic will automatically become a part of the Chinese federation, at their own will. The Mohammedan and Tibetan peoples, likewise, will form autonomous republics, attached to the Chinese federation.[8]

In short, Communist China under the leadership of Mao has changed almost everything done by Chiang Kai-shek and his Nationalist regime, but it has not changed the "maps" of the historic Chinese Empire. The Chinese Communist claims to what are at present portions of the Soviet territory are in large part a revival of the old irredentist and nationalistic dream of the twentieth-century power elites.

Both before and after the establishment of Communist rule in mainland China, Mao Tse-tung harbored many resentments and much bitterness against the Soviet Union, especially Stalin. Mao perhaps remembered that Russian (both czarist and Communist) encroachment on Chinese territorial sovereignty continued *long after* the period of imperialistic expansion on the part of other European powers had come to a close. Also, Mao apparently remembered that during the Second World War Joseph Stalin, for reasons of national security, deported thousands of Chinese workers from the Soviet Maritime Province to remote exile in western or northern Siberia, from which they have never returned.[9]

Also serving as an irritant to Mao in the 1940's was Stalin's predatory stripping of Manchurian industrial facilities as "war booty" at the expense of both the Nationalists and the Communists—a step that was hardly consistent or compatible with the professed anti-imperialistic revolutionary credentials of the Soviet Union as the "fatherland of the world proletariat." The Pauley Commission, which investigated in May and June 1946, estimated that the damage to the Manchurian economy during the Soviet occupation totaled $858 million, or $2 billion replacement value.[10] In addition, the Soviet troops had confiscated $3 billion in bullion and $850 million in Manchurian *yuan,* and the note issued had been doubled in occupation *yuan.*[11] Moscow's systematic stripping of the Manchurian industrial complex came after the Nationalist Chinese rejected outright the Soviet demand for fifty-fifty Soviet-Chinese operation of 154 industrial and mining establishments, comprising 80 percent of Manchuria's heavy industry.[12]

Mao was undoubtedly disgusted with the Soviet leaders who, aside from failing to give the Chinese Communists active support in the civil war against the Chinese Nationalists, had occasionally indulged in making derogatory remarks about the Chinese Communists in public statements. In June 1944, for instance, Stalin told W. Averill Harriman, then American ambassador to Moscow, that "the Chinese Communists are not real Communists. They are margarine Communists."[13] A similar statement was given to United States Secretary of State James F. Byrnes at Potsdam in July 1945.[14] V. M. Molotov, one of the Soviet leaders, expressed this identical view in talks with various Americans (e.g., Patrick J. Hurley, Donald M. Nelson) by saying:

> The Soviet Government could bear no responsibility for international affairs of developments in China for which at times it had been unjustifiably held responsible. . . . In part of that country the people were half starved and miserable; and thus they called themselves "Communists," but they had no relation to Communism; they used the name as a way of expressing their discontent over their conditions; but if these were improved, they would forget that they were "Communists"; and so, if the United States helped these unfortunate people, there would be fewer "Communists" in China. . . . The Soviet people would be very glad if the United States helped China.[15]

What was even worse, Stalin, bent on re-creating the traditional Russian spheres of influence in the Chinese borderlands by keeping China divided and weak, was ready to sell out the Chinese Communist cause in 1945, urging the Chinese Communists to forget about revolution, to disband their armies and join Chiang Kai-shek's anti-Communist government as a minority.[16] In his secret speech made to the Tenth Plenum of the Eighth Central Committee of the Chinese Communist Party at Chungnanhai in Peking on September 28, 1962, Mao said:

> The roots [of the conflict between the Soviet Union and Communist China] were laid long before. They [the Soviet Communists] did not allow China to make [Communist] revolution. This was in 1945, when Stalin refused to permit the Chinese [Communist] revolution by saying that we should not engage in any civil war and that we must collaborate with Chiang Kai-shek. Otherwise, the Republic of China will collapse. At that time, we did not adhere to that, and the revolution was victorious.[17]

Mao doubtless remembers that the Soviet Union was the last country to withdraw its ambassador from the dissolving Nationalist government in 1949.

The historically well established fact is that Mao Tse-tung has always hated the Russians. Stalin, for his part, liked Chiang Kai-shek better than Mao, and it is possible that the

Soviet dictator would have preferred to deal with a weak China under Chiang Kai-shek. According to a U.S. Department of State document released in 1969, Mao Tse-tung and Chou En-lai in 1945 had repeatedly tried to establish relations with the United States, probably in order to pursue an independent, "Titoist" course.[18] But not only did Washington rebuff these efforts, it also suppressed all information about them for two and a half decades.

Even after the victory of the Chinese Communists in 1949, Stalin's uncomradely disposition toward them continued to be manifest. In the winter of 1949–1950 Stalin imposed on Mao another "unequal" treaty.

In December 1949, Mao Tse-tung paid his first visit to the Soviet Union; and during his unusually long nine-week stay in Moscow, a number of important Sino-Soviet agreements were concluded.[19] Mao, dealing with Stalin from weakness, got very little of what he wanted for Communist China's modernization, and, to make matters worse, he had to make one-sided concessions on a major scale.

Most important of these agreements was the thirty-year Treaty of Friendship, Alliance, and Mutual Assistance, signed on February 14, 1950. In this treaty of political and military alliance (which, to all intents and purposes, is now dead), the Chinese and Soviets agreed that if either ally were "attacked by Japan or any states allied with it" (e.g., the United States), the other partner would "immediately render military and other assistance by all means at its disposal." By a separate agreement, the Soviets gave Communist China economic backing through a five-year 300-million-dollar loan. During the same period, important trade and other economic agreements were also worked out.

In return for Soviet support, Mao had to make major concessions to Stalin. The Soviet dictator was still insistent upon preserving Russia's old "special rights" in China. Thus, another set of agreements signed on February 14, 1950, provided for joint Sino-Soviet administration of the Chinese Changchun Railway (i.e., the combined Chinese Eastern and South Manchurian railways) in Manchuria, as well as for joint use of the naval base at Port Arthur and the commercial port of Dairen, either until a peace treaty with Japan could be concluded or, at the latest, until the end of 1952. Subsequent agreements regarding the railway and the naval base may be summarized as follows: The two governments agreed on September 15, 1952, that the Soviet Union would return the Manchurian railway system to sole Chinese management by the end of 1952, as agreed upon in 1950.[20] However, on the same date in 1952—during the Korean War—the 1950 agreement on Port Arthur was amended to extend the Soviet base rights beyond 1952, allegedly at Peking's "request." [21] On October 12, 1954, the Soviet Union agreed to terminate its base rights completely by May 31, 1955.[22]

Among the concessions made to the Soviet Union by China on February 14, 1950, was an agreement to recognize the independence of Outer Mongolia.[23] Another set of agreements concluded between the two countries in the spring of 1950 called for the establishment of several long-term joint-stock companies to operate mostly in China's borderlands, where the Russians had traditionally pressed for special rights. Those included two companies to exploit petroleum and non-ferrous mineral resources (probably including uranium) in Sinkiang, a company to build and repair ships in Dairen, and a civil aviation company to provide services between China and the Soviet Union.[24]

In Mao's eyes, the 1950 agreements between Moscow and Peking clearly demonstrated that the Soviet Union had not yet fully renounced the traditional czarist expansionism, for they were not drastically different from those agreed upon between the Manchu court and Czarist Russia in 1898 and between the Chinese Nationalists and the Soviets in August 1945. In 1950, in short, Stalin acted like the "new czar" and the typically greedy capitalist. Harrison E. Salisbury describes the situation very well by saying:

Imagine! China had just got the international capitalists off her back, and now Moscow came along and took their place! The new companies were just like the old European capitalist concessionaries —no better, maybe worse. And these were China's Communist comrades who were exploiting her.[25]

According to Polish sources, Nikita S. Khrushchev, in a speech in Warsaw after his decision to promote "de-Stalinization," specifically accused Stalin of having been responsible for serious strains in Sino-Soviet relations between 1949 and 1953.[26] According to Khrushchev, Stalin and Mao were on the verge of a full split in 1950. The Soviet dictator forced Mao to make a series of economic concessions smacking of colonialism and insisted that he must have the same final say over the development of Communism in China as he had become accustomed to having in other countries of the Soviet bloc.[27] Mao was extremely embittered by Stalin's insistence on preserving Russia's "special interests" in China and refused to submit to Stalin's authority over internal Chinese Communist affairs.[28]

The Khrushchev remarks in Warsaw were later confirmed by Mao himself. In his secret speech to the Tenth Plenum of the Eighth Central Committee of the Chinese Communist Party on September 28, 1962, Mao described his difficult relations with Stalin by saying:

Even after the victory of the Chinese Communists Stalin feared that China would become a Yugoslavia and I would become a Tito. Later on, I went to Moscow in December 1949 to conclude the Chinese-Soviet Treaty of Alliance and Mutual Assistance [of February 14, 1950], which also involved a struggle. Stalin did not want to sign it, but finally agreed after two months of negotiations. When did Stalin begin to have confidence in us? It began in the winter of 1950, when our country became involved in the Resist-America Aid-Korea Campaign [the Korean War]. Stalin then believed that we were not Yugoslavia and not Titoist.[29]

Incidentally, what Mao failed to mention in his secret speech was that Communist China had to repay every penny it owed to the Soviet Union for Stalin's military assistance in the Korean War, although the Chinese people had made great sacrifices.[30]

In short, during the initial period of relations between the People's Republic of China and the Soviet Union from 1949 to 1954, there was good reason to believe that Stalin and Mao secretly hated each other. But the common interests of the two Communist powers outweighed their different and, at times, conflicting interests. Furthermore, Mao respected Stalin as the world Communist leader, and Communist China did need the Soviet Union's military, diplomatic, economic, and technical aid at the time of its weakness. Accordingly, the Chinese Communist leaders chose not to disrupt Communist unity by public discussion of their differences with the Soviet Union on "unequal" treaties and the territorial matter.

In fact, Peking entered into extensive cooperation with Moscow along their common border. The Amur River, marking the northern Manchurian boundary, became the "River of Friendship," and in the friendlier 1950's Chinese and Soviet boats traded across the Argun, Amur, and Ussuri rivers and there were soccer matches. In 1951, Moscow and Peking established the joint Sino-Soviet Commission for Navigation on Boundary Rivers, which was to set up navigational procedures and to supervise shipping along the Amur, Ussuri, Argun, and Sungacha rivers and Lake Khanka. These were the waterways separating China's northeastern provinces from the Soviet Far East.[31] Between 1951 and 1967 the commission met fifteen times, alternately in Chinese and Soviet territories. In August 1956 the two countries negotiated an agreement on the joint investigation and comprehensive utilization of natural resources in the Amur valley, including the planning and building of a 13-million-kilowatt system of hydroelectric power.[32] In December 1957 they also signed a new friendly agreement aimed at simplifying the rules governing commercial navigation and shipping on border rivers and lakes.[33] The agreement provided for the full reciprocal navigation rights of the two countries in border areas, and restrictions on movement of crew and passengers were kept to a minimum.[34] No restriction was placed on carrying weapons or on using radio or radar. As Harald Munthe-Kaas correctly notes, "customs and other formalities for ships entering and leaving ports along the border rivers were very lenient and relaxed." [35] The treaty also stipulated that Moscow and Peking should "take measures in providing gratis whatever transit services are possible for the merchant ships of the two countries . . . any time of the day as well as night during the navigation season" and "mutually provide preferential treatment." [36]

Shortly after 1949, in the meantime, Chinese dissatisfactions with the present Sino-Soviet frontiers in Asia were manifested in many directions.

Numerous maps published in China under Communist rule provided evidence that the Chinese Communists had not abandoned China's traditional interest in the "lost territories" in Asia.[37] For example, a Chinese history textbook published in 1954 contained a map that showed China's old frontiers as including a large part of the Soviet Far East, parts of Kirgizia, Tadzhikistan and Kazakhstan as far west as Lake Balkhash, and other areas in Asia, e.g., Assam, Burma, Thailand, Bhutan, Sikkim, Laos, Vietnam, Korea, and such far-off bits as the Sulu Islands.[38] This map undoubtedly alarmed some Russians and many Asians, particularly Indians. Contending that the map was an unofficial one, the work of historians, China officially disassociated itself from the 1954 map, but the map continued to circulate. On this matter, the Soviet Union gave the Chinese the ominous silent treatment.

When Nikita S. Khrushchev and Nikolai Bulganin visited Peking in 1954, Mao Tse-tung quietly tried to discuss the status of Outer Mongolia with them but failed to receive any response.[39] In January 1957, Khrushchev again refused to discuss territorial questions concerning Outer Mongolia with Peking's Premier Chou En-lai.[40]

Meanwhile, in the early 1950's, particularly after Stalin's

death in March 1953, China put increasingly heavy pressure on the Soviets to liquidate their economic interests in the Chinese borderlands. During his visit to Peking in October 1954, Khrushchev agreed to relinquish Soviet "special interests" in Sinkiang in the form of the joint-stock companies and to return Dairen and Port Arthur to sole Chinese control by the end of 1955.[41] By 1955, therefore, nothing remained of the Soviet special rights and presence in Manchuria and Sinkiang.

With the elimination of the last vestige of Soviet intrusion into China in 1955, China began to speed up the program already started of establishing firm Chinese control over its borderlands.[42] Northeastern Manchuria (Heilungkiang Province), Inner Mongolia, and Sinkiang—all three areas, significantly, adjacent to the Soviet Union—became the targets of intensive settlement, colonization, Sinification, and economic development.[43] In this connection, a massive migration of Han Chinese from China proper into the remote regions of borderland China was carried out, nomadic minority tribes were resettled, Chinese-style education, culture, and government imposed, and new agricultural and industrial resources exploited.

As mentioned in Chapter 1, Chinese settlement of both Inner Mongolia and Manchuria began in the middle of the nineteenth century. But in the 1950's Chinese colonization had reached massive proportions, and now Peking's ethnic dominance is maintained in the two border areas. As far as Manchuria is concerned, the goal of true ethnic and cultural amalgamation now appears to have been achieved.[44]

An area of 178,996 square miles, Heilungkiang Province in 1957 had a population of 14,860,000 out of the total Manchurian population of 51,500,000 or about 29 percent,[45] while Liaoning Province had 47 percent, and Kirin Province had 24 percent.[46] During the period from 1940 to 1957 Heilungkiang Province had experienced a high rate of population increase, in part as a result of the expansion of agriculture and the development of new resources and industries in northern Manchuria.[47] In 1956, for example, over 26,000 immigrants were reported to have settled in the province.[48] The discovery of the Taching oil field in northwest Heilungkiang in 1958 gave a further big boost to the economic development of the province and brought about the immigration of additional Chinese (both civilian engineers and army veterans) from China proper.[49] According to Peking's official statement, over 100,000 demobilized soldiers of the Chinese People's Liberation Army had been settled along the Amur, Ussuri, and Sungari rivers since the early 1950's.[50]

Like four other regions of Communist China, Inner Mongolia is theoretically an "autonomous region" but, in practice, is under direct control of the central government in Peking.[51] The Mao regime has sought to exercise and formalize its tight grip on the non-Han minority peoples in China.[52] In the early 1950's, Peking bolstered border defense of Inner Mongolia to prevent clandestine penetration by Outer Mongolian agents into the area, accelerated the mass influx of Chinese into the Mongolian minority province, continued to obliterate or suppress Mongolian nationalism, and attempted to assimilate the Mongol minorities into the new Chinese Communist order of things. As a result, the ratio of Han Chinese to non-Han minority races in Inner Mongolia was altered from four to one in 1953 (total population, 6,000,000) to seven to one in 1961 (total population, 9,200,000).[53] China's grip on Inner Mongolia seemed secure in 1960 when the Sino-Soviet ideological conflict came into the open.

Immediately following the relinquishment by the Soviets of their stake in 1955, the Peking regime began to extend Chinese power into Sinkiang by radically transforming it to fit into the new Chinese Communist model as an integral part of China. Peking has always been suspicious of Sinkiang's numerically dominant indigenous Uighurs, Kazakhs, and other Moslem minorities who, historically, have often rebelled against Chinese rule and who have had closer ties with kinsmen across the Soviet border in Kirgizia and Kazakhstan than with the Han racial majority in China.[54] These nomadic Moslem peoples traditionally moved freely over the frontier between Chinese Sinkiang and Soviet Central Asia, mixing with their clans on the Soviet side of the border, with whom they had a common race, language, and history. Accordingly, the Mao regime has been particularly sensitive to the trouble Moscow could stir up in Sinkiang.

In an effort to redistribute Sinkiang's population internally, the Chinese Communist regime has poured a flood of permanent Chinese immigrants, forced as well as voluntary, into almost every corner of the province (i.e., into cities, towns, villages, oases, and pasturelands). Between 1953 and 1965, the population of Sinkiang had risen from 5,000,000 to 7,500,000, with its increment exclusively Chinese.[55] The Chinese component in Sinkiang's population rose from 6 percent (300,000) to 40 percent (3,000,000).[56] In 1965, for the first time in history, the Han Chinese constituted a major population in Sinkiang, as against 5,000,000 Uighurs, Kazakhs, and other Moslem peoples combined.[57] In the same year, however, the local Moslem tribal population in the province still outnumbered the Chinese, despite a harsh Sinification program, and were reportedly Soviet-oriented.

In the 1950's and 1960's Chinese settlers in Sinkiang tended to concentrate along a strategically drawn east-west zigzag line cutting directly across the center of Uighur-Kazakh territory between Lop Nor and the oil fields, where main highways and key cities and oases are found. Chinese are most densely congregated in Urumchi, the capital of Sinkiang, where they form over 50 percent of the population.

Since the mid-1950's, the Peking regime has tried to Sinicize the local Moslem minorities of Sinkiang by modifying their language and customs, regulating their religion, controlling their marriage practices, and surrounding them with Chinese immigrants. Many of the Chinese brought to the province have been socially isolated on state farms, however, and

Peking's efforts to promote intermarriage in relatively integrated areas have reportedly failed to erase the self-conscious local nationalism of the Moslem peoples.

In December 1959, Communist China carried out a language reform in Sinkiang, adopting the Latin alphabet for the local Moslem peoples rather than the Cyrillic used across the border in the Soviet Central Asian republics.[58] This measure was designed partly to set up a wall of separation between the Moslem peoples of Sinkiang and their cousins across the border.

Furthermore, in 1959 the Chinese Communists, bent on the Sinification of Sinkiang and the destruction of the pro-Soviet orientation of the majority of the local Moslem tribes, broke the long-established nomadic and oasis patterns of life by sealing the Sinkiang border off from the Soviet Union and seeking to impose fixed residence on the fiercely independent, rebellious, and nomadic tribesmen.[59] The Chinese troops have since garrisoned the frontier points tightly.

The Sinification of the borderlands intensified the resentment and resistance of the non-Chinese minority population, who felt that their areas had become a "Chinese colony." This tendency was particularly strong in Sinkiang, as well as Tibet.[60] The non-Chinese minority races resisted the imposition of an unfamiliar and often unpleasant Chinese Communist form of government upon them, and also resented Peking's often-manifested "great nation chauvinism" and Chinese attempts to weaken their traditional patterns of life.[61] The continuing existence of the age-old discrimination and oppression served to increase the resentment of the local non-Chinese people.[62] These difficulties seem to have led to the occurrence of major anti-Chinese Moslem rebellions in Sinkiang in 1958, when Mao's Great Leap Forward and the people's communes led to economic distress. These revolts were immediately followed by Peking's heaviest purge of "local nationalists" there, and the large-scale exodus of some 6,000 Uighurs and Kazakhs into Soviet Central Asia in 1962, which exacerbated already deteriorating Sino-Soviet relations.[63] It would not be too wide of the mark to assume that, as Communist China officially charged in September 1963,[64] Soviet intrigue, Soviet agents, Soviet propaganda and machinations may have played a role in these events.

The Soviet Union by no means lost interest in Sinkiang even after Khrushchev's relinquishment of Soviet influence there in 1955. Right after Sino-Soviet relations began to deteriorate in 1960, Moscow reverted to the same tactic that it adopted in 1944—that of exploiting Moslem resentments against the growing chauvinism of Chinese rule. Playing on Moslem hostility to the Chinese, Soviet agents in 1961 encouraged Sinkiang's Moslems to stir up the native groups by comparing their bad treatment under Chinese rule with better conditions in the Soviet Union and exhorted them to move into Soviet territory. In the spring of 1962 about 6,000 Uighurs and Kazakhs fled across the border, impelled not only by poor living conditions but by the disastrous Great Leap Forward and an increasingly oppressive Chinese policy.[65] Chinese attempts to halt the exodus led to riots, deaths, and widespread arrests.[66] Soviet trucks picked up the refugees, while Russian troops sometimes covered their escape. It was during this period that China decided to close the Soviet consulates in Sinkiang, at Urumchi and Kuldja.[67]

After the 1962 events, the border between Chinese Sinkiang and Soviet Central Asia began to become a serious trouble spot between the two Communist giants.

For about a decade following their takeover of China in 1949, the Chinese Communists had no overt border complaints. In the wake of deteriorating Sino-Soviet relations in the early 1960's, however, the respective Communist powers became more nationalistic, and frontier frictions began to develop as the momentous Sino-Soviet split started to widen in other spheres. Therefore, different and conflicting sentiment as well as interests, which had been largely dormant in the first stage of the alliance, have now made themselves increasingly felt in present Sino-Soviet relations.

At first the Sino-Soviet quarrel remained in the realm of

ideology. But as relations deteriorated from friendly alliance into angry polemics, another element entered the picture— China's territorial claims—and the dispute intensified to the point of flare-ups along the frontier. The open break on the territorial (or boundary) issue came on March 8, 1963, as only one symptom of sharper and more fundamental differences between the two Communist powers. At present, the territorial dispute adds fuel to the fires of the hotter Peking-Moscow rancor.

After the Cuban crisis of October 1962, Khrushchev's agreement to withdraw Soviet missiles from Cuba in November 1962 was denounced by Communist China as a reprehensible capitulation before United States "blackmail." The Chinese attacked Khrushchev as an "adventurer" for putting nuclear weapons in Cuba and as a "capitulationist" for then withdrawing them under the American "paper tiger's" nuclear threat.[68] Peking made its strongest public defense of its "hard-line" policy toward the United States and defended the Maoist thesis that war was "necessary." Describing Khrushchev's diplomacy of "peaceful coexistence" as "absurd," the Peking regime said the Soviet backdown in Cuba could only be regarded as "100 percent appeasement, a 'Munich' pure and simple." [69]

In his December 12, 1962, speech to the Supreme Soviet, Khrushchev struck back hard after a Chinese Communist attack on his "adventurism" and "capitulationism" in Cuba, saying that the "American paper tiger" had its "nuclear teeth." To refuse to back down in Cuba, he said, might have invited a thermonuclear war with the United States.[70] At one point in his speech, in an obvious thrust at Communist China, Khrushchev asserted that the "ultra-revolutionary loudmouths," as he called the Chinese Communists, had not "liberated" Hong Kong and Macao.[71] Communist China's concession to the British and Portuguese "colonialists" was, according to him, not "capitulationism" or "a retreat from Marxism-Leninism," but rather the same sort of good common sense he practiced in securing a peaceful solution to the Cuban crisis.

In mid-January 1963 the Communist Party of the United States came to Khrushchev's defense by taking issue with the Chinese Communist position on the Cuban crisis. In its open letter to the Chinese Communist Party, it said:

The Communist Party of the United States regretfully finds it necessary to take sharp public issue with the policy of the Chinese Communist Party in respect to the Caribbean crisis and in respect to its wrong position on peaceful co-existence in general. . . .

One could say at this point that our Chinese comrades, who set an example of flexibility in their heroic struggle for liberation, are even today, correctly, not following the adventurous policy in Taiwan, Hong Kong, and Macao that they advocate for others. Why this double-standard approach? [72]

The Chinese Communist leaders reacted sharply to these counterarguments. In their famous letter of March 8, 1963, addressed to the Communist Party of the United States, but unmistakably meant for Khrushchev, they publicly declared that they would not accept the continuing validity of nine so-called "unequal" treaties of the nineteenth century, by which Chinese territory was ceded to various European powers (including Czarist Russia) and Japan.[73] On that day the editorial of *Jen-min Jih-pao,* the official organ of the Chinese Communist Party, said:

During the hundred or so years preceding the victorious Chinese Communist revolution, the colonial and imperialistic powers—the United States, Great Britain, France, Czarist Russia, Germany, Japan, Italy, Austria, Belgium, the Netherlands, Spain and Portugal—became unreservedly engaged in a campaign of aggression against China. They imposed on the various regimes of the old China numerous unequal treaties: the Treaty of Nanking in 1842, the Treaty of Aigun in 1858, the Treaty of Peking in 1860, the Treaty of Ili in 1881, the Convention for the Extension of Hong Kong in 1898, the Treaty of 1901, etc. . . . By virtue of these unequal treaties, they annexed Chinese territory in the North, South, East and West; or they caused territories to be ceded to them on lease along the coast of China and even in the Chinese heartland. . . . When the People's Republic of China was founded in 1949, our government clearly stated its intention of eventually reexamining all the treaties concluded by previous Chinese regimes with foreign governments and according to their respective texts either recognizing, denouncing, revising, or renegotiating them at the appropriate time.

You are not unaware that such questions as those of Hong Kong and Macao relate to the category of unequal treaties left over by history, treaties which the imperialists imposed on China. It may be asked: in raising questions of this kind, do you intend to raise all questions of unequal treaties and have a general settlement? Has it ever entered your heads what the consequences would be? Can you seriously believe that this will do you any good? [74]

As already seen in the previous chapter, three of these nine "unequal" treaties listed above were imposed by Czarist Russia—in 1858, 1860, and 1881. These three treaties have defined important sections of the present Sino-Soviet border in the Asian heartland for almost a century. Therefore, Peking's public declaration of March 8, 1963, clearly indicated that the Chinese would lay historical claims to the southeastern part of Siberia, the Maritime Province and at least 500,000 square miles of Central Asia, which are now ruled by the Soviet Union but which were wrested from Imperial China by the Russian czars in the nineteenth century. The Chinese asserted that their territorial losses deriving from the old "unequal" treaties were the "outstanding issues" which, when the conditions were ripe, should be settled peacefully through negotiations, and that pending a settlement the status quo of the present border should be maintained.[75]

Peking subsequently demanded a blanket admission from Moscow for the public record that the present Sino-Soviet boundary is the result of "unequal," and therefore illegal treaties, imposed by the czars.[76] At the same time, it wanted a comprehensive reexamination of the entire question of the Sino-Soviet boundary—although it was prepared to take the existing treaties as a basis for negotiations—and insisted that a new, "equal" treaty should be signed to replace the old, "unequal" ones.[77]

In the fall of 1963 the Soviet Union countered the Chinese claims by denying that the nineteenth-century border treaties were "unequal." The Soviets flatly declared that they had no territorial conflicts with any of their neighboring states.[78] On these grounds, Moscow refused to enter comprehensive boundary negotiations and was only prepared to discuss certain sections along the boundary where disagreements had arisen.[79]

It is an open secret that thousands of border incidents or clashes have taken place between the two Communist powers since March 1963, particularly after the advent of the Cultural Revolution in 1966. Up to the bloody armed clashes in the Ussuri River in March 1969, however, both sides had apparently believed it prudent not to play up or publicize these incidents to the delight of the outside "capitalist press."

The first major border trouble flared on September 6, 1963, when Peking publicly charged that Moscow had carried on "large-scale subversive activities in the Ili region of Sinkiang and enticed and coerced several thousands of Chinese citizens [Moslems] into going to the Soviet Union in April and May 1962." [80]

On September 23, 1963, the Soviet Union replied to the above Chinese charge and published its version of the border incidents of 1962 in Sinkiang.[81] It said that about 6,000 Uighurs and Kazakhs had fled to the Soviet Union, partly because of the famine in Sinkiang and partly because of Peking's anti-Moslem discrimination and persecution, and had been given asylum.[82] It charged that the Chinese Communists themselves had "systematically" violated the Soviet border in Central Asia about 5,000 times in 1962 alone to halt the exodus of Moslem refugees and warned that if they continued on their present course of illegal trespass, they could expect a "most vigorous rebuff" from the Soviet Communist Party and the Soviet people.[83]

Immediately following this event, Sinkiang became the focus of harsh propaganda warfare between Moscow and

Peking, and both sides reinforced their garrisons in the border regions. Soviet propaganda spoke of arbitrary evacuation of the local Moslem people from their centuries-old homelands and subsequent resettlement of them into concentration camps in lifeless deserts, of persecution of minority leaders, armed suppression of the native population, and cruel Sinification of the province.[84] Since 1962 Moscow has been inciting anti-Chinese ferment among the Moslem minority groups in the area, even to the extent of openly promoting a Free Turkestan movement aiming for the "liberation" of Sinkiang from China. Activities of this secessionist movement, which has been set up in, and operating out of, Alma-Ata, capital of the Soviet Central Asian republic of Kazakh, adjoining Sinkiang, have been stepped up with the deterioration of Sino-Soviet relations in the early 1960's.[85] According to a refugee leader from Sinkiang, Isa Yusuf Alptekin, who is now president of the Eastern Turkestan Refugee Association with its headquarters in Istanbul, the Soviet Union recently set up a secret military school for Moslem refugees to teach them guerrilla warfare, commando tactics, and public administration.[86] The Moscow-supported 60,000-man Moslem refugee army, called the Turkestan Liberation Army, includes members of the former Sinkiang Fifth Corps Army who fled to the Soviet Union during a major anti-Chinese uprising in 1962. The army is led by Zunum Taipov, a Uighur, who was one of the leaders of the Moslem revolt of 1944 against the Chinese Nationalist regime. A former major general in the Chinese Communist army, he also defected to the Soviet Union in 1962.[87]

China accused the Soviet Union of fomenting large-scale subversion and sabotage in Sinkiang, occupying more Chinese territory, provoking border incidents, spreading big lies about the leadership of the Chinese Communist Party, and distorting the history and conditions of Sinkiang through press and radio. China warned the Soviets not to "dare to stretch out their evil hands" to the province.[88] As border incidents increased along the northwestern section of the Sino-Soviet boundary in recent years, Peking sent substantial troop reinforcements to Sinkiang in 1964 and fortified a buffer zone along hundreds of miles of the troubled border to seal its frontiers against the flight or reentry of Moslem insurgents and against the entry of foreign agents, and above all to prevent extensive contacts between domestic dissidents and potential foreign supporters. It should be noted that Sinkiang is particularly important to China as a uranium-rich province and as the home of its nuclear testing grounds (at Lop Nor) and its missile range.

In 1963, Communist China was undoubtedly not serious about pressing claims to its "lost territories" actively (or by military means), given Moscow's wealth of nuclear weapons, missiles, and bombers. Instead, it decided to use the border dispute as a major anti-Soviet political propaganda weapon to achieve five objectives.

First, Peking attempted to put Moscow on the defensive by portraying itself before the eyes of other "fraternal" Communist countries and parties, as well as of many anti-Communist countries, as the victim of Soviet duplicity in every field.

Second, Communist China intended to inflame or provoke the irredentist passions of other Communist and non-Communist countries, such as Japan, West Germany, Poland, Rumania, and Finland, which had actual or potential territorial disputes with Moscow.[89] At the same time, the Chinese Communists sought to put the Soviets in a tight spot by generating a series of similar border conflicts between Moscow and the above-mentioned non-Soviet powers. In addition, they perhaps attempted to appeal subtly and implicitly to these non-Soviet countries for the formation of a united front against Moscow. Curiously enough, the only support for Communist China in this effort came from a rightist and militantly anti-Communist Munich newspaper, *Deutsche National Zeitung und Soldaten Zeitung*.[90]

Third, the Chinese Communist leaders desired to demonstrate to the Afro-Asian world that the Soviets were the direct successors of Czarist Russia and also were merely another group of the white colonialists in Asia. No doubt, this move was intended to put the Soviets on a par with the Western colonial powers in the eyes of the anticolonial Afro-Asian countries, to isolate Moscow diplomatically from the "nonaligned" third bloc.

Fourth, the territorial dispute also served Peking's internal psychological and political needs. The Mao regime could utilize it to arouse a strong anti-Soviet anger in the Chinese people and also to amplify the old Manchu image of foreign "white devils" by playing on their nationalistic and chauvinistic sentiments. Also, it would unify the country and make Peking's task of border consolidation a lot easier.

Fifth, the Chinese perhaps also hoped to check Soviet intrigues and subversion among the non-Han population of Sinkiang by emphasizing their claims and grievances against the Soviet Union.

On December 31, 1963, Khrushchev addressed a letter to heads of state and governments, calling for all countries to sign a new international treaty renouncing the use of force to resolve territorial disputes or border problems.[91] This proposal was clearly made with the Sino-Soviet territorial dispute in mind.

Peking could not afford to give Moscow the propaganda edge. One and one half months later, China and the Soviet Union agreed to negotiate their boundary questions. The first open reference to such talks came when Peking's Premier Chou En-lai told Edgar Snow on January 23, 1964, that "we [the Chinese] have reached an agreement with the Soviet Union that negotiations be held on Sino-Soviet boundary questions." [92] The Chinese Communist Party's open letter to the Soviet Communist Party on February 29 said that the two Communist powers had started boundary negotiations in Peking on February 25, 1964.[93] The letter also said that Communist China was willing to take the old "unequal" treaties as the basis for Sino-Soviet border discussions.[94]

Before the Sino-Soviet border negotiations of 1964 started, Communist China had signed boundary agreements with Burma,[95] Outer Mongolia,[96] Nepal,[97] Pakistan,[98] and Afghanistan.[99] India and the Soviet Union were the only two neighboring countries with which the Peking regime failed to sign a new boundary agreement by early 1964.

Evidence suggests that the 1964 border negotiations were broken off without any tangible result. This was publicly confirmed by both the Soviet Union and Communist China in March 1969.[100] The border negotiations were not resumed until October 1969. The two countries had started from fundamentally different premises on a border settlement and complete deadlock was a foregone conclusion. Peking was understood to have demanded a comprehensive reexamination of the entire Sino-Soviet boundary, but Moscow appeared to have insisted on a narrower formula under which the negotiations would be confined strictly to minor adjustments of the frontier. This was confirmed by Mikhail Suslov's report to the Central Committee of the Soviet Communist Party on February 14, 1964, in which he said in part:

The Soviet government has taken the initiative in the holding of consultations relating to defining the frontier between the Soviet Union and Communist China on certain of its sections. In doing so, we proceed from the fact that no territorial disputes exist between the two Communist countries, that the Soviet-Chinese border developed historically and that there can be a question only of a certain clarification of the border where this may be necessary.[101]

Even before the 1964 border negotiations ended in failure, Chairman Mao Tse-tung entered the dispute himself publicly for the first time. He attacked the Soviet Union for its "territorial ambitions and expansionism" in Asia and Europe in his July 10, 1964, interview with a delegation of the Japanese Socialist Party in Peking. In this interview, he said:

There are too many places occupied by the Soviet Union. In accordance with the Yalta agreement, under the pretext of assuring the independence of [Outer] Mongolia, in fact the Soviet Union brought this country under its domination. Mongolia occupies a far greater area than the Kurile Islands. In 1954 when Khrushchev and Bulganin came to China, we raised this question but they refused to talk to us. They have misappropriated part of Rumania. In cutting off part of East Germany, they drove the local population into West Germany. In detaching part of Poland, they included it into Russia and as compensation they gave Poland part of East Germany. The same thing happened in Finland. They detached everything that could be detached. Some people have said that the Province of Sinkiang and territory to the north of the Amur River should be included in the Soviet Union. The Soviet Union is concentrating troops on her frontier.

The Soviet Union occupies an area of 22 million square kilometers, while its population is only 200,000,000. It is time to put an end to this allotment. Japan occupies an area of 379,000 square kilometers, and its population is 100,000,000. About a hundred years ago the area to the east of Baikal became Russian territory and since then Vladivostok, Khabarovsk, Kamchatka, and other areas have become Soviet territory. We have not yet presented our bill for this list. As regards the Kurile Islands, for us the answer is clear. They should be returned to Japan.[102]

Peking's Premier Chou En-lai reechoed Mao's position on the territorial matter, in his July 19, 1964, interview with a Mr. Osaka, a Socialist member of the Japanese Diet.[103]

The Mao interview with the Japanese Socialist delegation was not published in Communist China. But the Soviet Union published it, along with a violent rejoinder of its own.[104] In reply to Mao's irritating statement of July 1964, Moscow countercharged that Mao's territorial demand was reminiscent of those of his "predecessor" (obviously Hitler) for *Lebensraum*.[105] The pro-Soviet Outer Mongolian leaders also attacked the Mao statement along the same line presented by Moscow.[106]

Khrushchev lost no time in replying to the Mao interview personally. In his September 15, 1964, interview with members of a Japanese parliamentary delegation in Moscow,

Khrushchev said that if Czarist Russia had been expansionist, so had been the Middle Kingdom that seized Mongolia, Tibet, and Sinkiang.[107] He himself singled out Sinkiang for special comment and said:

> Let us take Sinkiang for example. Have the Chinese been living there from time immemorial? The Sinkiang indigenous population differs sharply from the Chinese ethnically, linguistically, and in other respects. They are Uighurs, Kazakhs, Kirghizes, and other peoples. Chinese emperors conquered them in the past and deprived them of their independence.

He not only defended the right of Outer Mongolia to independence, but hinted that Inner Mongolia was a Chinese colony. As he saw it, the Chinese-Russian frontiers were a product of imperialist history. The imperialism of the czars and the imperialism of the Chinese emperors should cancel each other out.

Though the Chinese Communists attributed the Sino-Soviet conflict and the border troubles to Khrushchev, they fared no better with his successors. During 1965, Khrushchev's successors seemed to be conciliatory toward Peking, and the Sino-Soviet frontiers appeared to be quiet. But frontier tensions began to aggravate with the advent of Mao Tse-tung's anti-revisionist (anti-Soviet) Cultural Revolution. The Cultural Revolution reduced what was left of Sino-Soviet relations to ashes. Border incidents, always frequent, were reported in the thousands by both sides.

The Cultural Revolution extended into the Chinese borderlands, and during its initial Red Guard stage many native leaders in Inner Mongolia, Tibet, and Sinkiang who had achieved important rank as Communists were purged partly on the charge of having promoted "counterrevolutionary nationalism." [108] At the same time, Peking accelerated the Sinification, continued to obliterate "local bourgeois nationalism," and reinforced its border defense against Soviet intrigue, subversion, and sabotage.

Soon after the Cultural Revolution started in mainland

China, the incidents of conflict were frequent along the Sino-Soviet boundary, particularly along the river boundaries between Manchuria and the Soviet Far East (i.e., along the Amur and the Ussuri) and in the northwestern section between Sinkiang and Soviet Central Asia.

Peking abandoned joint efforts to develop the resources of the Amur valley in contravention of its agreement with Moscow of August 1956. It also virtually scrapped the 1957 Sino-Soviet agreement on boundary and transit services by merchant ships on border rivers and lakes.[109] In the spring of 1966 the Peking regime promulgated a set of unilateral regulations governing foreign (mostly Soviet) vessels on the border rivers. These regulations were undoubtedly intended to reduce drastically, if not to stop altogether, Sino-Soviet cooperation in the border regions.[110] These new regulations were apparently designed partly to irritate Soviet ships, because they were required to fly the Chinese flag when they were entering a Chinese river port, and partly to create friction with Soviet citizens, because the crew and passengers of Soviet vessels were forbidden to take photographs, make maps, or take soundings; they were also forbidden to swim, fish, or hunt on the Chinese side of the border rivers and in Chinese ports.[111] The fourteenth regular meeting of the joint Sino-Soviet Commission for Navigation on Boundary Rivers was not held as scheduled in 1967. According to Moscow, Peking simply wrecked this conference.

During the early stage of the Cultural Revolution, many Red Guards had moved into Sinkiang and organized mass rallies there to demand the return of China's "lost territories." [112] In 1966, as a security measure, Peking cleared a twelve-mile border strip along the Sinkiang border and pumped in Chinese immigrants to farm—and defend—the territory.[113] In early 1967, Communist China denied overflight rights to the Soviet government airline Aeroflot over Sinkiang and Tibet.[114] It also organized several so-called production and construction corps, made up of 50,000 to 60,000 men each.[115] While these corps concentrate on opening new lands to cultivation, building roads, and reforestation, they also have weapons and operate under the control of the Chinese People's Liberation Army.

In 1966 the Soviets used troops to evict Chinese squatters who had moved to some of the disputed islands in the Amur River on the northeast border of Manchuria, near the city of Khabarovsk.[116] As soon as the Cultural Revolution started in 1966, all Soviet border zones were normally closed to persons without special permission, and residents near the borders were instructed to be on the alert for suspicious activities. When Nikolai Podgorny, a member of the top echelon of the Soviet hierarchy, visited Khabarovsk on June 1, 1966, he implicitly warned Peking against any attempt to seize chunks of Siberia by force.[117]

When the Red Guards unleashed a new wave of political and religious persecution in Sinkiang in late 1966 and thus created unrest and disorder in this sensitive province, Moscow decided to take advantage of the turbulence. The Soviets began to publish lurid accounts of Chinese persecution of the province's Moslem minorities. They increased their propaganda appeals to disaffected Moslems to defect to the Soviet Union. It is reported that during 1966 about 200,000 Moslems fled from Sinkiang to Soviet territory.[118] In some instances, Moscow encouraged Soviet-based Moslem guerrillas to raid Chinese frontier posts in Sinkiang. According to a refugee leader from the province, the Soviet-supported Moslem refugee army made 5,000 guerrilla raids into the Sinkiang area in 1966 alone.[119]

In an effort to seal the escape route across the Tien Shan mountain range, the Chinese rushed more and more troops to the Sinkiang border. The Soviet Union also moved several divisions to the area to counterbalance the Chinese military buildup and retain an edge over the Chinese in the psychological warfare now waged by both sides in Central Asia.

When the Cultural Revolution started, the Soviet Union's

position on its territorial dispute with China was unmistakably clear; it was prepared to uphold the historical validity of the present Sino-Soviet boundary at all costs. On October 29, 1966, Moscow announced its plan to build a showcase city on the Soviet frontier quite near Communist China. It said that the city of Blagoveshchensk, just across the Amur River from Chinese territory, would have factories and skyscrapers by 1970,[120] indicating Soviet confidence that any Chinese threat to the area could be safely contained. The expansion of Blagoveshchensk undoubtedly underlined Soviet determination to control and develop the Soviet Far East, despite Peking's territorial claims to the area.

On December 15, 1966, the Soviet government announced that its military budget for 1967 would total 14.5 billion rubles ($16 billion), up 1.1 billion rubles ($1.22 billion) over 1966.[121] This was 13.2 percent of the total national budget for 1967. An increase in the military budget for 1967 was also partly to cover increasing Soviet military aid to North Vietnam. Although Moscow officially blamed "aggressive" United States policies and the war in Vietnam, its announcement of an 8.2 percent increase in defense spending for 1967 was undoubtedly related partly to strengthen defense along the Sino-Soviet boundary.

In July 1967, Moscow adopted a special nine-year economic plan for developing Siberia, and the execution of this extraordinary regional economic development plan was emphasized as a top priority. In connection with this project, the west Siberian "capital" of Novosibirsk was being developed into a "science city" (or "academic village," as the Soviets call it) with an elite population of 30,000 grouped in twenty scientific and technological institutes and a university that would recruit the country's most talented youth.[122] The institutes housed not only an atomic reactor, cyclotron accelerator, vast computers and other glamour equipment, but also some of the Soviet Union's keenest minds.[123] The academic village of Novosibirsk, which was formerly the Siberian division of the Soviet Academy of Sciences, already has a dozen branches throughout Siberia (including a virtual second center at Irkutsk, grouping eight existing institutes).[124] Now Soviet scientists from Novosibirsk and Leningrad are at work creating a new academic village for the Soviet Pacific region at Vladivostok.[125]

In the mid-1960's, by and large, the Soviet Union was displaying conspicuous haste in planning to develop the vast and thinly populated region of Siberia by pouring in substantial amounts of capital and a large number of people. This policy clearly indicated the Soviet Union's long-term goal to turn Siberia into a bastion against the Chinese. The long-term potential of Siberian development is enhanced by the fact that the area's mountains, tundras, and steppes are extraordinarily rich in minerals (especially gold), timber, and hydroelectricity. Its diamond mines are believed to be richer than those of South Africa.

Only 15 percent of the Soviet population lives in Siberia. For the past decade, the Kremlin has made feverish efforts to attract a large number of permanent settlers, particularly technicians and laborers, to Siberia by giving them bonuses and other inducements. This policy has had very limited success, however, due chiefly to Siberia's extremely cold weather, inadequate living conditions, shortage of food and consumer goods, and poor cultural facilities and services. People apparently still find the area a place of barren, often frozen exile. According to *Pravda*'s January 28, 1970, report, four million people went to develop Siberia in the past seven years—and four million got fed up and left there.[126] This exchange cost the Soviet Union nearly a billion rubles.[127] As of this writing, the Soviet government nevertheless still continues to encourage migration to Siberia, but without good result.

Partly for the above reason, and partly because Siberian development is too costly for the overtaxed Soviet economy to bear alone, the Soviets in recent years were doing their utmost to lure Japanese involvement in an ambitious program for the joint development of Siberia.[128] Obviously, this move was politically motivated as well; that is to say, one aim of the Soviet leaders was to build up and use Japan as a countervailing force and partner in Siberia against possible future encroachments by China. In the summer of 1966, in fact, they were very receptive to Japanese proposals for joint development of natural resources and industry in Siberia, including an oil pipeline to the vast coast of the Sea of Japan. In August 1968, Moscow and Tokyo concluded a major new agreement for joint development in Siberia.[129] According to the terms of this agreement, Japanese banks would grant a $133 million five-year loan (mostly in machinery and equipment) at the annual interest rate of 5.8 percent to enable the Soviets to develop Siberian timber-cutting. In addition, a consortium of thirteen Japanese companies, including such big trading firms as Mitsui and Mitsubishi, would be allowed to sell $30 million worth of consumer goods to Soviet settlers in Siberia. As repayment of the loan and to cover its interest, the Soviet Union would ship eight million cubic feet of timber to Japan over a five-year period.

This agreement may be the first step in a much broader joint development undertaking in Siberia, possibly to include oil, iron, and coal. In fact, the Soviet Union was already proposing that Japan might like to lend another $40 million to build a pipeline from Siberia's Okha oil fields to the Sea of Japan and perhaps to participate in a $1.2 billion program to develop copper mines near Lake Baikal. Japan, which is poorly endowed with raw materials and forced to import oil from the Middle East and copper from Africa, will probably be interested in these and other ventures.

The Soviet-Japanese accord of August 1968 will no doubt have far-reaching political as well as economic significance. Not surprisingly, the Peking regime attacked the Soviet opening of Siberia to Japanese investment.[130] It said that the Soviet Union and Japanese "monopolists" were cooperating

in "filthy" conspiracy to encircle the Chinese on their northern flank.[131] Furthermore, China contended that Soviet-Japanese "collusion" in Siberia was part of a gigantic anti-Chinese
conspiracy, in which the United States was deeply involved.

Immediately following the ruthless Soviet invasion of
Czechoslovakia in August 1968, the nervous Mao regime
reinforced its border regions with more regular troops. The
Chinese Communists appear to have been badly shaken by the
Soviet occupation of Czechoslovakia and the accompanying
Moscow enunciation of the Brezhnev Doctrine, which says
that the Soviets can afford to proclaim their own right to
decide when the common interests of Communism are in
danger in any allied Communist countries, and to use military
intervention to forestall such danger.[132] Peking seemed quite
worried that the Soviets, who were nagged by the nightmare
of Chinese hordes pouring into vacant Siberia in search of
living space, might stage a similar military thrust or even a
preemptive nuclear strike against the Chinese mainland on
the same grounds that the Kremlin employed to justify the
subjugation of Prague.

Since the increase of anti-Soviet virulence in Communist
China generated by Mao's radical Cultural Revolution, the
Soviet Union had been preparing for the possibility of a
serious armed clash with Peking in the regions along the
border. After late 1965, the Kremlin leaders launched a major
indoctrination campaign to dispel any lingering doubts of
Soviet citizens about the gravity of Peking's current anti-
Soviet anger and the possibility that dangerous events would
lie ahead along the Sino-Soviet boundary.[133] The Soviet propaganda machine was also making increasing references to the
"great khan chauvinism" of the Chinese and trying to create
a sense of another "Yellow Peril" in the minds of the Soviet
people. Soviet officials in the frontier areas continued to drop
unambiguous hints in public speeches about a connection
between Communist China's Cultural Revolution and the
threatened security of the Soviet frontier. From the Soviet

border areas came reports of intensified military training for the civilian population, and a campaign was under way to rally patriotic sentiment and to sharpen military preparedness among the people of the Soviet Union's three Central Asian Republics—Kazakhstan, Tadzhikistan, and Kirgizia.[134]

Before the spring of 1969, by and large, both Moscow and Peking had faced each other across their long boundary with a continual risk of incidents and armed incursions. Then, bloody border clashes between the two Communist giants suddenly took place in the Ussuri River in March 1969.

CHAPTER 3

The Ussuri Border Clashes of March 1969 and Thereafter

After thousands of minor border incidents and provocations had taken place, the Sino-Soviet boundary finally burst into flames in March 1969, and the world was treated to the spectacle of the two giant, "peace-loving, Socialist champions of the oppressed" shooting it out over a tiny island in a frozen river at the far reaches of their territories.

As expected, each side accused the other of being the aggressor. Needless to say, it was in the interest of each side to portray the other's belligerence in lurid terms. From the totally conflicting accounts, it is impossible to tell precisely what happened on the disputed island of Damansky, or Chenpao, in the Ussuri River on March 2, 14, and 15, 1969. (See Introduction.)

The size of the forces involved—there were several hundred men—demonstrated without doubt that the border episode of March 1969 in the Ussuri River was something beyond a purely routine border patrol. The speed of complaints showed that the Soviet Union and Communist China were both alert to possible border trouble.

Only Moscow had offered the world a reasonably detailed —but doubtless in part self-serving—account.[1] The shifts in Moscow's version of the armed border clashes tended to invite suspicion. In their first official protest, the Soviets spoke of having been attacked by "200 Chinese soldiers," but the Moscow press later amended this to an armed "crowd" of people and finally a Soviet Foreign Ministry account claimed that 330 Chinese troops were involved, with another 200 hidden in ambush.[2]

Peking's version was at least consistent, and it did not stoop to self-serving atrocity stories such as those published by the Soviet Union.[3] The cocky Chinese Communists, however, were not innocents. They were quite capable of starting an incident or of goading the Soviets to open fire.

The scene of the Sino-Soviet armed border clashes in March 1969 was an inhabited island in the ice-bound Ussuri River. The Amur and Ussuri rivers, which wind 2,000 miles along the eastern part of the Sino-Soviet boundary, are dotted with hundreds of small islands. Some belong to the Soviets, some to the Chinese, and many are disputed. This island, a mile long and a third of a mile wide, was not identified on the most detailed maps available up to that time. To complicate matters, it had two names: Damansky, the Russian name, and Chenpao ("Treasure"), the Chinese.

The riverine boundaries in the eastern sector of the Sino-Soviet border area are clear in their general alignment, but create some problems and disputes because nature plays tricks by making the Amur and Ussuri rivers change course.

The Ussuri River, for example, is about half a mile wide and forms part of the eastern frontier between Manchuria and the Soviet Far East, meandering northward through a broad, sparsely populated flood plain between ranges of low hills. It freezes over in winter. In spring, when the ice melts again, the Ussuri rampages and regularly floods its low-lying banks, shifting its main navigation channel, abandoning old river arms, changing the location of islands in the river, flooding old islands, and forming new ones that change configuration from year to year. As a result, frequent navigational disputes and the problem of the ownership of many small islands at the confluences in the Ussuri River arise from the lack of agreeable point control. This was one of the causes of the March 1969 armed border clashes.

The disputed island, Damansky (or Chenpao), is one of many islands created by the meandering of the Ussuri River, which has frequently changed its course since the frontier between Manchuria and the Soviet Maritime Province was delineated in 1860. As seen in Chapter 1, the Ussuri River became the border between Czarist Russia and Manchu China under the Treaty of Peking in 1860. By the terms of the treaty the Manchu Chinese ceded all the land east of the Ussuri to the Russians. This old treaty took no account of the shifting water course and the consequent question of jurisdiction over some islands. Hence the course of the boundary in the Ussuri River was never precisely delimited. The treaty referred only to lands on the north and the south bank but never to the river itself. That is to say, quite contrary to the Chinese Communist contention that the Peking treaty of 1860 awarded Damansky, or Chenpao, Island to Manchu China,[4] the island itself and a number of others in the meandering Ussuri were not assigned to either country by the treaty, and have been in dispute for many years.

According to established principles of international law in the case of navigable boundary rivers, the middle of the main channel or strongest current downstream, known technically as the *thalweg* in international law,[5] forms the boundary line. But the difficulty with meandering rivers subject to flood, such as the Ussuri, is that—aside from disagreement as to which arm of the river constitutes the main navigable channel—the *thalweg* may shift over a period of time, changing the location of islands and thus bringing the issue of their sovereignty into question. This may explain why Damansky/Chenpao is claimed by both the Soviet Union and Communist China. Peking recently asserted that in 1964 the Kremlin had acknowledged that the island was Chinese territory, but the Soviets denied that they had made any such admission.[6]

They insisted that they would yield no territory to Communist China.

By and large, a new and detailed treaty defining the precise alignment of the riverine boundaries in the eastern sector of the Sino-Soviet borderlands and providing for the regulation of traffic, customs, water rights, and ownership of many islands at the confluences in these rivers is an obvious necessity. Given goodwill, teams of surveyors, and sufficient patience and time, agreement could be reached easily on many disputed tiny islands in the Ussuri and Amur rivers. But there has been only shouting, spitting, and animosity backed by quickly available military force, and the islands have become a perfect seedbed for trouble. Indeed, the bloody border clashes over a useless piece of real estate in the Ussuri River were a good indication of the frigid relations prevailing between Moscow and Peking in March 1969.

Western diplomats had no precise information as to who was the guilty party in the armed clashes. According to a recent annual survey of the Institute of Strategic Studies in Great Britain, it was the Chinese who initiated the fighting at Chenpao, or Damansky, Island on March 2, 1969, seemingly in reaction to a long period of harassment in the area by the Soviets. And following the initial attack, according to the report, indications are that Moscow's counterattack was responsible for the subsequent border clashes. The Soviet reaction was apparently intended to teach the Chinese a lesson and to provoke a war of nerves with them.

But more significant than precisely who did what to whom was the lavish way in which both Moscow and Peking put these incidents to propaganda use in the noisiest exchange of public insults and recriminations since their ideological split erupted in 1960. Up to March 1969, both sides had played down thousands of border clashes. Suddenly, however, they decided to play up the Ussuri incidents and give them world attention instead of suffering them in silence. In politics, timing is very important.

Rather than letting tempers cool, the two Communist giants had made an extravagant effort to dramatize the Ussuri clashes in their daily newspapers, trading denunciations and striving hard to vilify each other's leaders to the outside world. Throughout China, millions of people had been engaged in the biggest display of national indignation and hatred ever organized against a foreign country. In the Soviet Union, too, one sensed the deep and passionate rage that nations feel only toward their deadly enemies. The massive anti-Chinese demonstrations held in front of the Chinese embassy in Moscow in March 1969 were rated as the largest since the Bolshevik Revolution of 1917. Needless to say, these angry rallies, parades, and demonstrations were carefully choreographed and manipulated by the respective governments.

These vigorous and unprecedented hate campaigns inside the two Communist countries suggested that both sides were making the most of the incidents for domestic and external purposes at the moment. In both countries, it appeared to be politically useful for their leaders to have a monstrous enemy abroad, thereby arousing widespread suspicion that both regimes welcomed the opportunity to solidify things at home and abroad. If this hypothesis is correct, what political advantages did Moscow and Peking expect to extract?

Speculation as to Moscow's motives can cover a wide area of possibilities. Any or all of the following speculations may be valid:

1. For the Soviets, who were anxious to build European Communist sympathy and support for the international Communist conference scheduled for June 1969, the March border clashes offered proof of Chinese intransigence, and the Soviet Union wanted to turn the conference into a forum to expel the Chinese from the world Communist movement.

2. Many hawkish Soviet politicians and generals in recent years have toyed with the idea of solving the "Chinese problem" once and for all by a quick attack or a war. Accord-

ingly, the Kremlin hawks may have staged a provocation aimed at providing an excuse for at least a limited preemptive attack on Communist China, possibly with a view to destroying Peking's nuclear installations in Sinkiang and overturning the Mao Tse-tung regime.

3. Moscow perhaps wanted to utilize the Ussuri clashes to mobilize Soviet opinion and to blacken China's name abroad. It could also use the clashes as evidence before the world that an obstinate Maoist China was a major threat to world peace.

4. The Soviet Union was deeply worried about Berlin, where in early 1969 East Germany was harassing traffic on the western access route to the city and also threatening to embroil Moscow in a showdown with the United States. One way to get off that limb without excessive loss of face was to murmur that the Soviets wanted to get tough with the West over the provocation the West Germans had caused by electing a president in West Berlin. Yet they could not act because of the aggressive and uncontrollable force of Peking threatening in the rear.[7] It is significant to note that the Ussuri River frontier clashes took place just three days before the West German presidential election in West Berlin. Perhaps the Soviet blasts at the Chinese in connection with the Ussuri clashes were also oblique warnings to the East Germans to restrain their troublemaking activities around Berlin.

5. The Soviets could use the clashes to intimate that Mao and his radical colleagues in Peking were stark raving mad. The Soviets also hoped to use the Ussuri incidents to persuade Communists at home and abroad that Peking was flirting with "U.S. imperialism" [8] because the Chinese had timed the border clashes to coincide with the convening of the West German Electoral Assembly in West Berlin.

6. It was apparent in early 1969 that the Soviet ruling elite had lately been divided on a wide range of policy issues.[9] Therefore, it is conceivable and even plausible to argue that

the Soviet leaders, resorting to an old diversionary ploy, chose to escalate border tensions with China in order to paper over their personal differences on Czechoslovakia, Berlin, Stalinism, and other questions.

7. The Soviet Union perhaps provoked the border incidents in an attempt to distract Soviet citizens from their country's domestic problems, and also to deflect their interest from one of 1969's major and still unexplained mysteries—the January 22 shooting at the Kremlin.

8. By condemning the Chinese as aggressors in the Ussuri River skirmishes, Moscow hoped to buy world sympathy for the Russians, and, coincidentally, to dull further the world's continuing, though waning, outrage about the Soviet invasion of Czechoslovakia.

9. For the Soviets, the Ussuri clashes seemed to be useful in their attempt to lessen or head off the likelihood of any rapprochement between Communist China and some Western nations—Canada, West Germany, Italy, and Belgium—which had talked about establishing or had recently established diplomatic relations with Communist China.[10]

Establishment of diplomatic relations with these non-Communist European nations would mean a reduction in Communist China's isolation—a development contrary to the Soviet Union's power-political aims. Therefore, there is good reason to suspect that Moscow's vicious diatribes against Peking and some Soviet ambassadors' promotion abroad of Moscow's harsh, anti-Chinese version of the Ussuri border skirmishes were intended to cause the above-mentioned Western nations some misgivings about new rapprochement with Communist China.

10. It is also likely that the Soviets hoped that their condemnation of the Chinese as aggressors might gain them favor in American public opinion and also raise questions or second thoughts in Washington on the advisability of seeking better Sino-American relations if the price might be a decline in American-Soviet relations.

11. By flexing their muscles at Communist China, the Soviets perhaps attempted to make a favorable impression on Nationalist China, India, and other countries of Asia that had reasons to oppose the Mao regime in Peking. India, for example, also has a territorial dispute with Communist China. Surprisingly enough, the Chinese Nationalists in Taiwan, who sided with Peking during the 1962 Sino-Indian border war, now appeared to be partial to the Soviet Union as well and, more important, were trying to improve their diplomatic relations with the Soviet Union.

12. Moscow possibly believed that continued friction with Communist China along the common frontier might eventually drive a wedge between Mao and the pragmatic and professionally-minded Chinese army officers[11] who wanted at all costs to avoid a disastrous conflict with the Soviet Union. By dramatizing the danger of the possibility of a wider conflict on the Sino-Soviet boundary, especially through its recent rocket-rattling against Peking,[12] Moscow was evidently striving to alarm the senior Chinese army officers who had been troubled by the disastrous effects that Mao's wild Cultural Revolution had on Peking's military capabilities. No doubt the design behind this effort, if pressed far enough, would prompt these officers to oust Mao and come to terms with the Kremlin.

13. It seemed certain that the Kremlin leaders wanted to use the March 1969 border clashes to arouse anti-Chinese animosity in the Soviet Union and also to resurrect the horror of the "Yellow Peril" without actually using the words. Moscow may fear the possibility that China's swelling population may one day spill over into the Soviet territory of Siberia and Central Asia.

Coupled with this, the high-pitched Soviet campaign to depict China as a monstrous and cruel enemy was possibly designed in large measure to prepare the Soviet people for the possibility of more serious border incidents.

China's motives were equally devious. Peking, or whatever faction was directing events, had been in need of a red-hot foreign devil to display to the Chinese people and to any elements favorably inclined toward the Soviet Union, in connection with the Cultural Revolution. Now that American pressure in Vietnam was tapering off, the Chinese Communist leaders might have felt it safer and easier to escalate their feud with Moscow within controlled limits. Mao Tse-tung seemed to be banking on the proposition that the Soviets would not do anything really drastic on the eve of their scheduled meeting with world Communist leaders in June 1969.

1. Like Brezhnev, Mao found it convenient to do a bit of foreign dog-baiting in order to divert the Chinese from the internal chaos caused by the Cultural Revolution—and xenophobia has always been Peking's tonic to put Mao in a position to denounce Soviet supporters or sympathizers as traitors in China.

2. At the same time, by mobilizing millions of Chinese in anti-Soviet demonstrations, Peking appeared to be engaged in a massive effort to depict Communist China as a strongly cohesive nation ready to withstand alien assaults. That is to say, the Sino-Soviet border conflict served as a kind of safety valve for internal Chinese emotions, or as a useful tactic in factional power struggles in Peking.

3. The object of this anti-Soviet exercise was, in part at least, to appeal to Chinese patriotism in hopes of unifying the country, which had been badly disrupted during the past three years by Mao's radical Cultural Revolution.

4. The Maoist radicals in Peking had another and perhaps stronger reason for promoting the anti-Soviet hate campaigns—their army. As a result of the turbulent Cultural Revolution in early 1969, the Mao regime was counting on Defense Minister Lin Piao's army to keep the whole power structure from falling apart. Lin, in turn, was looking for some issue to hold the Chinese People's Liberation Army together. Chairman Mao and Defense Minister Lin (who

was Mao's officially chosen heir) probably thought that they had found an issue in the propaganda line that the Soviet Union, in harness with "U.S. imperialism," was violating China's "sacred territories."

5. In particular, by leaning as heavily as they were on the anti-Soviet theme, the Maoist leadership had evidently desperately sought to attain national cohesion in preparation for the then forthcoming Ninth Congress of the Chinese Communist Party. The Ninth Party Congress had been delayed for many months as a result of internecine political squabbles. The fact that the Ninth Party Congress was held in Peking several weeks after the Ussuri border incidents is highly instructive.

6. Stirring up the nationalistic fervor that spilled blood has provoked is always good for a group battling to stay in power. Accordingly, Peking tried to use the Ussuri incidents at the Ninth Party Congress to show that China was truly surrounded by foes. Furthermore, Peking hoped to emphasize that national unity behind the leadership of Mao Tse-tung was now a necessity as never before. In addition, the Ninth Party Congress was used as a forum for a detailed denunciation of the Soviet Union, for an attack against Soviet revisionism, and, finally, for writing Mao's anti-Soviet line into a new Party constitution.

7. Communist China wanted to present the March 1969 border skirmishes as dramatic proof of the need to carry out Mao's instruction to "grasp revolution and promote production and preparedness against war." The cry in the spring of 1969 was for "concrete actions" in the factories and communes. Workers in the steel, coal, and petroleum industries were exhorted to regard production as the "battle-front against imperialism and revisionism." Peasants were also urged to support frontier guards by "going all-out" to level land and improve farm buildings.

8. By equating Soviet savagery on the Chinese border in March 1969 with the Soviet invasion of Czechoslovakia in

August 1968, the Chinese Communists hoped to convince the Communist bloc and the Afro-Asian countries that the "revisionist renegade clique" in power in Moscow were merely "the new czars," bent on subjugating and exploiting their neighbors and guilty of "big power chauvinism" and "social imperialism." This pitch was evidently timed to influence the outcome of the international Communist conference in Moscow that was to be held in June 1969.

9. Still another Chinese motive was to humiliate the Soviet Union over the recent Berlin crisis by creating a second front in Asia. In so doing, Peking would be able to find a good moment to attack the credibility of the Soviets on anything involving "anti-imperialism" or "anti-Americanism."

10. Peking perhaps calculated that the bloody Ussuri clashes of March 1969 would serve a useful purpose: they would frustrate the current Moscow plan of Siberian development by frightening thousands of Soviet "pioneers" in the area to pack their belongings and flee back to their homes in the European part of the Soviet Union and also by discouraging Japanese capitalists from cooperating with the Soviets for joint development of Siberia's vast economic resources.

11. Rightly or wrongly, the Mao regime seemed convinced that the Kremlin leadership had been divided between the reactionary "revisionists" in power and the "authentic" Marxist-Leninists ("neo-Stalinist" conservatives). By escalating Sino-Soviet border tensions within controlled limits in the spring of 1969, it hoped to help the neo-Stalinists in Moscow to overthrow the Brezhnev-Kosygin regime, for the Soviet neo-Stalinists would be more accommodating with the Chinese Communists if they were to come into power. Thus Peking, as well as Moscow, hoped to use the explosive frontier situation to its advantage in various ways.

On March 29, 1969, Moscow, in calm tones, called on Peking to join in steps to "normalize" the frontier situation and suggested that the two sides resume the border talks that had been broken off in 1964.[13] The Soviets followed up on April 12 with another call for a meeting.[14] These Soviet moves were undoubtedly designed in part to demonstrate to the world that it was China and not the Soviet Union which was aggressive and unreasonable, thereby gaining a distinct propaganda advantage.

No immediate Chinese response came to the Soviet calls for border negotiations. Shortly after the Ussuri border clashes, Peking's posture on the territorial dispute with Moscow had remained adamant. On April 4, China's diplomatic mission in London distributed a map identifying the eastern Soviet cities of Vladivostok and Khabarovsk with the Chinese names of Haishenwei and Poli respectively.[15] In large letters the Amur River was referred to exclusively as the "Heilungkiang River." The map marked out the territory taken from China by Czarist Russia through the old "unequal" treaties and held by the Soviet Union in spite of an apparent pledge by the Soviets in 1920 to return all of it to the Chinese people.

During the spring and summer of 1969 the Mao regime had been showing a mainland Chinese audience numbering scores of millions a new motion picture entitled *The Anti-Chinese Crimes of the New Czars*.[16] The film was a documentary portrayal, from the Chinese point of view, of Russian relations with China concerning boundaries from the seventeenth century through the outbreak of the Ussuri border skirmishes of March 1969. No doubt, the objective of this anti-Soviet propaganda movie was to arouse intense national and chauvinistic emotion against the present Kremlin regime.

On May 11, China suddenly accepted the Soviet proposal of April 26 that the fifteenth regular meeting of the joint Sino-Soviet Commission for Navigation on Boundary Rivers (which had not met since 1967) be held in Khabarovsk in May. However, China made a counter-proposal of mid-June for the date, to allow "good preparations to make the meeting a success." [17] It should be noted that this commission was not empowered to touch on the whole range of disputes over the lengthy Sino-Soviet boundary. Its function was limited to talks on the question of navigation on the Ussuri, Argun, Amur, and Sungacha border rivers and on Lake Khanka. On May 23 the Soviet Union suggested June 18 as the date to begin the fifteenth regular session of the joint commission.

Thus Peking moved to ease slightly the extreme tension that had prevailed along the Sino-Soviet border in the spring of 1969. China's willingness to meet with Soviet delegates in June of that year to discuss navigational problems along the border rivers was the first positive response the Kremlin had received to its pleas for border negotiations since March 29.

But the Mao regime apparently took care not to ease border tension too much. Accordingly, a Chinese statement of May 11 had charged the Soviets with "slander" for having accused Peking of evading participation in the regular meeting of the joint commission in 1967, expressed "doubt" about the extent of Soviet sincerity in convening the forthcoming meeting, referred to the meeting place by its old Chinese name, Poli, rather than its modern Russian name, Khabarovsk, and emphasized Peking's intention to promote and preserve normal navigation on the border rivers.

On May 24 the Chinese expressed a willingness to begin preparations for new general boundary talks as Moscow had suggested on March 29, but they set the condition that the Soviets first had to halt artillery and machine gun fire at various disputed points along the border.[18] It charged that the Russians were continuing to direct their troops to open fire on Chinese soldiers at the site of the March border incidents on Chenpao Island, called Damansky by the Soviets.[19] The Chinese further warned the Soviet Union that they would be ready to fight to a finish rather than bow to what they called Soviet nuclear blackmail and armed provocations.[20]

The keynote of accommodation and reasonableness contained in Peking's replies of May 1969 to the Soviet calls for border talks was apparently intended partly to prevent the Ussuri border clashes from degenerating into full-scale hostilities and partly to disprove Soviet charges that Communist China was so unreasonable and intransigent that it would not even agree to negotiate. In so doing, the Mao regime hoped to block any anti-Chinese resolution at the world Communist conference planned for June 5, 1969, in Moscow, which was boycotted by Peking. Like Moscow, in short, Peking was more interested in swaying world public opinion than in promoting border talks.

On June 7 the Chinese government announced that it had accepted a Soviet proposal of May 23 to reopen meetings of the joint Sino-Soviet Commission for Navigation on Boundary Rivers at Khabarovsk on June 18.[21] It also said that China would send a ten-man delegation led by Chang Chan-teh. The Chinese announcement came as Soviet Communist Party chief Leonid Brezhnev attacked China at the world Communist conference in Moscow.

On June 13 Moscow Radio called on China to resume talks toward normalizing the situation on the border in the next two or three months.[22] The Soviets emphasized their point: in order that a businesslike atmosphere might prevail and that constructive discussions might be held, the border negotiations must be undertaken without any preliminary conditions.[23] The Soviet statement rejected territorial claims contained in the Chinese statement of May 24 as well as what it termed Peking's "slanderous insinuations" against the Soviet people. It called attention to Peking's continuing provocations on Soviet frontiers and the promotion of an "unbridled anti-Soviet campaign" in mainland China.

During the summer of 1969, while the Soviets and the Chinese had managed to hold low-level talks on border river navigation and the stage seemed to have been set for more significant border talks, a new series of border incidents had taken place along the eastern and western sectors of the Sino-Soviet boundary. Then Peking and Moscow exchanged serious charges and countercharges.[24] On June 6, for example, Peking's protest note to Moscow said that during the period

from March 29 to May 31, 1969, Soviet aircraft, including
bombers, fighters, and reconnaissance planes, "wantonly in-
truded into China's airspace for harassment and reconnaissance." [25] It said that Soviet planes had made up to 57 sorties,
and that some planes had penetrated about forty miles into
Chinese territory.[26] On August 19 a protest note from the
Chinese Foreign Ministry was handed to the Soviet Embassy
in Peking. The note asserted that the Soviets had made as
many as 429 provocations along the entire Sino-Soviet border
in June and July, ranging from intrusions of Soviet aircraft
into Chinese territory to ground attacks by troops.[27] On September 10 Moscow countered by charging China with 488
deliberate violations of the Soviet frontier between June
and mid-August.[28] The Soviet statement said that a total of
2,500 Chinese soldiers had participated in the violations. It
offered documentary evidence seized by Soviet frontier guards
from "Chinese provocateurs," and warned that further Chinese encroachments "will be most resolutely rebuffed." [29]

The clash between Moscow and Peking forces on August
13, 1969, along the border between China's Sinkiang Province and Soviet Kazakhstan, in which both sides reported
many dead and wounded, appeared to be the most serious
Sino-Soviet clash since the March 1969 Ussuri incidents. This
battle took place only five days after the two powers, meeting
in the Soviet city of Khabarovsk, had reached an agreement
to carry out, during the 1969 navigation season, certain measures necessary to improve the shipping situation along the
Amur, Ussuri, Argun, and Sungacha rivers and Lake Khanka
—the waterway system that makes up the Far Eastern frontier.[30] Furthermore, the two sides had agreed to meet again
the following year in China. The August 13 battle on the
Sinkiang-Kazakhstan border took place in the vicinity of the
Dzungarian Gates, the ancient traders' pass that had been
the scene of two brief but bitter encounters in June and
July 1969. According to Peking's protest note to Moscow, the
Soviets sent helicopters, tanks, armored vehicles and several

hundred armed troops to intrude deliberately into Sinkiang, wounding and killing many of the Chinese frontier guards.[31]

While it is possible that the border battle of August 13 was a case of accidental escalation, the circumstances suggested that the Soviets took the initiative in deliberately starting the skirmishes. By keeping the Sinkiang-Kazakhstan border stirred up, the Soviet Union wanted to accomplish two limited objectives. They wanted to keep the Chinese off balance—by reminding them that they had soft spots along their Sinkiang border inhabited by many non-Chinese minorities—and they wanted to prevent Peking from starting new trouble along Moscow's more remote and vulnerable Far Eastern border.

Following the battle of August 13, 1969, on the Sinkiang-Kazakhstan border, the Soviet Union stepped up psychological warfare against the Chinese to frighten them out of rash action along the border and also to compel them to enter into meaningful discussions of Sino-Soviet differences, with the implicit threat that the alternative was a nuclear war in which China had everything to lose. At the same time, the Soviets were toying with the idea of preventive nuclear strikes against China's nuclear weapons plants and dropped hints that such strikes had been recommended to the Kremlin leadership by its principal military advisers.

On August 28 a long editorial in *Pravda* for the first time publicly and directly raised the possibility of nuclear war between the Soviet Union and Communist China.[32] The border clashes, it said, were "a link in the chain of hostile actions taken by the Peking leaders, who have not given up their absurd territorial claims against the Soviet Union." [33] "The Maoists' military arsenals are filling up with all the latest weapons," *Pravda* said. "If a war were to break out under present conditions, with the armaments, lethal weapons and modern means of delivery that now exist," a Sino-Soviet war would inevitably involve the use of nuclear weapons and also would not spare a single continent.[34] The *Pravda* editorial solemnly warned that "all attempts to speak to the Soviet

Union in the language of weapons and to encroach on the interests of the Soviet people, who are building Communism, will meet with a firm rebuff." [35]

Shortly after the above *Pravda* editorial was published, Soviet Deputy Defense Minister Matvey Vasilyevich Zakharov raised the specter of a preventive war against China by saying that Soviet action against the Mao-Lin regime might take the form of a surprise blitzkrieg.[36] This undoubtedly indicated that the Kremlin leadership contained many hawkish politicians and generals who were itching for a crack at China.

Then there were unconfirmed reports that in late August 1969 the Soviets had been sounding out Eastern European countries and pro-Soviet Communist parties of the world on what they would think of a preemptive rocket strike by Moscow against Peking's expanding nuclear facilities.[37] There was, however, no report on the responses received.

As part of a broadening war of nerves by Moscow against Peking in September 1969, there appeared a dispatch from Soviet journalist Victor Louis, a controversial correspondent of *The London Evening News* and apparently also a high-ranking operative in the Soviet propaganda apparatus, bluntly stating that Soviet nuclear missiles were already zeroed in on significant areas in China.[38] Louis' dispatch, which undoubtedly reflected the official Kremlin line, said:

Some circles in Eastern Europe are asking why the doctrine [i.e., the Brezhnev Doctrine] that Russia was justified in interfering in Czechoslovakia's affairs a year ago should not be extended to China. Events in the past year have confirmed that the Soviet Union is adhering to the doctrine that socialist countries have the right to interfere in each other's affairs in their own interest or those of others who are threatened.

The fact that China is many times larger than Czechoslovakia and might offer active resistance is, according to these Marxist theoreticians, no reason for not applying the doctrine. Whether or not the Soviet Union will attack Lop Nor, China's nuclear center, is a question of strategy, and so the world would only learn about it afterwards.[39]

Probably echoing the arguments of military circles in Moscow, Louis' dispatch said that the Soviets would prefer using nuclear rockets to manpower.[40]

Indications in the latter half of 1969 were that the Chinese had reacted in the belief that Moscow's threat of a preemptive nuclear strike against their country was genuine. They were clearly worried about the danger of a violent showdown with the Soviet Union.[41] Because of a fanatic Maoist rigidity of self-righteousness, however, Peking was unable or unwilling to back away on the border dispute and in the ideological conflict. In other words, the Peking regime was walking a very tight rope. It could not afford to push Moscow around too much, but it was equally unable to capitulate. China risked Soviet military action in either case—in response to excessive Chinese provocation or in response to evidence of Peking's weakness. To extricate itself from such a painful dilemma, there seemed to be only one solution: to maintain an essentially defensive posture toward the Soviet Union while agreeing to resume border talks simply to buy time to get through a highly dangerous phase in the conflict. That would be in line with one of Mao Tse-tung's dictums: "To defend is directly to preserve oneself but at the same time it is also a means to supplement attack or to prepare to turn to attack." [42]

Soviet Premier Aleksei Kosygin, while returning from Ho Chi Minh's funeral in Hanoi, had made an unannounced detour and held an airport consultation in Peking with his Chinese counterpart, Chou En-lai, on September 11, 1969. The meeting had been hastily arranged at Kosygin's request.[43] Chou and Kosygin agreed in the course of their three-hour talk to resume boundary negotiations and to take other steps to ease frontier tensions.[44]

Following the Kosygin-Chou meeting, frontier incidents on the Sino-Soviet border, which had occurred almost daily during the spring and summer of 1969, virtually ceased. Also, both sides decided to halt for a while their hostile propaganda exchange, which had likewise been intense for months previously.

On October 7, 1969, China announced that an agreement had been reached with the Soviet Union to open negotiations aimed at resolving their bitter border conflict.[45] The Peking announcement said that the negotiations would be held in Peking at the deputy foreign ministers' level at a date still to be decided.[46] The statement was firm but not bellicose and expressed the hope that the Soviet government "will truly take a serious and responsible attitude" toward border negotiations. The border issue should be "settled peacefully," the statement went on, adding, "Even if it cannot be settled for the time being, the status quo of the border should be maintained and there should definitely be no resort to the use of force."[47] The Peking announcement reiterated the Chinese position that China did not demand the outright return of territory that Czarist Russia had annexed in Siberia and Central Asia during the nineteenth century under what the Chinese contended were "unequal" treaties.[48]

The Chinese decision to open border negotiations with Moscow was plainly prompted by Peking's fear that the "hawks" in the Kremlin leadership were preparing to launch a preemptive nuclear strike against mainland China. This point came through quite clearly in Peking's October 7 statement agreeing to talks: "Should a handful of war maniacs dare to raid China's strategic sites in defiance of world condemnation, that will be war, that will be aggression."[49] Plainly reflecting Chinese apprehension at the prospect of Soviet military intervention, the statement said: "There is no reason whatsoever for China and the Soviet Union to fight a war over the boundary question."[50]

It is possible that Moscow's nuclear and military superiority and the Soviet hints of preventive nuclear attacks in the summer of 1969 convinced Peking's moderates, led by Premier Chou En-lai, that the Soviets meant business and that the time had come to face reality and respond to Soviet

Premier Kosygin's conciliatory gesture. Presumably, the moderate faction's advocacy of a more pragmatic, flexible approach to the Soviets was endorsed by some of China's senior military leaders, including Chief of Staff Huang Yung-sheng,[51] who knew very well which side would win in a showdown with the Soviet Union. This helped Chou En-lai's moderate faction to persuade hawkish Peking leaders (Maoist radicals led by Mrs. Mao) to consider a temporary truce in the Sino-Soviet conflict to avert full-scale hostilities. To be sure, in the tug-of-war that has been going on in Peking ever since the Cultural Revolution began in 1966, between a moderate or pragmatic faction and a hard-line radical clique,[52] neither side has yet emerged as the clear and final winner.[53]

The North Vietnamese and the Eastern European Communists, particularly the Rumanians, apparently played a mediating role and pressured Moscow and Peking into healing the breach between them.

A last testament by Ho Chi Minh, released during his funeral in Hanoi, deplored the Sino-Soviet rift and urged the two countries to settle their differences.[54] At the time of Ho's funeral, Hanoi's statements publicly appealed to the Soviets and the Chinese to repair their rupture, and Ho's successors apparently pressured Soviet Premier Kosygin into inviting himself to Peking for a healing of the wounds. After Ho's funeral, Kosygin flew from Hanoi, via Calcutta and Tashkent, to Peking for the surprise meeting with Chinese Premier Chou En-lai which later led to resumption of Sino-Soviet border negotiations.

At the Moscow conference of world Communist leaders held in June 1969, Rumania's President (and Party chief) Nicolae Ceausescu fought successfully against a condemnation of China. In his report to Rumanian Communist Party Congress of August 1969, Ceausescu specifically urged high-level meetings between Moscow and Peking. Earlier, in April 1969, he had indicated that while his country sought continued good relations with the Soviet Union, it would not lend the Soviets military and other support in case of war with China.[55] In the light of these efforts, it was quite likely and logical for Rumania adroitly to seize the opportunity presented by Ho's death and funeral to arrange a high-level Sino-Soviet conference to ease border tensions.[56]

Eastern European Communist leaders reportedly put pressure on Moscow to take the initiative in making at least one more serious effort for resumption of the Sino-Soviet dialogue before the border crisis passed beyond the point of no return. This perhaps prompted Soviet Premier Kosygin to arrange his brief meeting with Chinese Premier Chou En-lai in September 1969 and to deliver a warning to Peking that Soviet patience on the issue of border clashes was wearing thin.

Peking's response to the Soviet bids for border negotiations in October 1969 was undoubtedly designed in part to accomplish one important objective—to prevent too intimate and far-reaching a Soviet-American rapprochement. The Communist Chinese have repeatedly made it clear that they fear "collusion" between Moscow and Washington. Shortly after Peking's October 7 statement, in fact, the Mao regime began to show interest in Washington's flirtation, no doubt to break its own fear of two-front encirclement. In so doing, it apparently wanted to play off Moscow against Washington to achieve maximum negotiating leverage at the border talks.

The prospect of border negotiations did not substantially diminish the hostility between the two Communist powers over ideological, border, and power rivalries. The proposed border talks, as far as Peking was concerned, amounted to little more than a search for a *modus vivendi,* an attempt to back away from the brink of nuclear war. It may be supposed that Peking also wanted to prevent Soviet propaganda from making headway with claims that Chinese intransigence was to blame for the Sino-Soviet border troubles. The Peking regime was fully aware that the Soviets would not make any significant concessions to them with regard to their territorial claims as long as Moscow maintained nuclear and military superiority over Peking. Therefore, the Communist Chinese themselves did not hold out much hope for more than a temporary or, at best, limited reduction of tensions with the Soviet Union. Peking's October 7 statement was frank: "The Chinese Government has never covered up the fact that there exist irreconcilable differences of principle between China and the Soviet Union and that the struggle of principle between them will continue for a long period of time." [57] But, the Chinese went on, "this should not prevent China and the Soviet Union from maintaining normal state relations on the basis of the five principles of peaceful co-existence." [58]

Moscow also seemed to be resigned to the fact that the Sino-Soviet differences were beyond any immediate solution. On the eve of the Sino-Soviet border talks in Peking, Mikhail Suslov, the Soviet Communist theoretician, writing in *Kommunist,* the Party's theoretical journal, attacked the Maoist type of Chinese Communism as an adventuristic departure from true Communism.[59] Maoism was doomed to an ill fate, he said. "Marxist-Leninists are convinced that sooner or later life itself will lead to a situation when the ideas of scientific socialism [i.e., of anti-Maoism] will inevitably triumph in China." He implied that the border talks in Peking were a government matter, so the two Communist parties were still far from being able to reconcile their views.

The current top-level Moscow-Peking border talks began on October 20, 1969, between delegations led by high-level diplomats, Soviet First Deputy Foreign Minister Vasily Kuznetsov and Chinese Vice Foreign Minister Chiao Kuanhua, meeting only two or three times a week in the Chinese Foreign Ministry building. In early July 1970 Kuznetsov returned to Moscow on the advice of physicians. He was replaced in August 1970 by Leonid Ilyichev, a top Kremlin ideologist known for his hard-line approach toward China. In addition to beginning top-level border negotiations, the two Communist nations also agreed on another round of second-level talks on joint navigation problems on the rivers that form a large part of the Far Eastern border. Such talks were held between July and December 1970 in Heiche in China's Heilungkiang Province.[60]

The Sino-Soviet border negotiations, which have been held intermittently in strict secrecy in Peking since October 1969, seem to have been deadlocked right from the start.[61] Each side apparently continues to repeat its own irreconcilable position without any actual negotiations. This deadlock has been accompanied by the full-scale resumption of the on-and-off propaganda war between the two Communist giants and the continuing military buildup along the Sino-Soviet boundary.

The major stumbling block thus far in the still continuing, but protracted, border negotiations has been the formulation of an agenda. In other words, the two sides have been in basic disagreement about what the talks are supposed to cover.

As mentioned previously, the Chinese entered into the negotiations mainly in order to defuse the border crisis that seemed to be escalating into a major conflict with the Soviets during the summer of 1969. Accordingly, the Chinese side wanted the talks limited to border questions along the Sino-Soviet boundary.[62]

China has proposed [63] that the first step in the current border talks should be an agreement on provisional peace-keeping measures, beginning with a mutual withdrawal of armed forces to a distance of sixty to eighty miles from all disputed sectors along the border.[64] Only after that, Peking is said to have told Moscow, can steps be taken for an all-around settlement of the Sino-Soviet territorial dispute.

The Chinese are prepared to take the old treaties forced on Manchu China by Czarist Russia in the nineteenth century as the basis for an overall settlement of the boundary question and insist that they do not demand the outright return of vast territories in Siberia and Central Asia annexed by the Russians under the treaties. For example, on October 7, 1969,

Communist China officially abandoned claims to 1.5 million square kilometers, or 600,000 square miles, of China's "lost territories." This new stand indicates Peking's new effort to make its position on the boundary question appear so sensible and reasonable that Moscow cannot continue to contend that Communist China is making a wild claim to hundreds of thousands of square miles of Soviet territory. But the Mao-Lin regime has adamantly demanded that the Soviet Union acknowledge for the record that the present Sino-Soviet boundary is the result of "unequal," and therefore illegal, treaties forced on China by the czars. It has demanded that the Soviets also agree to conclude a new "equal" treaty to replace the old, "unequal" ones. Until that is done, Peking says, the entire Sino-Soviet boundary line would be regarded as not formally delimited. In support of this position the Peking statements of both May 24 and October 8, 1969, quoted such Communist luminaries as Marx, Engels, and Lenin as having condemned the "unequal" treaties of czarist imperialism, and charged that the Brezhnev-Kosygin regime has "extolled" these treaties as being sacred and inviolable.

China also accuses the Soviets of having "illegally" expanded into Chinese territory in excess of the terms of the old "unequal" treaties. Peking demands that such additional lands be returned to the Chinese people unconditionally. However, Peking adds that "necessary adjustments" of these regions may be reached through "mutual understanding and mutual accommodation and in consideration of the interests of the local inhabitants." According to the Chinese, the area unlawfully seized by the Soviets beyond the stipulations of the old treaties includes 600 of the 700 islands in the Ussuri and Amur rivers between Manchuria and the Soviet Maritime Province (about 400 square miles) as well as 12,000 square miles of the Pamir mountain sector adjacent to the southern corner of China's westernmost province, Sinkiang.

Peking has repeatedly asserted that its northwestern boundary with the Soviet Union is the central line of the main channel of the Amur and Ussuri rivers. This would oblige Moscow to concede that 600 (including Chenpao/Damansky Island) of the 700 islands in the Amur and Ussuri rivers are in fact on the Chinese side of the central line of the main channel, do not belong to the Soviets, and should be returned to Peking. It is to be noted that Article 1 of the Sino-Soviet agreement on navigation and construction on border waterways of the Amur, Ussuri, Argun, and Sungacha rivers and Lake Khanka, signed on January 4, 1951, stated that traffic in the rivers would follow the main navigational channels regardless of their relationship to the state frontier.[65] This wording strongly implied either that Moscow and Peking did not agree where the state frontier was, or that it was not in the *thalweg*.

In claiming the Pamir mountain sector, the Chinese have contended that the region was unlawfully occupied by Russian troops in 1892 in violation of the 1884 boundary protocol.[66] The background of the dispute is as follows: In 1891, Czarist Russia dispatched troops to the eastern Pamirs to protect Russian scientific expeditions.[67] At this time, the Chinese-Russian frontier in the Pamirs had never been demarcated. The Manchu Chinese protested strongly against this Soviet advance but could not do anything about it because of their military weakness. In April 1894 the two countries exchanged notes and agreed to maintain temporarily the respective positions of their troops pending a final settlement of the Pamir question. This temporary frontier line has remained up to the present.

In contrast, the Soviet Union is reported to be trying to enlarge the border talks to include discussion of a wide variety of issues that have contributed to its conflict with Peking over the past decade.[68]

Moscow has refused to accept the Chinese demand to withdraw Soviet troops to a distance of sixty to seventy miles from disputed areas. Such a withdrawal, without a political settlement, would leave the Soviet border and Russia's vital

Far Eastern railroad (part of the Trans-Siberian Railway) dangerously exposed to Chinese incursions. Accordingly, the Soviets are said to have insisted that China first negotiate a frontier demarcation and other agreements aimed at improving Sino-Soviet relations.[69]

Maintaining that the Sino-Soviet boundary has been legally and historically fixed and that therefore a dispute does not exist along the entire frontier line, the Soviet Union has flatly refused to acknowledge publicly that the old nineteenth-century treaties signed between Manchu China and Czarist Russia are "unequal."[70] Also, Moscow has firmly ruled out either the comprehensive settlement of the Sino-Soviet border issue or the conclusion of a new, "equal" treaty to replace the old, "unequal" ones, as demanded by Peking. Were the Chinese view upheld, the Soviets said, Latin America would "return to the rule of the Spanish crown and the United States to the bosom of Great Britain while Greece, as successor to Alexander the Great, could lay claim to contemporary Turkey, Syria, Iran, India, Pakistan and Egypt."[71]

But the Soviets have indicated a willingness to make minor adjustments in particular frontiers where geography and boundaries are in obvious conflict. They are reported to have submitted a list of these minor "disputable" areas, which focus mainly on the strategic Sinkiang and Vladivostok regions.[72]

The Soviet Union has a different interpretation of the implementation of the 1884 boundary protocol between Manchu China and Imperial Russia. It denies that the Czarist Russians had seized extra land in the Pamir mountain region in circumvention of the old treaty.[73]

Concerning the river boundaries in the eastern sector of the Sino-Soviet borderlands, Moscow has maintained that the international boundary between Manchuria and the Soviet Far East runs along the Chinese banks of the Amur and Ussuri rivers, as demarcated by the 1861 protocol attached to the 1860 Treaty of Peking.[74] That is to say, the Soviets refuse to accept the doctrine of the *thalweg*. According to their view, 600 out

of the 700 islands in the rivers come legally under Soviet ownership and jurisdiction.[75] Certainly the historical evidence makes
this Soviet claim untenable, for the course of the boundary in
the Amur, Ussuri, and Argun rivers has never been precisely
delimited. As seen in Chapter 1, old treaties simply referred to
lands on the north bank and the south bank but never to the
river itself.

The Kremlin leaders apparently fear that some future Chinese regime, under pressure to find space to accommodate
China's huge population, may use Soviet acknowledgment of
the "unequal" treaties to lay claim to large parts of Siberia.
At the same time, they evidently realize that concessions made
to the Chinese could instantly or eventually encourage territorial claims by Japan, Rumania, and other countries that have
territorial disputes with the Soviet Union.

The present military balance between the two Communist
powers is heavily in favor of the Soviets, and the Soviet Union
has no intention of giving up the "sacred" territory of Mother
Russia. In recent months, the Soviet leadership and the Moscow press have repeatedly quoted Lenin's statement: "Vladivostok is far away—but it is ours."

One significant sign of Moscow's unwillingness to compromise with Peking on the territorial issue was the Soviet announcement of August 1970 that the Soviets had embarked
on an extensive "island reclamation" project in the Amur and
Ussuri rivers.[76] The "reclamation" project involves many hundreds of the very islands that the Chinese contend belong to
them.

Obviously, neither the Soviet Union nor China wants to be
the first to break off the talks, thereby allowing its enemy to
gain the propaganda edge against it while maintaining "correct" normal state relations.[77] Moreover, it appears that each
adversary regards the prolonged border negotiations as tactically useful or significant even if no progress is expected. For
different tactical purposes, then, both sides are striving to buy
time.

The Kremlin leaders seem to believe that a prolongation of

the talks may serve to exacerbate tensions between hard-line and pragmatic factions in the Chinese ruling hierarchy. They are also apparently convinced that Mao Tse-tung's twilight is nearing and his death in the coming years will bring to the fore a group of moderate Chinese Communist leaders who may be prepared to make pragmatic compromise and accommodation with the Soviet Union.

Soviet military leaders have long warned against the danger of a two-front war. The Brezhnev-Kosygin regime is fully aware that it cannot effectively deal with the Chinese Communist challenge unless and until it pacifies Russia's western European frontier. This makes détente with Western Europe an essential goal of Soviet foreign policy. The Soviet Union's recent friendship treaty with West Germany[78]—the country in Western Europe that is most dynamic, but most feared and disliked by the Soviets—fits into this pattern. So does growing French-Soviet accord.

Moscow perhaps calculates that its détente with the West may also serve to deter Western nations from a highly tempting ploy: that of forming ties with Communist China. The Soviets evidently hope that Western nations, and especially West Germany, which today is one of Communist China's principal trading partners, will soon feel so committed to the spirit of reconciliation that they will not wish to endanger their good and profitable relations with Moscow by flirting with Peking.

When the current border talks began in Peking in October 1969, the Chinese had no reason whatever to expect that their territorial dispute with the Soviet Union would be settled amicably. In other words, Peking was seeking to keep the border dispute with Moscow within controlled limits because it recognized Soviet military superiority and its own vulnerability. Peking hinted that the Chinese might at least accept some kind of *modus vivendi* for the sake of avoiding a direct military confrontation with the Soviets. If that can be achieved, China will have bought time.

On the eve of the border talks China had stated discreetly, through at least one provincial radio station in Nanking, that the talks were simply a time-gaining stratagem and would further "expose the ugly features of the enemy and place him in an even more isolated position." [79]

The threat of war with Moscow in the context of the territorial dispute is particularly useful and even beneficial for the Peking regime in the country's recent political upheaval, called the Cultural Revolution, in which Soviet "revisionism" was an important issue. The war scare pulls the nation together, makes it easier to demand and enforce loyalty and unity and to tighten up another notch in the national belt. It also enables Peking to stigmatize laggards and dissidents as "traitors."

Indications are that China is anxious to prevent the border talks from breaking off. The Chinese are apparently apprehensive that a collapse of the negotiations might provide the Soviets, especially hawkish elements in the Kremlin, with the pretext to resume their military threats and perhaps even take military action. Rightly or wrongly, the Peking regime may also believe that the Kremlin leaders took the initiative in calling for the current border discussions, knowing full well that the talks would fail and that, therefore, they would have a rationale for a military thrust against mainland China. In this connection, Peking also appears fearful that Soviet success in sealing the *status quo* in Western Europe through the strategy of détente will give Moscow a free hand in the East to threaten China.

At the present stage of the game, by and large, the Chinese leaders undoubtedly would much prefer to draw out the current border talks as long as possible and thus to avoid a clash with superior Soviet military power, but they are not sure whether their delaying tactics will work well over a long period of time. That is to say, they would prefer not to leave everything to chance by putting all their eggs in the negotiation basket. Plainly pessimistic about the future, they have been using the present breathing spell to embark on a campaign of war preparations for a possible clash.[80]

As a diplomatic maneuver to parallel its military preparations, the Peking regime has recently launched a new foreign policy of détente with the United States. This new policy resulted in President Nixon's trip to mainland China in the spring of 1972. Any sort of close tie between Communist China and the United States worries the Kremlin and is a trump card in Peking's hand. The Chinese are equally haunted by the nightmare of Washington-Moscow collusion against them. Playing off one enemy against another is a strategy as old as Chinese history. Traditional Chinese statesmen called the technique *i-i-chi-i,* which means literally "using barbarians to control barbarians." Assuming that the Mao regime can overcome the dogmatic rigidity of Maoism, the long-term prospect is that the Chinese Communist leaders by necessity would desire to develop a triangular diplomatic strategy in order to maneuver more effectively with the two nuclear superpowers, whom they view as threats to their national security and welfare.

By and large, the fundamental Soviet and Chinese positions on the territorial dispute have not changed, so it is safe to assume that the current top-level border talks in Peking will make no significant progress at all toward a satisfactory boundary settlement in the foreseeable future. Today the roots of discord between the two Communist giants—not only on territorial questions but on other issues as well—are very deep indeed. What is more important, these disagreements have already been transformed into matters of principle, and compromise has become that much more difficult.

The prospects for a settlement of the Sino-Soviet territorial dispute appear to be bright only if and when both sides in the talks modify their fundamentally irreconcilable stands without having recourse to war. One possibility of such compromise could be that the Soviets might offer to make minor concessions to the Chinese, granting them some of the disputed islands in the Amur and Ussuri rivers in exchange for a formal renunciation of Peking's historical claims to large areas of the Soviet Far East and Central Asia.

But mutual compromise is not the common language in the

highly explosive relations between Peking and Moscow, and it is doubtful that either side will make the concessions necessary to resolve their territorial dispute. In reality, deterioration of relations between the two powers has now reached the point where both adversaries would regard any kind of concession as a shameful defeat. Both Peking and Moscow seem to want the fruits of war against each other without war itself.

The boundary is quiet now, and hostilities have been shifted to less immediately dangerous warfare. But the continuing deadlock in the current Sino-Soviet border talks leaves the immense area along the boundaries enflamed and tense, obliging the two Communist countries to keep their armed forces on combat alert. At best, the Sino-Soviet territorial dispute will continue to be a war of words. At worst, it could spark fresh border clashes that, in turn—if rationality does not prevail on both sides—could lead to a full-scale armed conflict.

CHAPTER 4

Sino-Soviet War
in the 1970's?

Ever since the Sino-Soviet territorial dispute escalated into the bloody Ussuri clashes of March 1969, some commentators on world affairs have been wondering whether, in view of the increasing gravity of the rift, relations between China and the Soviet Union may someday explode. They assert that unless the Moscow-Peking relationship can be rebuilt on more solid foundations, a short-term accommodation to avoid a war would do neither side any good and is only a postponement of the inevitable showdown. For example, Harrison E. Salisbury, assistant managing editor of *The New York Times,* contends that war between China and the Soviet Union is inevitable unless the United States takes every possible active step to head it off or the death of Mao Tse-tung in the coming years paves the way for reconciliation.[1]

This author is inclined to estimate the chance of a Sino-Soviet war in the next ten years to be only one in ten—assuming that Mao is physically durable enough to live this much longer, and assuming the United States does not intervene directly or actively in the festering confrontation between the two Communist giants. The possibility of renewed outbreaks along the Sino-Soviet boundary, of course, still exists. Many arguments can be presented in support of the above contention.

First of all, the territorial issue between China and the Soviet Union is only a sidelight. It can be turned on or off as the overall political climate changes, and it holds too little value to warrant a major armed conflict between the two countries. Both sides must know that war between them would only benefit the United States, which may be tempted to fish in troubled waters. Therefore neither side has anything to gain politically. The potential dividends hardly seem to be worth the cost, and should a big war erupt, both Moscow and Peking will emerge as losers.

A Sino-Soviet war will inevitably involve the use of nuclear weapons. Differing on all else, the Chinese and the Soviets, according to their public pronouncements, agree wholeheartedly on one point: It is more than likely—indeed all but inevitable—that any local conflict will escalate into a nuclear war. Nuclear war is too dangerous and horrible to imagine, even for the Maoist Chinese who publicly proclaim that "a third world war would only send the whole pack of imperialists, revisionists and reactionaries to their grave." [2] Such a conflict would be futile, insane, counterproductive, and immensely dangerous for both Moscow and Peking, and neither could confidently expect the fruits of victory to be great.

Should a nuclear war erupt, there would be the obvious danger of radioactive fallout poisoning large inhabited areas, including mainland China and the Soviet Union. World public opinion would certainly condemn the two Communist powers for their crimes against humanity. As a corollary to this, it may be added that a Sino-Soviet nuclear war would do incalculable damage to Soviet and Chinese prospects of gaining, or retaining, influence in the Third World. Even theoretically, in short, one could not entertain the idea that the Soviet Union and Communist China are seriously considering mass murder as part of their military strategy.

Even if the Soviets succeed in completely destroying China's nuclear facilities and industrial centers with a quick first strike, they would be bogged down in a protracted and bloody human-wave conventional guerrilla war of uncertain outcome over the whole length of the border, a war which the Soviet Union could hardly limit and which it might find impossible to win. For Moscow, a protracted land war in the Asian heartland seems to make little sense from either the military or the political point of view and, in the words of Bernard Gwertzman of *The New York Times,* "would make the American involvement in Vietnam, by comparison, look like a minor skirmish."

No one can predict all the consequences of a death struggle between the two Communist giants, but it would, no doubt, not only undermine Soviet predominance in Eastern Europe but split the world Communist movement along racial lines and eventually destroy the movement itself without guaranteeing an end to the conflict.

Realizing these incalculable risks involved in a war with China, the Soviet Union has recently shifted to the more moderate and patient strategy of playing for time or sitting tight a bit longer in the hope, not such a remote hope, that the death of Mao Tse-tung in the near future will bring to the fore a group of moderate or anti-Maoist Chinese Communist leaders more favorably disposed toward the Soviet Union. The objective of this Soviet strategy is to eliminate from China's political arena Mao and his radical partisans who are dead opposed to a Sino-Soviet rapprochement, not to eliminate 750 million Chinese. It has been reported that Moscow has given refuge to anti-Maoist Chinese leaders (e.g., Wang Ming, a former secretary-general of the Chinese Communist Party) in exile as possible cards to play in a post-Mao era.

In large measure, the future prospect of war or peace at the Sino-Soviet border will probably depend more on China than on the Soviet Union, for the territorial claims are all on the Chinese side. The Chinese leaders genuinely fear the overwhelming superiority of Soviet power. It is therefore unlikely that they will seriously contemplate pressing their territorial claims against the Soviet Union by military force in the foreseeable future.

Contrary to some views widely held in the West, the Peking leaders are not mad, not irrational, but shrewdly cautious men able to weigh the costs and advantages of alternative policies. Mao Tse-tung's military strategy—which is influenced by the ancient Chinese military strategist, Sun Tzu[3]—emphasizes that the Chinese Communists will never fight unless they are sure of victory.[4] Mao knows when to advance and when to retreat. The history of the Chinese Communist movement under his leadership has been characterized by tactical flexibility and prudence. He exercises extreme caution in situations that could threaten him directly and is capable of retreating in the face of a superior enemy, without sacrificing his ultimate goal. In the late 1950's he spelled out the Maoist doctrine of flexibility and prudence in both domestic and foreign policies:

> In order to struggle against the enemy, we [the Chinese Communists] had formed the concept over a long period, namely, that strategically we should despise all enemies, and tactically take them seriously. That means that we should despise the enemy in the overall situation, and pay attention to him in every specific issue. If we do not despise the enemy in the situation as a whole, we will commit the mistake of opportunism.[5]

For the past twenty-odd years, the whole process of Communist China's foreign policy has followed closely and consistently this Maoist recipe for flexibility and prudence. And it will undoubtedly continue to do so in the 1970's.

The prudent way the Chinese Communists handle their foreign relations, when war or peace with the Soviet Union is involved, is clearly demonstrated by Peking's evident attempt to play down its latest nuclear tests and successful launching of China's first man-made earth satellite to avoid provoking a hostile reaction from Moscow. The Mao regime well knows that among the Kremlin leaders there are hawkish elements who would relish justification for preemptive strikes against China that would humble Mao Tse-tung, smash the Chinese nuclear establishment, and solve "the China problem" once and for all. Peking would logically and naturally be careful not to provide such a justification. While exploiting the nuclear tests and the satellite-launching to rally the populace behind the "invincible" leadership of Chairman Mao, to counter domestic factionalism, and to enhance China's global image, Communist China seemed to have been avoiding any direct reference to the military implications of these achievements, which would almost certainly be interpreted in Moscow as a provocation.[6]

While Peking's rhetoric sounds fierce, many senior military leaders who now rule the Chinese mainland in coalition with civilian political leaders appear determined to pursue basically prudent policies aimed at averting full-scale hostilities with the Soviets, which they know they cannot effectively handle. Many of the 2.5 million in the Chinese People's Army are still busy with civil administration of mainland China, for Mao's radical Cultural Revolution demolished much of the old ruling-party government apparatus.[7] These military leaders realize that the Soviets may feel it would be advisable to attack China while the fighting effectiveness of the Chinese troops is reduced by the nonmilitary tasks imposed on them.

As long as Mao Tse-tung keeps the Sino-Soviet border tensions below the threshold of a military showdown with the Soviet Union, his noisy anti-Soviet propaganda serves many useful domestic political purposes. Confronting Moscow, the Mao regime then asks: Why should China abandon the hot-words, cool-deeds control that pays such good political dividends?

For all these reasons, the prospect of real war between the two Communist giants in the foreseeable future must be discounted.

But the grim possibility of a major war between China and the Soviet Union cannot be *entirely* excluded from the range of possible future developments. Good common sense dictates action to prevent the Sino-Soviet territorial dispute from escalating into full-scale war. But there is no guarantee that both the Soviets and the Chinese will behave toward one another with rational restraint. Man, Communist or not, is not always rational. A Sino-Soviet war may break out, possibly under the following circumstances.

1. Moscow's recent high-risk "land reclamation" projects involving many disputed islands in the Amur and Ussuri rivers[8] is bound to be viewed as a provocation by the Chinese. It would also goad them into claiming these islands as their own or striking back at Soviet aggravations and showing by occasional minor thrusts and forays that they are ready to fight if pushed too far. Sooner or later, a mounting tension would explode into another big border clash—one in which commanders on both sides call in more and more reinforcements until at last the engagement becomes general. This, in fact, was precisely the pattern that developed into the undeclared war between Japan and the Soviet Union on the Manchurian borders in 1938 and 1939. In 1939, the Soviet army under Marshal Zhukov delivered a stunning blitz against the Japanese at Khalkin-gol in Eastern Mongolia.[9]

2. Despite his constant effort to keep the border conflict from getting out of control, Mao Tse-tung may be overplaying his hand in continuing to provoke the Soviets with pinpricks for whatever domestic political and propaganda purposes he may have, believing that the Soviet Union could never contemplate risking war with China until it stabilizes relations to the West, both in Europe and in the Middle East. Anything is possible. A new action-reaction cycle may be set in motion, and it could well flare into full-scale battle through miscalculation rather than design.

3. If and when Mao Tse-tung and his ideologues face the danger of being overthrown in the near future by their domestic opponents, or by the moderate and professional-minded army officers, the Maoist radicals might desperately seek to manufacture some dramatic external tensions along the Sino-Soviet border. In this way the Maoist hard-line faction could rally the nation behind its leadership in the name of national unity against the outside enemy. The Soviet Union would then decide to take advantage of Mao's domestic troubles and also

intervene militarily in China's domestic turmoil to topple the
Maoist extremists from power. If these things ever happen,
it would mean a wider war, with its incalculable risks.

4. In long-range, overall terms, the Soviets have been very
likely acting more aggressively along the frontier than the
Chinese, given their clear-cut military superiority over their
Chinese adversaries. A substantial portion of their military
potential is now advantageously deployed along the Chinese
borders. The Soviets are thus in a position to take calculated
risks, knowing that if a showdown occurs the odds are on their
side. Under the circumstances, the Soviet Union may be
tempted to provoke border incidents to achieve some useful
political and propaganda purposes at home and abroad, or to
press for concessions from Peking at the border talks, or to
exacerbate tensions between moderate and hard-line factions
in the Peking hierarchy. The Chinese would almost surely
respond in kind, and then full-scale combat operations could
evolve by a chain reaction.

5. Unable to bring about an end of the border conflict on
Soviet terms, hawks in the Kremlin may soon grow impatient
with the current deadlocked boundary negotiations. Presumably, the Kremlin's doves led by Premier Kosygin may not
have an unlimited length of time and political rope to pay out
in their effort to defuse, if not resolve, border questions. If, as
is only too likely, the Chinese drag the current border talks out
for years, as the Vietnamese Communists have done in Paris,
while the Chinese nuclear arsenal grows sufficiently strong to
threaten the Soviet Union, the Kremlin's hawks might succeed
in nudging the Soviet regime into taking the risks of a preventive nuclear attack against Peking's nuclear establishment
before China has acquired a second strike capability. If this
situation develops, the Mao regime would be cornered into
abandoning its present defensive posture toward the Soviet
Union and reacting violently, against its better judgment, to
Moscow's surprise attack.

6. In the Chinese borderlands of Sinkiang and Inner Mon-

golia, there are many non-Han ethnic minority groups who have close ties with cousins on the Soviet side of the border and in Outer Mongolia. Moscow may find it difficult to resist the temptation to stir these traditionally rebellious anti-Chinese minority races into causing major trouble for the Chinese by promoting a Vietnam-type national "war of liberation" movement, and a bloody repression of them by the Peking regime would increase the risk of direct Soviet intervention. This would mean a major war between the two Communist giants.

There is no doubt that Soviet and Chinese generals are laying contingency plans for actual fighting between them, which might break out under one or a combination of the above-mentioned circumstances. Indications are that both the Soviet Union and Communist China have been busily war-gaming a Sino-Soviet war in recent months. There is no assurance that such a war would be conducted solely with conventional weapons. There is evidence in earlier Soviet statements of a determination not to forgo nuclear weapons in fighting the hordes of China.[10] The Peking regime has stated that while it will never be the first to use nuclear weapons, it will use them if they are used against it. If and when China finds itself facing certain devastating defeat, Peking's temptation to use its small stock of nuclear devices would be too strong to resist.

It is estimated that Communist China now has enough fissionable materials on hand to produce about 300 Hiroshima-sized (20 kilotons) nuclear bombs (or warheads).[11] The primary means hitherto available to the Chinese to deliver nuclear bombs has been about 150 obsolete Russian-built IL-28 Beagle light bombers.[12] China is now reportedly producing its own medium-range two-engine jet bomber able to carry nuclear warheads in the 20-kiloton class to targets 1,500 miles beyond its borders.[13] This aircraft is a Chinese copy of the Russian TU-16 Badger, which has been in Soviet service in large numbers since 1955. China has reportedly deployed about twenty operational nuclear-tipped missiles of medium range (up to 1,000 miles) mainly in northwestern and northeastern China,[14] and is also preparing for more widespread deployment of eighty to one hundred medium-range missiles by the mid-1970's,[15] against the eventuality that the hot-and-cold border conflict with the Soviet Union might suddenly erupt into major war. Peking's successful launchings of its first (381-pound) earth satellite in April 1970 and its second (486-pound) earth satellite in March 1971 [16] caused China specialists and American defense analysts to speculate on the military implications of the two events. It remains unclear whether, for its satellite launchings, China is using the booster (or first stage) of its medium-range ballistic missiles (MRBM) or is testing the booster stage of an intercontinental ballistic missile (ICBM). The United States Department of Defense nevertheless estimates that the booster capability would permit China to test intercontinental ballistic missiles by the mid-1970's.[17] Some American China experts believe that by the middle or late 1970's the Chinese could have between fifteen and forty operational first-generation liquid-fueled ICBM's, each with a 3-megaton thermonuclear warhead and a 6,000-mile range.[18]

With such a capability, China would potentially have the means not only of inflicting an immense amount of damage on the Soviet Far East but of threatening sensitive communication and industrial areas in Soviet Central Asia and the heart of the Soviet Union in retaliation, if a Sino-Soviet war breaks out in the 1970's.

It is not an easy task to predict the pattern of a possible full-scale war between China and the Soviet Union. In the last analysis, the course of a Sino-Soviet war would be likely to depend largely on what kinds of contingency war plans the two Communist powers have for use against each other. There is no difficulty at all in puzzling out, at least in broad outline, these Soviet [19] and Chinese war plans.

The Soviet Union maintains undoubted superiority in technology, in the air, in firepower and mobility on the ground, in nuclear weapons (see *Table II*); these would almost surely enable the Soviets to deliver a fearful blow against the Chinese

Table II[20]

COMPARISON OF MILITARY POWER
(1971–72)

	The Soviet Union	Communist China
General Information:		
Area	8,647,249 square miles	3,690,546 square miles
Population	241,748,000 (estimate)	759,600,000 (estimate)
Gross national product	$490 billion	$90 billion
Total defense expenditure	$55 billion	$8.5 billion
Nuclear Forces:		
Intercontinental ballistic missiles	1,510	None
Submarine-launched ballistic missiles	400	None
Long-range bombers	200	None
Medium-range bombers	700	200
Medium- and inter-mediate-range ballistic missiles	700	Several
Conventional Forces:		
Army	2 million	2.5 million
Navy—		
Attack carriers	None	None
Helicopter carriers	2	None
Cruisers, destroyers	120	4
Nuclear-powered submarines	80	None
Other submarines	270	35 (only one equipped with ballistic missile tubes)
Air Force—		
Tactical	5,000	2,800
Transport	1,700	200
Interceptors	3,200	?

and also to win most of the early battles. In other words, the Soviets in the first phase of the war, following massive air raids at China's nuclear establishment, key industrial and communication centers, and important military bases, would be able to cut into mainland China and conquer North China (including Manchuria) and Peking in blitzkrieg fashion.

But Moscow would be facing an enemy who enjoys the advantages of both superior manpower (China has 150 million able-bodied males of draft age) and vast reserves of space. These are the very advantages the Russians in the past enjoyed against Napoleon and Hitler. Accordingly, the conquest of the Chinese mainland in the conventional military sense seems to have slim chances of success. In case of a Soviet nuclear attack on China, Peking expects that about 300 million Chinese would be killed and 500 million Chinese would still survive the attack. Mao Tse-tung could turn the entire surviving population into fighting guerrillas who would put up a formidable resistance against Soviet invasion by "drowning the enemy in a hostile human sea," to use his phrase, and Moscow would not be able to match the adversary's strength in men on the ground. Central and South China would then be able, despite the loss of the North, to launch a guerrilla war of unprecedented dimensions—a war that would last for years and be virtually impossible to win. Chinese guerrilla bands would hit the advancing Soviet columns from all angles, perhaps even crossing over Eastern Siberia to sever the Trans-Siberian Railway, which is the main link between the Soviet Maritime Province and the Russian heartland, and also to raid airfields, supply depots, and military bases. Above all, Mao Tse-tung, the master strategist of guerrilla warfare, and his military commanders would do their best to lure the invading Soviet troops deeper into the Chinese countryside with its complicated terrain where the Soviets would be vulnerable to a protracted guerrilla war of annihilation. If the Chinese succeed in this purpose of bogging the Soviets down more and more in a bottomless military and political quagmire, it may well prove that the fate of the Soviet invaders would be a thousand times more painful than the American involvement in Vietnam.

Moreover, Moscow's deep preoccupation with a massive guerrilla war in the Chinese mainland almost certainly would trigger popular (or national) uprisings in Eastern Europe on the Hungarian model. These would be welcomed in the West if they were quick and successful, and the temptation to intervene on behalf of these anti-Soviet freedom fighters would be immense for the West, particularly for West Germany.

It would certainly be surprising, therefore, if there were in the Kremlin and the Soviet high command no advocate of a single, quick, and massive strategic nuclear bombing designed to scare China into submission in the quickest possible time.

But it is doubtful that nuclear weapons alone would enable Moscow to win a quick victory against a country such as Communist China, which has a large population and territory, plus a complicated terrain. It is doubtful whether Moscow could crush the stubborn resistance of several hundred million Chinese or destroy their will to carry on protracted guerrilla warfare. It must be kept in mind that, even in the event of war with China, the Soviet Union must preserve a great portion of its nuclear capability against possible surprise nuclear attack or nuclear blackmail by the United States. In other words, the Soviets, even after nuclear bombing attacks, would have to deploy a large number of army divisions for securing the long border against Chinese infiltration attempts and guerrilla operations, and final Soviet victory over China would require a conventional army, regular weapons, and occupation.[21]

The eastern sector of the Sino-Soviet boundary is partly hilly and partly level and offers a terrain that, given a relatively highly developed communications network, is suited for operations by mechanized forces. It is estimated that Soviet strength in the Far Eastern Military District now totals some 250,000 regulars (20 divisions) in addition to special frontier guards.[22] By comparison, Communist China has about a half million men (28 divisions) deployed from Peking north through

Manchuria. In addition to long-range or intermediate-range strategic nuclear strike forces, the Soviet Union has now deployed many hundreds of tactical nuclear missiles and rockets along the eastern sector of the Sino-Soviet boundary, including the first deployment of a new solid-fuel mobile missile known to Western defense analysts as Scaleboard.[23] This missile is mounted on a tank chassis, has an estimated range of 500 miles, and carries a warhead of over one megaton, the equivalent of a million tons of TNT.

Manchuria would be an early Soviet target. After Manchuria the Soviets would probably try to capture Peking quickly by a pincers movement carried out from the north (through Manchuria) and the west (through Mongolia).

But a Russian thrust across the Amur-Ussuri river border would not be easy. The Chinese vastly outnumber the Soviets in the Far Eastern frontier area,[24] and their lines of communication are short, so the logistical advantages—speed of reinforcing troops, for instance—are on the Chinese side. The Soviet Union undoubtedly maintains strong military forces and substantial supplies in the Vladivostok-Khabarovsk-Irkutsk region, but the Soviet Far East is separated by thousands of miles from the main source of Soviet power in the European part of the Soviet Union. In eastern Siberia, the Soviets are dependent on the double-track Trans-Siberian Railroad which, in following the Amur River, runs for a long distance in the immediate vicinity of the Chinese border and which could easily be cut off by raiding Chinese guerrilla bands, especially in the long winter months when the Amur-Ussuri river borders are frozen. In view of the long distance between the territory east of the Ural Mountains and the Soviet Maritime Province (e.g., there are 4,089 miles between Omsk in western Siberia and Vladivostok) and the still inadequate capacities of the Trans-Siberian Railroad [25] and of airfields in Asiatic Russia, any Soviet attempt to match the numbers of troops that Communist China could put into the battlefield would be hopeless. It must be recalled that Russia lost the war with Japan in

1904–05 mainly because of the inability of the (then) single-track[26] Trans-Siberian Railroad to supply, reinforce, and provision the czar's troops in Manchuria.

In the field of conventional warfare in the eastern sector of the Sino-Soviet boundary, the Chinese would be expected to employ their overwhelming manpower superiority in the form of a human-wave sweep across the Amur-Ussuri river borders in an attempt to capture the Soviet Far East.

The central sector of the Sino-Soviet frontier encompasses the nearly unpopulated desert area of Mongolia (i.e., the Gobi Desert) and is suited for modern desert warfare similar to Second World War operations in North Africa. The Soviet Union today maintains 150,000 troops or 10 divisions in the area, and Communist China maintains 275,000 regulars or 18 divisions. (In the summer of 1969, Defense Minister Lin Piao announced that two Chinese Communist army corps were to be trained for desert fighting in Inner Mongolia.) Moscow has recently installed medium-range nuclear missiles inside the pro-Soviet Mongolian People's Republic (Outer Mongolia), which maintains one infantry division of its own.[27]

Peking's advantage in the eastern sector of the Sino-Soviet boundary would be matched by Moscow's advantage in the western, or Sinkiang, sector, where conventional infiltration tactics and guerrilla warfare would be possible but operations by mechanized forces would be difficult to carry on. Sinkiang is extremely vulnerable to Soviet attack, because the Soviets possess an enormous tactical advantage over the Chinese there; ample ground, air, and rocket forces are available and supply lines are short. The Soviet Union has deployed roughly 200,000 regular troops, or twenty-seven divisions, along the Sinkiang frontier, and Chinese strength there consists of 90,000 men, or four divisions, in addition to special frontier and militia units of dubious ability.

In Sinkiang, far from their main centers of power, the Chinese are not only militarily weak and lacking a good logistical link[28] but are also politically shaky because of the province's

predominantly Moslem ethnic minorities, who have traditionally disliked the Han Chinese. The Moslem minority races in
Sinkiang have frequently shown themselves receptive to Soviet
blandishments in their efforts to resist harsh Chinese cultural
assimilation, and it would not be difficult for Moscow to
manipulate them to rise up against Peking rule. Indeed, the
Soviet Union has been secretly aiding Moslem guerrilla bands
that are skirmishing against the Chinese inside Sinkiang.[29]

To the Soviets, Sinkiang is a considerable economic-military
prize, partly because it maintains Peking's nuclear establishment—uranium mines, gaseous diffusion works, nuclear test
sites (Lop Nor), and rocket range—and partly because it is
rich in underground treasures, ores of all kinds and petroleum.[30]

Because of their involvement in two major wars and many
minor military engagements in the Far East in the past half
century, the Soviets are extensively experienced in warfare
along the Chinese frontier. They know where China is weak
and strong and how best to strike. Moscow's battle plan for
the China war has unquestionably taken account of many
valuable lessons learned from previous military encounters
in Soviet Far Eastern frontier areas, particularly the most successful ones. The most successful Soviet military engagements
were (a) a ten-day battle at Khalkin-gol in August 1939 [31] and
(b) the Manchurian campaign of August 1945.[32] The success
of these engagements was due to several important factors: (a)
mustering and employment of superior forces at the end of a
four-thousand-mile land supply line from the heart of the
Soviet Union; (b) careful and secret preparations; and (c)
launching of a stunning blitz against the enemy, which in-
flicted savage casualties and had a severe psychological effect.
The memory of these victories, particularly the one at Khalkin-
gol, which is still celebrated in the Soviet Union,[33] is still
vivid and fresh in the minds of some Soviet generals. On
September 2, 1969, *Izvestia* published in abridged form an
article by Marshal Matvei V. Zakharov, chief of the general

staff of the Soviet armed forces. The article ostensibly dealt with the almost-forgotten Soviet military campaign against the Japanese in Mongolia thirty years ago.[34] It must be observed, however, that if the Khalkin-gol battle were of purely antiquarian, academic interest, *Izvestia* would hardly have wasted space on it. In this article, Marshal Zakharov said that the examination of the Mongolian campaign of 1939 had "an important significance for strengthening the security of the Far Eastern frontiers of our fatherland." [35] In short, there is good reason to believe that in the event of full-scale war with China, the Soviet high command would choose to fight on the same general pattern of the two most successful Soviet military engagements in the Far East.

If the Soviet Union were to face a military showdown with China in the 1970's, a Soviet version of Israel's Six-Day War would seem most likely to be the pattern of the war that the Soviet military are prepared to wage. This kind of strategy would aim at knocking out Peking's nuclear installations and crippling the main centers of Chinese resistance (though not at occupying all of China's territory). It would aim to deal China a military blow so savage and a psychological effect so severe that the Mao regime would be humiliated and forced to surrender or to undergo its own internal demise in the quickest possible time.

The Soviets have apparently convinced themselves that a Sino-Soviet war, if it ever occurs, would inevitably involve the employment of nuclear weapons and that China will use its nuclear arsenal.[36] The Soviet military voice would argue that, this being the case, Moscow must strike first and quickly paralyze China's capability for retaliation and resistance. Moscow's intention to use its missiles when necessary is partly evidenced by the appointment in August 1969 of Colonel-General Vladimir F. Tulubko, 57, first Deputy Commander of the Soviet Strategic Rocket Forces, as commander-in-chief of the Soviet Far Eastern forces. In early 1972 General Tulubko replaced Marshal Nikolai I. Krylov, who died on February 9,

1972, at the age of 69, as the new commander of the Soviet Union's strategic missile forces.

Along with this line of contemporary military thinking, the Soviet high command's war plan in the first phase of the war would call for a swift, overwhelming strike at China's nuclear capacity, industrial, communication, and arms production centers, important military and army supply bases (including airfields), as well as deployment areas of the several armored and artillery divisions on which the Chinese People's Liberation Army depends for its mobility and heavy firepower—and, if necessary, the Peking region itself. Such a fatal knockout blow is feasible because of the relatively small number of military and military-industrial-communication targets vital to any Chinese war effort, and the Soviet military intelligence certainly must know exactly where these targets are.

The second phase of the Soviet war plan would be to employ mainly nonnuclear forces in the Far East, with stress on amphibious and airborne operations. Soviet mechanized (i.e., tank) forces would cut the Chinese salient between the Amur and Ussuri rivers and roll several hundred miles across the Inner Mongolian plains from the Outer Mongolian border, to occupy North China and Peking. Such an operation would be a carbon copy of the Soviet conquest of Manchuria in August 1945 by a maneuver of three converging thrusts—from the west, north, and east.

The Soviets would invade Sinkiang and stir up a "war of liberation" for an independent "East Turkestan Republic" in the area, where Uighurs, Kazakhs, and other Moslem minorities are already restless under Peking's rule. The Sinkiang "liberation forces" would undoubtedly be supported and joined by their cousins in Soviet Central Asia. Inner Mongolia, which has been brutally Sinicized, also provides a vulnerable target for "liberation forces" from Outer Mongolia.

In the third phase of the war, after occupying North China and Peking in blitzkrieg fashion, thereby driving the Mao regime from its capital and also destroying its prestige as a legitimate government, the Kremlin leaders would be extremely reluctant to keep their troops in China for an indefinite period of time or to send them any farther south than Peking with the intention of conquering mainland China in the conventional military sense. The Soviets, fully aware that such a large-scale general land war would be long and costly, would try instead to launch a psychological-political type of warfare designed to subvert the Mao regime. And their purpose in so doing would be totally political: to discredit Mao Tse-tung and his anti-Soviet regime and to establish a pro-Soviet "legitimate" government along China's northern tier. If they did so, they would simultaneously call upon the Chinese people (through round-the-clock broadcasts and leaflet-dropping) to overthrow the "illegitimate" Mao regime and save themselves. Or they may hope, with a good deal of logic, that if this were done, the Chinese mainland would simply come apart at the seams, and the central government that Mao has imposed over the past two decades would collapse completely and be replaced by regional military warlords. All in all, Soviet national interest would be far better served by a weak, divided China than by a conquered China (assuming that to conquer China were militarily feasible).

During the third phase of the war, when its deadly Communist rivals are pressed militarily in Central and South China, Chiang Kai-shek's Nationalist China on Formosa might find it difficult to resist the temptation to intervene and might possibly invade its "lost homeland," even with Moscow's tacit encouragement or acquiescence. The Indians, who were humiliated by the Chinese Communists in the 1962 border war, might be tempted to even the score with the Mao regime and also to help Tibetan "liberation forces." [37]

If and when China were massively attacked on Chinese soil by the Soviet Union, Chinese strategy would probably be to retreat before superior Soviet forces and draw the invading enemy into the depths of the countryside for a protracted guerrilla war of annihilation rather than to fight a frontal engagement—as described earlier in this chapter. This strategy is consistent with Mao Tse-tung's theory that China's best defense in case of attack is to wage a protracted guerrilla war (or "people's war") rather than to attempt to fight a conventional war against any enemy superior in firepower.[38] The essence of the Maoist thesis of a protracted guerrilla war is to draw an invading enemy into the depths of China and then, as he has put it, to "drown the foe in an ocean of humanity." [39]

But there are indications that Mao and his professional-minded army officers[40] may, as repeatedly in the past, be divided in a major debate over how best to handle the menace and aggression of the Soviets. They also disagree about how political or professional the armed forces should be. Mao wants the army politically oriented and controlled; military professionals demand technical expertise. The problem of political control of the army versus exclusive military professionalism has troubled Mao for the past forty-odd years, and has usually brought about a hot debate inside the Peking hierarchy, as Alice Langley Hsieh correctly observes, "at a critical juncture in Chinese decision-making [on national security] or in a crisis situation." [41] For, while Mao has consistently stressed that "political power grows out of the barrel of a gun," he insists that "the gun must never be allowed to command the party." [42]

A similar debate occurred in early 1965, when United States escalation of the Vietnam War seemed to threaten mainland China. Prior to this debate, Defense Minister P'eng Teh-huai, a member of the Chinese Communist Party's Politburo, attacked Mao's military doctrine at the Party's Politburo meeting and Central Committee plenum held in July and August 1959.[43] Mao weathered the challenge and purged P'eng and his chief subordinates in the Defense Ministry in September 1959.[44]

During early 1965, a faction of professionally oriented army officers led by (General) [45] Lo Jui-ch'ing, then chief of the general staff of the Chinese Communist army, favored a greater emphasis on professional military training and a limited reconciliation with the Soviet Union in order to deter a possible American attack on China.[46] Lo also insisted on the strategic importance of nuclear weapons in modern warfare, considering the Maoist military doctrine of a "people's war" dangerously anachronistic as the defense strategy for China in the nuclear age.[47]

In contrast, Mao and his chief lieutenant, (Marshal) Lin Piao, who was later to become Mao's officially designated heir during the Cultural Revolution, advocated reliance on the Maoist thesis of guerrilla war. Rejecting the primary importance of nuclear weapons and technology, Mao and Lin argued that China's best defense was to lure the enemy to penetrate deep into Chinese territory and then to "drown him in an ocean of people." [48] They also contended that professional specialization represented dangerous and poisonous bourgeois revisionism and that Communist China would return to capitalism unless this evil could be suppressed and eradicated. (Defense Minister Lin Piao disappeared from the political scene in the fall of 1971. According to the official announcements made by the Peking regime in the summer of 1972, Lin had led a plot to overthrow and assassinate Mao Tse-tung and was killed in a plane crash in Outer Mongolia while fleeing to the Soviet Union right after the abortive coup in September 1971.[49])

Lo Jui-ch'ing was purged in the course of Mao's radical Cultural Revolution on charges that he harbored "bourgeois military thinking" as P'eng had done in 1959.[50] The purge of Lo undoubtedly strengthened the hands of the Maoist doctrinaires vis-à-vis the military professionals. During the height of the Cultural Revolution, the Mao-Lin regime in Peking had renewed the drive to crush all bourgeois military ideas and lines within the army. At the same time, a publicity campaign to inculcate and immortalize Mao's military thinking had been launched with unprecedented vigor. For example, *Chieh-fang Chün-pao* (*Liberation Army Daily*), the

army newspaper, which was controlled by Defense Minister
Lin Piao, said bluntly on September 20, 1966, that officers
and soldiers "must think and act in accordance with the
teachings of Mao Tse-tung. If Chairman Mao says it is so,
then it is so, and if he says it is not so, then surely it is not
so."

The Cultural Revolution apparently did not succeed in
eliminating potential sources of tension between Mao and
the military professionals. Available evidence suggests that
professionals such as P'eng and Lo still exist in the Chinese
Communist army. With the Sino-Soviet territorial dispute
edging toward the brink of full-scale war in 1969, reports
from Communist China suggested that these professionals were
challenging Mao's "people's war" thesis and claiming instead
that purely military preparations should be given priority
over ideological considerations.

Such an anti-Maoist, military-professional viewpoint was
publicly aired on December 9, 1969, when the *Liberation
Army Daily*, one of the authoritative Maoist publications in
China, published an important article written by its editorial
department, which, by the brilliant use of double-talk, coded
words, and veiled allusions—the Aesopian mode of communication—unmistakably gave support to a "treasonable"
military professional viewpoint. Asserting that the United
States and the Soviet Union threatened Communist China
with a "large-scale aggressive war," the *Liberation Army Daily*
article called for greater attention to military preparations to
"defend the socialist motherland." In so doing, it paid token
obeisance to Mao's military thought that ideology is more
important than weapons, and that therefore "politics must
command military affairs." But it also stressed, "We [the Chinese people] should not think that by putting politics in
command, military affairs can be neglected. . . . We must not
think that being good in political and ideological work is
everything." Accordingly, it underlined the need for "daily
practical [i.e., professional] training" in military technique in

order to harden troops for "fighting big and fierce battles and fighting under the most difficult circumstances." In an obvious thrust at the Maoist ideologues, who insist on intensive political indoctrination of the army, it said: "It will not do to rely solely on [political] lectures [based on the Maoist scripture]. More time must be given to [professional military] training."

In an apparent gibe at Maoist proletarian military principles, which were averse to the existence of bourgeois-type military ranks,[51] the *Liberation Army Daily* referred to "relations between higher and lower levels of command" and "between officers and men," urging that they be made "harmonious and close."

It is conceivable that many senior military officers who now rule Communist China in coalition with civilian political leaders are keenly aware that their army would be unable to win in a showdown with the Soviet army. These officers may be urging caution toward the Soviet Union. Presumably, they endorsed Premier Chou En-lai's advocacy of a more pragmatic approach to Moscow—recall, for example, the Kosygin-Chou meeting at the Peking airport in September 1969 to reopen the border negotiations. Indications are that, behind the protective shield of these senior military leaders, military professionals have recently been reinforcing their voice within the Chinese military establishment.

The Maoist response to the *Liberation Army Daily* article of December 9, 1969, has been swift, direct, and intense—a renewed major broadside against military professionalism.[52] The Maoist press and Chinese internal broadcasts, since December 10, 1969, have renewed the campaign to canonize Mao's military thought and have leveled severe attacks on the "bourgeois military viewpoint" advocated previously by P'eng and Lo. Recently, one Maoist publication said bluntly: "Chairman Mao's military thinking is the magic weapon in defeating the enemy." [53]

The dispute between Mao and the modernizing military professionals about how best to deal with the Soviet menace and possible attack (and also the related problem of political control of the army versus exclusive military professionalism) covers many specific but interrelated issues. As it has evolved, the dispute is, quite contrary to the exaggerations and distortions of Maoist propaganda, not a simple black-and-white or "proletarian" versus "bourgeois" argument, but a debate over emphasis or priority. Professionally-minded military officers tend to view military problems in the nuclear age essentially from the professional rather than the political standpoint.

Professional army officers, many of whom experienced overwhelming U.S. firepower during the Korean War, stress the importance of nuclear weapons and modern military technology. They argue that, in modern warfare, the material and technological factors are more important than the human and political factors. By implication, this view rejects the validity of Mao's military thought that men, not weapons, are decisive in war,[54] as well as the cardinal Maoist principle of putting politics in command in military affairs.[55]

In line with this argument, China's military professionals want more professional, up-to-date armed forces equipped with ultramodern military weapons as a deterrent to Soviet attack on their country. They place the highest priority on the development of a strong nuclear capability, even at the expense of economic development.

Chinese military professionals believe that it is China, and not the Soviet Union, that is a "paper tiger," doubting the ability of the Chinese army to respond effectively to an attack by superior Soviet forces. They also realize that, in the event of war with Moscow, China can do very little against the Soviet Union's deadly nuclear strike force combined with a quick and massive armored and conventional attack. In other words, the Soviet Union can blast the Chinese people back to the Stone Age and this would require a hundred years to repair. In short, the stakes are too high to warrant the risk of fighting the Soviet Union.

China's professional army officers believe that the Maoist military doctrine of guerrilla warfare is not now the "magic" formula for defeating Moscow. They believe that to speak strong but empty language when the country is in reality not strong would invite immediate danger and extinction.[56] They assert that at a time when science, technology, and military knowledge are rapidly advancing, Mao's military thinking is outmoded by at least twenty or twenty-five years as far as wars against the world's two superpowers are concerned.[57] They accuse Mao of underestimating Moscow's military strength with easy pride, undue optimism, and arrogance and also of treating military affairs in this nuclear age as something to toy with. Viewing any possible future war between China and the Soviet Union primarily as a one- or two-strike affair, they contemptuously reject the argument for Mao's defensive strategy of protracted guerrilla warfare by proclaiming that, in modern warfare, offense is strategy, while defense is only a stratagem. For example, they argue that in the event of a Sino-Soviet war, the Soviets would be smart enough not to run the risk of becoming bogged down by land battles in a country with a large population and territory. Accordingly, they assert, it is small wonder that discussion of contemporary military affairs by those who dogmatically refuse to appreciate the military implications of the nuclear age leads to a topsy-turvy view of what is right and wrong.

These military professionals, who believe that China's military strength is too weak to allow Mao to talk lightly of war with Moscow, contend that the Mao regime is not justified in playing the dangerous game of confrontation or brinksmanship with the Soviet Union over the territorial issue until Peking develops a sophisticated and credible nuclear capability. Unless and until such an effective military posture is acquired, they believe that Peking should deescalate the current tense boundary conflict with the Soviets, enter into protracted diplomatic negotiations, or even seek a compromise with Moscow on outstanding boundary and other issues.[58] Alternatively, they suggest that an effort be made to seek a rapprochement with the United States, chiefly in order to keep Moscow off balance and thus to help deter a Soviet military move against China along the lengthy common boundary. This move would also strengthen Peking's bargaining position at the current Chinese-Soviet border negotiations being held in Peking.

Professional army officers resent or even oppose excessive political interference in their command by the Party and its political commissars. They argue that the business of conducting modern warfare is too scientific, technical, and complex for civilian party leaders (including Mao himself) and political commissars to comprehend, and that the principle of having politics in command of military affairs is incompatible with the important requirement of functional, technical, and organizational efficiency in modern warfare. They favor a single chain of command and control rather than the present dual political and military command structure in the Chinese People's Liberation Army, which, in effect, means abolishing the tightly controlled leadership of Mao and his Communist Party over the army.[59]

Modern-minded professional officers dislike the intensive political indoctrination program for the armed forces. They assert that their splendid revolutionary past and their membership in the party[60] should exempt them from all ideological reforms and indoctrination and that they should be left alone to improve their own military proficiency.[61] They are appalled at the amount of time being wasted by the entire army on the study of the Maoist scripture and other forms of ideological indoctrination. They are in favor of reestablishing a proper or equal balance between political education and technical military training, and they also assert that, even within this balance, professional training is the best preparation for war.[62]

Military professionals also oppose the Maoist idea of "a

multipurpose army," i.e., the employment of troops for non-military purposes, such as farming, operating factories, constructing highways and dikes, digging canals, and doing political propaganda work to spread the thought of Chairman Mao. They contend that such employment depresses army morale, dissipates troops' energy, and interferes with the military training program. They resent having the talents and energies of their men diverted to nonmilitary tasks at a time when they are charged with the responsibility of preparing for a possible conflict with the Soviet Union, which has superior military hardware.

Military specialists disagree strongly with Mao and his party on the idea as well as the utility of the militia.[63] They argue that the militia is professionally deficient in military training and technology, economically wasteful, and militarily useless in times of war. The militia is an unwanted burden to many army officers, who apparently lack the patience to train amateur soldiers. Therefore, they advocate that the militia should be abolished so that the resources allocated to it could be diverted to the regular armed forces.

Today's professional army officers strongly dislike Mao's policy, in effect since May, 1965, of abolishing all military ranks and badges in the Chinese army.[64] This leaves officers as faceless as their men while the power of the already powerful political commissars is enhanced. They fear that this policy affects the authority and prestige of the officers, weakens army discipline, and impedes the work of the military command, thereby leading eventually to a sharp decline in professional standards as well as in the combat effectiveness of the armed forces.[65] They assert that a modern war and a modern army require a tightly centralized, disciplined, hierarchical military organization and technical professionalism, rather than proletarian democracy and the heroic individual initiatives that were valuable in the prenuclear Yenan days of guerrilla warfare against the Chinese Nationalists and the Japanese.

Mao Tse-tung flatly rejects the viewpoints of the military

professionals and approaches military problems essentially from a political angle. Both Mao and the professional officers are fully committed to military modernization of their country in the face of Soviet threat, but each tends to see matters in a different light.

Mao and his radical ideologues have not been unaware of both the strategic importance of nuclear weapons in modern warfare and of China's vulnerability to nuclear attack or blackmail by the Soviet Union and the United States. Thus China's fear of war with Moscow—expressed in a new austerity drive with programs for building shelters, bunkers, and slit trenches on a vast scale, dispersing industry and developing regional self-sufficiency—is real. In fact, Mao and the Maoists have made a determined effort to develop China's nuclear capability both to deter an American or Soviet attack and to wield increased influence in world affairs. But they realize that China has many years to go before she possesses a dependable and sophisticated nuclear striking capacity. During Peking's present nuclear weakness the effective substitute is the Maoist strategic doctrine of a "people's war"—the "spiritual atomic bomb." [66] As Mao sees it, a huge but poorly developed land such as China has a unique source of strength—its vast "ocean of [nearly 800 million] people" that will suffocate and drown several million invading Soviet troops.

The Maoist military doctrine believes in the inherent superiority of man over machines or weapons. It is not the gun, Mao insists, but the man behind the gun who is decisive in the outcome of war.[67] Furthermore, this inherent superiority of man can be materialized only if and when every soldier is properly inspired, motivated, and conditioned through intensive political indoctrination. The Chinese Communist Party alone is competent to do this important job by applying the canonical thought of Mao Tse-tung.

Armed with superior political morale, will, and revolutionary consciousness, a technically inferior Chinese army can overcome all sorts of obstacles to defeat its superior enemy.[68] The revolutionary and political indoctrination of people's hearts, not military technique, is what decides victory or defeat in war.[69] Hence, politics (or the political and ideological preparations of the people, based solely on the thought of Mao Tse-tung) should take priority over technical professionalism. In short, Mao's military thinking is far superior to nuclear weapons.[70]

Peking's continuing heavy emphasis on the superiority of man and politics over modern weapons of mass destruction reflects the fact that Mao and his partisans find compensation for Communist China's nuclear weakness in the iron will and discipline they learned during the long, difficult period of their revolutionary struggle for power against the superior forces of their Chinese Nationalist enemies and the Japanese invaders. In this connection it may be recalled that the Soviet Union also depreciated the role of nuclear weapons in modern warfare when the United States held its atomic monopoly right after the Second World War.[71] At the present time, therefore, the Maoist military doctrine of guerrilla warfare is well tailored to Communist China's internal strengths and weaknesses. The constant reiteration of the man-over-weapons thesis raises the morale of the populace and the armed forces in the face of potential enemies who possess far superior military weapons and technology, breaks down the fear of the Chinese people and the army about nuclear weapons and the Soviet threat while Peking is developing a credible nuclear deterrent, sustains the validity of Mao's military thought, justifies Mao's tight political control of the army, rationalizes China's heavy emphasis on the major role of conventional ground forces in modern war, and finally hopes to convince powerful adversaries that an attempt to invade, defeat, and conquer the Chinese mainland would be too costly.

As do the professionally-minded officers, Mao and his loyal supporters fear that the Soviet Union would or might attack the Chinese mainland as a result of escalation of the boundary conflict. For such an eventuality, the Maoist military doctrine presupposes the feasibility of a protracted guerrilla-type "defense in depth" (*chung-shen-p'ei-pei*) of the vast territory of China, the outcome of which would be decided by close-range hand-to-hand combat, day and night, within two hundred meters between soldiers using primitive conventional weapons such as bayonets, hand grenades, knives, axes, and picks.[72]

Mao insists that the Soviet Union would not be able to defeat China solely by a massive nuclear attack (even if this were combined with bacteriological and chemical weapons) because of the latter's large territory and population and its complicated terrain. For final victory, therefore, Soviet ground forces would still have to invade and occupy the Chinese mainland, and the Soviet invasion would only plunge the enemy into "the escape-proof net of a great, just people's war against aggression." [73]

In case of a Soviet nuclear attack on the Chinese mainland, Mao expects about 300 million Chinese to be killed, leaving about 500 million survivors, who would "dare to lure the enemy deep into a battle of annihilation." The surviving highly mobilized Chinese masses—regular forces, a massive militia, and local forces—would attack the Soviet invaders in caves, bunkers, mountains, forests, ditches, tunnels, and houses—that is to say, practically from all sides.[74] They would combine mobilized, large, and set-piece conventional battles with well-coordinated, widespread, intensive, and independent guerrilla warfare, and the invading Soviet enemy forces would be "bogged down in endless battles" and "drowned in a hostile human sea." Their readiness to fight with primitive conventional weapons at the close range of two hundred meters would nullify the Soviet advantage in military technology and weapons systems. In such an event, the Maoist Chinese assert, the "people's war" magic taught by Mao Tse-tung during the previous war against Japanese invasion would certainly be able to exhaust and, finally, defeat the Soviet Union.[75]

If and when the Soviet Union were to "stretch out all its ten fingers" and become hopelessly bogged down in protracted, large-scale and demoralizing "people's wars" over the whole length of the border and inside the vast area of mainland China, Mao predicts, it would signal the collapse of the Brezhnev-Kosygin regime in Moscow, as well as national disaster for the Soviet Union.[76] Many "suppressed" non-Russian ethnic minorities in the Soviet Union would then launch Vietnam-type "wars of national liberation" against the oppressive Kremlin regime in Central Asia, Georgia, the Ukraine, Latvia, Lithuania, and other places—practically everywhere in Soviet territory. The genuinely revolutionary-minded (i.e., Maoist-type) Mongolians would overthrow the pro-Soviet "reactionary puppet" regime of Outer Mongolia under Premier Y. Tsedenbal and launch a war of national independence against the Soviet Union, even with Chinese Communist help. If the Mongolians are unable, or refuse, to do this, the Chinese Communists would invade and occupy Outer Mongolia, overthrow its pro-Moscow "revisionist" regime in Ulan Bator, incorporate the country into "the Chinese federation," [77] and use Mongolian manpower for a war against the Soviet Union.

Troubled at home and in the world's "heartland" of Asia, the Soviet regime would have to withdraw Soviet troops from Eastern Europe to put down non-Russian domestic rebellions and reinforce troops in China and Outer Mongolia where more and more troop sacrifice would be needed. Finding the Soviet Union powerless in Eastern Europe, the Germans would seize the occasion to reunite their nation (possibly with the overt help of the United States). The withdrawal of Russian troops from Eastern Europe would encourage the process of "de-Sovietization" of the area. Separately, or perhaps more likely in unison, the German "revanchists" and "de-Sovietized" Eastern Europe, i.e., Hungary, Poland, and Rumania, would then press demands against Moscow for the return of their "lost territories" seized by Stalin. Finland and Japan would be tempted to join these countries' irredentist movements against Moscow. Japan might go so far as to occupy Sakhalin Island, the Kurile Islands, and even parts of Siberia for its imperialistic gain.

Amid this flurry, the Kremlin regime would not be able to carry on the war against China and at the same time to maintain law and order at home and would consequently "lose all control" over the country. Eventually, one final stroke—a battlefield defeat in the Asian heartland—would topple the Brezhnev-Kosygin regime and the Soviet Union would dissolve into anarchy, hate and violence, as Czarist Russia did in 1917.

In this "victorious people's war" against Soviet aggression, the Maoist military doctrine maintains that the militia would complement the regular armed forces and would be expected to play a major role in the defense of the homeland against the invading enemy forces. It is chiefly on this ground that Mao justifies the maintenance of the militia system in China. In actuality, the militia is more than a service army force that can be expected to defend mainland China. Among other important functions that it performs are included carrying out "Hate the Soviet Union" campaigns, aiding production drives in the economic field, helping the secret police, transmitting intelligence reports, and protecting state properties. Mao maintains that the militia constitutes no great burden on the national resources and treasury, since its members are largely self-supporting.

The Maoist Chinese are opposed to the demand of professional army officers that Peking's nuclear capability be improved at the sacrifice of economic modernization. They assert that the building of a highly developed economic base is a prerequisite for strong national military capability.[78] They charge that the military professionals are guilty of putting the cart of military modernization before the horse of economic modernization.

Mao is firmly opposed to a truce or compromise with the Soviet Union in the Sino-Soviet rift and boundary dispute. He argues that there can and will be no compromise between "truth" and "error." [79] Mao maintains that Sino-Soviet rapprochement is possible only if and when Moscow accepts the militant Chinese version of Communism and when the Soviet Union returns to China its "lost territories" that were grabbed by Czarist Russia. He is afraid that slavish reliance on and emulation of the Soviet Union will have a harmful effect on China's military modernization. Therefore, heavy emphasis is placed on the greatest possible self-reliance and self-sufficiency.

As for the idea of Sino-American rapprochement, Mao asserts that there is no need for China actively and hastily to seek rapprochement with the United States unless and until the Nixon Administration demonstrates its good faith and settles the Taiwan question on Peking's terms. But he is not opposed to the idea of opening communication with the United States chiefly for the purpose of making Moscow nervous. He argues, as he did at the time of his invitation to President Nixon to visit the Chinese mainland in February 1972, that the Chinese Communists must always distinguish between their major and their minor enemies at a given time; thus a temporary accommodation with the minor against the major enemy is tactically permissible.

As for the use of the Chinese army for nonmilitary purposes, Mao contends that Communist construction in the Chinese mainland is everybody's business, and that therefore the political loyalty of the army should be transformed into productive efficiency. He also insists that the army is a great school not only for the defense of the homeland, but for political training as well. Therefore, its active participation in political and economic activities will raise the ideological standards and the Communist revolutionary consciousness of the troops. [80]

Mao and his ideologues justify their policy of abandoning all military ranks and insignia in the armed forces on the grounds that military ranks are a harmful "bourgeois" and "revisionist" evil and that the change was merely a return to the army's old tradition when all ranks were "comrades." [81] They maintain that the preservation of the old guerrilla spirit of the Yenan period, which emphasized the principle of proletarian democracy, will strengthen rather than weaken the morale, discipline, and combat effectiveness of the entire army.

By and large, Mao envisions a truly classless society in which each Chinese is part poet and peasant, part soldier and factory worker, and most important of all, a Maoist "revolutionary."

For the past five years the Soviet Union has lost no time in intervening openly in China's Cultural Revolution with a propaganda campaign aimed at discrediting and subverting Mao's radical antirevisionist (anti-Soviet) campaign. As part of this campaign, Moscow has recently been meddling in the dispute that has been going on between those who hold to Mao's military doctrine and those who advocate military professionalism. Moscow has sought to turn the Chinese army, especially its senior officers, against Mao.[82] In a quite recent Chinese-language broadcast, Moscow derided the Chinese People's Liberation Army with "equipment a decade old or even dating from World War II," and ridiculed Mao's people's war strategy.[83] The Soviet Union appears to be trying to undermine the morale of the Chinese people and soldiers with the threat of its superior military strength and, at the same time, to help China's military professionals stiffen their opposition to Mao and his military thought. Moscow is also trying to use China's military weakness to extort concessions from Peking on the territorial dispute. Accordingly, the Soviets are likely to continue to exert pressure along the Sino-Soviet boundary, while maintaining a tougher or intransigent position in the current border negotiations in Peking.

As long as Mao Tse-tung is alive and rules Communist China, it is highly unlikely that military professionalism can prevail over Mao's classic military thought. Even more unlikely is the prospect that, as Moscow hopes, the Chinese army, particularly its professionally-minded officers, would turn against Mao, because of the myth of Mao, his prestige and charisma, and Chinese nationalism. China under Mao will remain intolerant of military professionalism.

However, the arrogant pretension of Maoism to all-time infallibility carries within it the seeds of its own frustration. Mao's genius lies more in wrecking an established order he dislikes than in building and managing a sophisticated and complex society. What Mao scornfully calls "revisionism" or "professionalism" is a concomitant of the industrialized and militarily powerful Communist society he himself has sought to build since 1949.

As China moves further toward economic and military modernization, Mao's military thought will no doubt become increasingly irrelevant. History's logic weighs against Maoism. With China changing, Mao may already have outlived his time. After Mao and other doctrinaire Chinese fade away from the scene, military professionalism will inevitably and gradually prevail over Mao's classic strategy of guerrilla warfare.

Conclusion

The Soviet Union and Communist China still show no signs of wanting to relax their guard in dealing with each other. They repeatedly make their mutual animosity clear. There has been no progress whatever in the current high-level Sino-Soviet border negotiations in Peking. The Soviets have not shown any disposition to abandon the fruits of czarist imperialism, nor are the Chinese willing to drop and forget their territorial claims against the Soviet Union. Even as the border discussions go on, both sides are steadily building up their military forces within reach of the border. Moscow now maintains forty-four divisions in the Sino-Soviet border area and in the Soviet satellite state of Outer Mongolia—a quarter of the entire Soviet army. The Chinese undoubtedly suffer from "Russophobia," and have been meeting this Soviet reinforcement with a military buildup of their own.

One hundred and fifty-odd years ago, Karl Marx felt that the world proletariat could win victory only through unity, yet world Communism today is more fragmented than ever before in its history. Communist China and the Soviet Union vilify each other in terms as harsh as either uses against the capitalist world. Today Moscow has replaced the United States in the minds of the Chinese Communist leaders as the chief threat and as public enemy number one. Peking's late Foreign Minister Chen Yi reportedly said to a European ambassador in 1968 that the Americans were "bastards but honest bastards," while the Soviets were "liars and traitors." [1]

The Soviets are apparently not content with defending their northern and western borders against Chinese incursion alone. Although thwarted at their first try, they are still striving to create "a system of collective security" in Asia. The Soviet proposal for an Asian collective security arrangement was first broached obliquely by the Soviet Communist Party's Secretary-General Leonid I. Brezhnev on June 7, 1969, in his speech to the world Communist conference in Moscow.[2] Soviet Foreign Minister Andrei A. Gromyko followed up in an address to the Supreme Soviet on July 10, 1969, saying that "discussion and consultation among interested states" on such a system was necessary.[3] The Brezhnev proposal was obviously motivated by a double Soviet desire: to contain and isolate China, and to fill the power vacuum being created in Asia by the gradual British and, particularly, American military withdrawal from the area. That is to say, it would run counter to the Sino-Soviet alliance treaty of February 1950,[4] which has never been formally abrogated by both partners although it has long been a dead letter. Furthermore, it appears to be part of an evolving Soviet policy for Asia after the Vietnam War to counter the American-Chinese rapprochement symbolized by President Nixon's recent visit to the Chinese mainland.

The Soviet concept of an Asian collective security system remains as vague as ever, but the Soviet Union appears to want the alignment to embrace the largest possible number of Asian nations, both Communist and non-Communist.[5] The Kremlin also reportedly envisages an alignment involving nonaggression pacts, mutual respect for the inviolability of borders, non-interference in one another's internal affairs, and mutual economic and other kinds (e.g., military) of cooperation.

In the fall of 1969 the Soviet Union launched a campaign to implement the Brezhnev proposal for a collective security arrangement in Asia. Moscow is now moving quietly and steadily to make friends, influence people, and advance its interests in eastern, southern, and western Asia, while Soviet and Chinese representatives are meeting in Peking to resolve their border (and, possibly, other) disputes. In recent months, for example, the Kremlin has improved its relations with Turkey, Iran, and Iraq, where United States influence has been strong. It has concluded a treaty of peace, friendship, and cooperation with India. In the recent Indo-Pakistani war it strongly supported India. It is increasing its influence in the new state of Bangladesh.[6] Yet even while championing the independence of Bangladesh, the Soviets appear to have successfully normalized their relations with Pakistan, which were strained to the breaking point during the Indo-Pakistani war, as indicated by Pakistani President Zulfikar Ali Bhutto's recent visit to Moscow.[7] Major commercial programs are being pushed in Singapore, Malaysia, Ceylon, Afghanistan, Nepal, Indonesia, Thailand, and Burma.[8] The Soviets are seeking to establish diplomatic relations with the Philippines—as indicated by their recent dispatch of the Bolshoi Ballet to Manila and the warm welcome accorded to Mrs. Imelda Marcos, wife of the country's president.[9] The Soviets are even flirting with Nationalist China.[10] In the spring of 1971 the Soviet leaders gave military aid to the Ceylonese government to help its effort to crush an uprising by about 10,000 young Maoist revolutionaries. The Soviet Union has gone out of its way to make a noisy and demonstrative show of support for North Vietnam and North Korea and thus to increase its influence in these two Asian Communist nations at a time when their relations with Peking are strained because of the Nixon visit to the Chinese mainland. In Indochina, in particular, it has been backing the Hanoi regime in its war against South Vietnam, Laos, and Cambodia more actively than before. Moscow is working assiduously to improve its relations with Japan and also to push forward Soviet-Japanese cooperation in the development of Siberia.[11] During his recent visit to Japan Soviet

Foreign Minister Andrei Gromyko reportedly told Japanese Prime Minister Eisaku Sato that his country would like soon to conclude a peace treaty with Japan formally terminating the Second World War.[12]

But the Soviet proposal for an Asian collective security system has made little headway in its implementation, and seems to face many obstacles in the future. For one thing, many Asians, i.e., the Indians, Pakistanis, and Afghans, still prefer to stick to the diplomacy of "nonalignment" in world politics, refusing to get caught with the "evil" of military alliances sponsored either by the United States or the Soviet Union. Some Asian leaders, as they observe a gradual reduction of United States commitment in Asia in accordance with the Nixon Doctrine, are understandably distrustful of the promises of protection and cooperation by another alien white giant whose motives are primarily guided by nothing but self-interest. The Soviet Union is distrusted by anti-Communist Asian governments, especially those threatened by Communist subversion and terrorism within their countries, because of the Kremlin's treacherous two-track efforts to maintain good relations with them while simultaneously covertly or overtly backing Asian Communist revolutionaries who are striving to destroy the established bourgeois authorities. Meanwhile, Asians are becoming increasingly aware of the necessity of self-reliance and self-support in the form of regional cooperation for their national survival and security. Moreover, even some conservative Asian nations on the periphery of mainland China, e.g., Thailand, are evidently anxious to keep open their options, hoping to reach a modus vivendi with Communist China if the latter adopts a more tolerant, good-neighborly, live-and-let-live attitude toward them. Despite their interest in the joint development of Siberia—because of their hunger for its resources—the Japanese clearly wish not to antagonize the Peking regime by enlarging their diplomatic and economic ties simultaneously with Moscow and Peking. The two other Asian Communist countries, North Korea and North Vietnam, are loathe to dance when the Soviets show a desire to encircle Communist China, partly because they desire to play off the two Communist giants against each other for their maximum political advantages and partly because they realize that they have little choice but to coexist with their powerful Chinese neighbor.

Mao's China indignantly denounces the Soviet scheme for a collective security system in Asia as "something Russia picked up from the garbage heap" of the late U.S. Secretary of State John Foster Dulles and says that it is doomed to failure.[13] Peking is actively taking various countermeasures to spoil Soviet efforts in Asia. At the same time, it is seeking a new coalition or a "united front" of governments of varying political complexion in Europe, Latin America, Asia, and Africa that will inhibit the power of the world's two superpowers—the United States and the Soviet Union. Political cynicism in world affairs is not the monopoly of the Soviet Union. In an attempt to strengthen its position in many parts of the world and also to increase its foreign policy options, the Peking regime is matching if not outdoing Moscow's Machiavellian cynicism, as exemplified by its recent decision to woo Tito's "revisionist" Yugoslavia after long years of outright hostility.

As regards the Sino-Soviet rift, Richard M. Nixon has said repeatedly that the United States is not interested in siding with either of the two Communist giants against the other. Consistent with this stance, he wants to normalize relations with mainland China by ending the mutual hatred and hostility that has separated Washington and Peking during the past two decades. Ironically, it is Nixon himself who rode the crest of the "Who lost China?" witch hunt in the early 1950's and subsequently built his political career largely on the basis of his fervent anti-Communism. This old American baiter of Communists has changed and mellowed since then. With this policy of evenhandedness on the part of the United States, the world has formally edged away from the simple bipolar confrontations of the Cold War into a new geometry of interlocking power balances. In the decade of the 1970's the Moscow-Washington-Peking triangular game is likely to be the dominant factor in the power politics of our time.

Sino-American relations began to warm up after President Nixon, in the fall of 1969, started sending Peking diplomatic signals—e.g., the suspension of the Taiwan Strait patrol by the U.S. Seventh Fleet, and a stage-by-stage elimination of restrictions on travel and trade between the United States and Communist China[14]—and after an indirect Soviet threat of a preemptive nuclear strike against the Chinese mainland following the bloody Ussuri border clashes of March 1969.[15] It was during 1971 that the two countries plunged into their behind-the-scenes efforts for mutual bridge-building, culminating in Nixon's recent historic trip to China.

Nixon must realize that the United States is best placed to hold the center of the triangle, partly because the two Communist giants share a long, hostile boundary and partly because America is less fettered by doctrinal prejudice than the others, having no need for permanent adversaries and seeking none. Accordingly, the United States should be in a better position to play off the two corners of the triangle against each other, thereby enhancing its bargaining position and diplomatic posture with both Peking and Moscow on a wide range of issues. It should also be better able to react to the hostility of each of the two major Communist powers as well as to the current explosive animosity between them, in order to bring about world equilibrium.

Reciprocally, Communist China has a great deal to gain from its policy of rapprochement with the United States, at little cost to itself. The most important motivation behind Peking's interest in establishing and maintaining amicable relations with the United States is probably its increasing awareness of the peril and promise of its triangular relationship with Washington and Moscow. The Chinese Communists desire to keep their communication with the United States open, partly to prevent possible anti-Chinese collusion between

Washington and Moscow and partly to signal the Kremlin that they are keeping their American options open—just in case. More specifically, Peking wants to use the prospect of improved Sino-American ties partly as a counterweight to the military threat posed by the Soviet Union along their common boundary and partly as a ploy to maneuver the Soviets into making concessions at the currently deadlocked high-level boundary talks in the Chinese capital. In short, China's extensive experience in using the centuries-old technique called *i-i-chi-i* ("using barbarians to control barbarians") is becoming even more pertinent today.

Obviously, the campaign against mainland China is today a major Soviet obsession. Accordingly, the Soviets are plainly nervous about the possibility of Washington-Peking détente. The Soviet Union, in public and informal statements, has made no secret of the fact that the improving relationship between Washington and Peking, as exemplified by the recent Nixon visit to Peking, is regarded with suspicion, jealousy, and anger verging on the hysterical. Undoubtedly, the possibility of a Washington-Peking rapprochement is emerging as the single most important problem for Soviet foreign policy in the years ahead. The question now for Moscow is how to influence the developing relationship between the United States and China in such a way that it does not become a threat to the Soviets. What are the options open to the Soviet Union?

There are four possibilities. Moscow can foster reconciliation with China by agreeing to many or all of the major demands of Peking. Or it can assume that Peking demands too big a price and come to terms with Washington on all major questions, more or less along the lines suggested by the United States. Or it can try to play off Washington against Peking. Or it can become reconciled to the eventual hegemony of the United States in Europe and of Communist China in Asia. Beyond these, there are no practical alternatives available. Of these, the only realistic course that Moscow shows signs of accepting, as demonstrated by the cordial welcome given to President Nixon when he visited the Soviet Union in May 1972, is that of trying to play off China against the United States. In a new, three-sided world, the Soviet Union has to be more careful and restrained than it was in the old, two-sided world.

By and large, the international political game in the 1970's is no longer two-handed poker played with concealed cards. Instead, it is a three-sided form of chess in which all the pieces are visible and can move themselves in a complex assortment of variations. Each of the three players dislikes and fears the other two and aims to reduce collusion between them to a minimum by playing on their mutual dislikes and fears and by seeking to maneuver them against each other. The surest way for any of the three to provoke the other two into fateful collusion is to display undue aggressiveness. The political beauty of the triangle is that each of its members is antagonistic to the two others, although, precisely because they form a triangle, their mutual antagonism may be modified in different sets of circumstances. All three players are nuclear powers, and the collective might of the triangle could easily wipe out human civilization, but all (even China, behind its fierce rhetoric) dread nuclear war and all must live in a common-law alliance against nuclear war. That is to say, none of the three players—without risking nuclear destruction—dares to withdraw from, or break, that relationship of the three-sided global chessboard even as their fairly traditional contest for power, influence, and other gains continues around the world.

Documents

Document 1

GEOGRAPHIC BACKGROUND
OF THE SINO-SOVIET BORDER

The Sino-Soviet boundary arbitrarily cuts across the principal physiographic regions of central and northeastern Asia. In the west, the boundary begins at the Afghanistan tripoint on the edge of the Pamirs, often referred to as the "roof of the world." This tangled knot of high mountain ranges surrounding a generally flattened plateau comprises the central core of the mountain system of Central Asia. From the Pamirs, the world's loftiest mountain ranges radiate in all directions. To the south and southeast lie the Karakorum, Himalaya, and Kunlun mountains which separate Pakistan, Kashmir, and India from Sinkiang and Tibet. To the northeast a complex pattern of mountain systems extends across and along the frontier.

The Pamirs, although of great elevation, are characterized

Excerpts from International Boundary Study No. 64, Feb. 14, 1966, *China-USSR Boundary* (Issued by the Geographer, Office of Research in Economics and Science, Bureau of Intelligence and Research, United States Department of State, Washington, D.C.), pp. 1–3. Reprinted by permission.

by a general flatness of both ridges and valleys and have been described as a "partially peneplaned area in which wide, mature valleys are separated by residual ridges." In general, elevations increase westward, where the highest peaks attain 25,000 feet or more in elevation. The parallel valleys vary from 5 to 10 miles in width and have an average elevation of 12,000 to 13,000 feet. The intervening ridges which are aligned generally east-west extend about 4,000 to 5,000 feet higher than the valley floors. The melting snows and glaciers have all but removed any evidence of soil from the ridges leaving only a mantle of rock and glacial debris. The valley floors, in contrast, have collected the alluvium resulting in flattish, but rock-strewn, floors.

Northward into the Alai ranges the same general "pamir" characteristics dominate. However, unlike the true Pamirs, the lateral extension of the mountain ranges is relatively limited. To the east and west extend lowlands—in the case of China the Tarim Basin, while in the U.S.S.R. it is the steppe and basin region of Kirghizia and Fergana. The mountains descend steeply to the lowland leaving the principal passes at great relative and absolute elevations. The major routes through the mountains are in the neighborhood of 13,000 to 14,000 feet. The major peaks lie at 23,000 feet, while the mean elevation of the lowlands is about 3,000 feet, although many parts of Russian Turkestan are much lower.

After crossing the Alai group, the frontier joins the Tien Shan, the northermost of the great ranges which radiate from the Pamir knot. The alignment, being generally east-west, soon leads the range away from the frontier to divide Sinkiang into its two component physical parts: the deserts of the Tarim basin to the south and the steppes of Dzungaria to the north. The Tien Shan is comprised of old limestone and slate rock formations which have been sharply folded and faulted into a series of parallel ranges alternating with shallow basins. Abrupt rises in elevation occur, attaining 10,000 feet locally. However, the basins generally lie about 10,000 feet in elevation while the ridges average only 3,000 to 6,000 feet higher. The highest peaks measure about 25,000 feet, most of them concentrated in the southern part. To the north, the ranges are lower and the valleys are much wider. The lowlands of the Tekes and Ili rivers form distinct natural routes across the frontier zone. North of the Ili, the Tien Shan give way to the Alatau, one of the block mountain systems of Central Asia, and the lowlands of Dzungaria.

The Dzungarian Basin is a triangular wedge of lowland projecting between the Tien Shan to the south and the Altai Mountains to the north. On the west, the Basin is closed off by the Dzungarian Alatau, the Birlik Tau, the Saur, and the Tarbagatay, most of which are boundary ranges. Primarily a steppe region, Dzungaria links western China and Soviet Central Asia through the famous Dzungarian Gate. The strategic pass is actually a ten-mile long gorge lying at 700 feet above sea level between the Ebi Nur and Alakol' lakes. It is through this pass that the Chinese Communists and the Soviets had planned to link their Turkestan railroad systems. The actual "Gate" of the great historic migrations is considered to be the lowland area to the north in the vicinity of Chuguchak. Beyond the Tarbagatay a third major route-way, the lowland valley of the Chernyy Irtysh, also cuts across the frontier.

The Turkestan sector of the frontier terminates in the Altai Mountains along the Mongolian frontier. The Altai are neither a very high nor a very spectacular range of mountains. However, their location, alignment, and elevation combine fortuitously to produce heavy precipitation in the form of rain and snow. The surrounding region, as a result, is relatively well watered and many streams rise on the flanks of the range along the Sino-Mongolian frontier.

East of Mongolia, the frontier region is less complex. The Khingan Mountains and their northward continuation, the Stanovoy, form a steep escarpment to the lowlands of Manchuria and a barrier to the maritime influences of the Pacific. Rising to approximately 6,000 feet in the south, elevations on the ranges decrease slowly northward to about 4,000 feet. The fall to the east, however, remains abrupt to the high plains of Manchuria, creating for the range a more mountainous character than the elevations would deem. The range is important as the interior limit of the maritime and monsoonal influence in climate and vegetation. It forms, as a result, a cultural boundary as well. To the east, the Han Chinese and their intensive agriculture have become established while to the west there exist the nomadic and/or extensive settlements of the Mongols.

East of the Khingan, the frontier region is a lowland—the Amur-Ussuri plains. Elevations are relatively low and the dominant landforms are gently rounded and forested hills alternating with poorly drained riverine plains. The large area of forest has been an economic attraction to the Chinese. Excellent stands of pine, larch, cedar, and spruce are found along the Amur while hardwoods, particularly oak and maple, grow along the Sungari and Ussuri rivers. Extensive swamps occur at the confluence of the Amur and Ussuri and around the upper Ussuri in the south. Primarily, the development and utilization of the valuable region suffers from its isolation from both the Soviet and the Chinese centers of production and communications.

Document 2

NERCHINSK TREATY OF PEACE AND BOUNDARIES, SIGNED AT NERCHINSK ON AUGUST 27, 1689

Article I

The river Gorbitza, which joins the Schilka from its left side near the river Tchernaya, is to form the boundary between

From *Treaties, Conventions, etc., Between China and Foreign States*, 2d ed. (Shanghai: Statistical Department of the Inspectorate General of Customs, 1917), Vol. I, pp. 4–7. Translated from the Russian by a member of the Chinese customs service.

the two Empires. The boundary from the source of that river
to the sea will run along the top of the mountain chain [in
which the river rises]. The jurisdiction of the two Empires
will be divided in such a way that [the valleys of] all the rivers
or streams flowing from the southern slope of these mountains
to join the Amur shall belong to the Empire of China [lit., of
Han], while [the valleys of] all the rivers flowing down from
the other [or northern] side of these mountains shall be similarly under the rule of His Majesty the Czar of the Russian
Empire. As to [the valleys of] the other rivers which lie between the Russian river Oud and the aforesaid mountains running near the Amur and extending to the sea, which are now
under Chinese rule, the question of the jurisdiction over them
is to remain open. On this point the [Russian] Ambassadors
are [at present] without explicit instructions from the Czar.
Hereafter, when the Ambassadors on both sides shall have returned [to their respective countries], the Czar and the Emperor of China [Han] will decide the question on terms of
amity, either by sending Plenipotentiaries or by written correspondence.

Article II

Similarly, the river Argun, which flows into the Amur, will
form the frontier along its whole length. All territory on the
left bank is to be under the rule of the Emperor of China
[Khan of Han]; all on the right bank will be included in the
Empire of the Czar. All habitations on the south side will be
transferred to the other.

Article III

The fortified town of Albazin, built by His Majesty the Czar,
is to be completely demolished, and the people residing there,
with all military and other stores and equipment, are to be
moved into Russian territory. Those moved can take all their

property with them, and they are not to be allowed to suffer loss [by detention of any of it].

Article IV

Fugitives [lit., runaways] from either side who may have settled in the other's country previous to the date of this Treaty may remain. No claims for their rendition will be made on either side. But those who may take refuge in either country after the date of this Treaty of Amity are to be sent without delay to the frontier and at once handed over to the chief local officials.

Article V

It is to be understood by both Governments that from the time when this Treaty of Amity is made, the subjects of either nation, being provided with proper passports, may come and go [across the frontier] on their private business and may carry on commerce [lit., buy and sell].

Article VI

All the differences [lit., quarrels] which may have occurred between the subjects [of each nation] on the frontier up to the date of this Treaty will be forgotten and [claims arising out of them will] not be entertained. But if hereafter any of the subjects [lit., traders or craftsmen] of either nationality pass the frontier [as if] for private [and legitimate] business, and [while in the foreign territory] commit crimes of violence to property and life, they are at once to be arrested and sent to the frontier of their own country and handed over to the chief local authority [military], who will inflict on them the death penalty as a punishment of their crimes. Crimes and excesses committed by private people on the frontier must not be made the cause of war and bloodshed by either side. When cases of this kind arise, they are to be reported by [the officers of] the side on which they occur to the Sovereigns of both Powers, for settlement by diplomatic negotiation in an amicable manner.

If the Emperor of China desires to engrave [on stone] the Articles of the above Treaty agreed upon by the Envoys for the determination of the frontier, and to place the same [at certain positions] on the frontier as a record, he is at liberty to do so. Whether this is to be done or not is left entirely to the discretion of His Majesty the Emperor of China.

Document 3

BUR TREATY: BOUNDARY PROTOCOL
EXCHANGED AT ABAGAITU HILL
ON OCTOBER 12, 1727

(Partial Text)

This letter is exchanged between Glazunov for Russia, Hibit for China and Najantai for the Mongols and confirms the agreement concerning the boundaries which was reached on the 20th of the August, 1727, on the Bur River.

The *majk* (border lighthouses) were erected beginning from the southern side of Mt. Burgutei. From its crest to the notable of Diret we set up 4 majk, each one against one of the 4 border outposts of the Chinese Empire which are located at Keransk, Chiktai, Arakuodur and Arahadain-Uus. We have counted part of the River Chikoi for a border and on the southern side of the River Chikoi we have set up 6 majk, two of which are majk for the location of Russian winter quarters. One of these two garrisons already stands on the upper portion of the Glen Sharbug, on the southern bank of the Chikoi River, near the newly erected majk. The second garrison was located at the

From *Treaties, Conventions, etc., Between China and Foreign States*, Vol. I, pp. 18–24. This translation was made from the Russian by Glen G. Alexandrin of Villanova University, Villanova, Pennsylvania.

mouth of the Arookood-Uur River on the southern bank of the Chikoi River. The border commissar of the Russian Empire, following the peaceful agreement that the border be cleared, destroyed this garrison building. Similarly, he transferred those Russian citizens, called *bratz,* who were following the garrison of the Chinese Empire along the Kudur River, with their belongings, to the northern bank of the Chikoi River.

With regard to these 6 majk, set up along the bank of the Chikoi, in order to discontinue the quarrels, the border commissars have agreed that Russian citizens should not cross to the southern riverbank to look over these majk and an order was issued to the border guards of the Chinese Empire at Zangin about the guarding and the repair of these majk.

In the area from the border marker of Arahadain-Uus to Oobur Hadain-Uus and to Tsagan-Ola, on the strength of a peaceful agreement between the citizens of the Russian Empire who live in these peripheral domains and the garrisons of the Chinese Empire, wherever there was empty land this land was divided. Thus 48 majk were erected on obvious mounds, on the ridges of extinct volcanoes, and on other sorts of outstanding geographical features such that they were near to the properties of the citizens of the Russian Empire. Similarly and equitably, in the area where the garrisons of the Chinese Empire already existed and on top of Chindagan where the Tungoose Ker, citizens of the Chinese Empire, live a nomadic life, the majk were set near their dwelling places. And these nomadic people, following the agreement, together with their belongings, were transferred to the Chinese side, by the Commissar of the Chinese Empire, to the area extending from the border garrison on Tsagan-Ola to the source of the Argun River near which there are 5 majk of the Chinese Empire. And they have declared this to be the border, decreeing that no one shall cross it and giving strong commands to the garrisons of both Empires to that effect.

And in this fashion, all along the border, it has been agreed that the previous quarrels should cease and so that thieves do not carry the border marks from one place to another we have written posters in Russian and Mongolian and have affixed these to the wood between the two border marks. We have also secreted these in the earth, indicating in these notes where the border marks are erected, by number, and how one follows another in terms of ridges, mountains, and rivers, thus describing the border from Mt. Burgutei and from the Grebenj Crest to the source of the Argun River. And this is as follows:

The 1st majk was set on the southern side of Burgut mound, the last mound in the Grebenj Range. The 2nd majk was erected on the southern side of the mound east of the Burgut mound, opposite Lake Tsadam. Opposite this salt lake and to the south at the end of the southern slope of Hoorlik Crest is the 3rd majk. Opposite the notable area of Diret Gap and opposite the Chikoi River, on top and on the eastern side of the mound is the 4th majk. At the upper end of the Chikoi River and on the Glen Sharbug is the 5th majk. At the mouth of Chiktaj River and on the mound atop the bank of the Chikoi was erected the 6th majk. The 7th majk was erected on the bank of the Chikoi where the Hazaj flows into it. On the bank where the Arkdour flows into the Chikoi was erected the 8th majk. At the mouth of the Ooilga where there is a flood meadow, on the bank of the Chikoi, was erected the 9th majk. The 10th majk was erected on the bank of the Chikoi where the Arahadain-Uus flows into it. An old majk stands on the point between the Arahadain-Uus River and the Liliej River. On the northern bank of the Liliej River is now erected the 11th majk. To the north of the old majk on Uboorhadain-Uus was erected the 12th majk. The 13th majk was erected to the north of the old majk on the Koomoorouin Ridge. The 14th majk was erected north of the old majk on the River Kooii opposite the end of the Koomoorouin Range. The 15th majk is north of the old marker on Gungurtai River and at the end of the Koomoroon Range. The 16th majk was erected on the northern bank of the Onon River in the vicinity of the Ashang

River, at the same height as the border garrison and on the top of the northern slope of the Range. The 17th majk was erected on the mound which is north of and in the vicinity of the empty majk of Harjagoot. On the northern bank of the Hasoolak River and north of the Hasoolak border garrison, on the mound atop the mountain, is set the 18th majk. On the right-hand side of the empty majk of Baldjee-Batookhad, toward the north and on top of the mound called Monko, was set the 19th majk. On the mound on the spit of land on the southwestern side of the River Baldzihan across to the north from the Kumulejski garrison's majk is the 20th majk. The 21st majk was erected on a mound called Belchir on the northern side of Mt. Galdatajski next to the unoccupied Galdatajski majk. The 22nd majk was erected on the crest of the left bank of the Kirhun River and north of the unoccupied Kirhun border garrison. The 23rd majk was erected on the tall ridge of Hall which is on the left bank of the Bookookoon River and north of the empty majk. The 24th majk was erected on top of the mound Bain Dzurik north of the Gilbir border garrison on the Gilbir River. The 25th majk was erected north of the empty majk of Altagahn and on the ridge of Boojukt. The 26th majk was erected to the north of the Argatsuj border garrison on the Hormoch River opposite the last mound of the Streloshnoj. The 27th majk was erected on the main ridge of the southern bank of the Gozolot River and north of the empty Nikur majk. The 28th majk stands atop the Ardarg mound on the northern bank of the Kerju River and toward the northwest of the border garrison of Tabun Tologoj. The 29th majk was erected on the mound to the north of the empty majk called Hongar. The 30th majk was erected north of the border garrison of Ulhootzk on top and at the end of the mound called Bugr and near the "Virgin" stone. To the left of the border garrison of Ulhootzk and opposite the northern bank of the Onon River and to the left (eastern side) of Arabaine Dzurik, atop a mound was erected the 31st majk. The 32nd majk was erected on top of the ridge of Chernoj Black Mound and to the north

of the empty majk Ubur Bain Dzurik Bituken. To the north
of the Birkin border garrison and on top of the ridge of Birk
was erected the 33rd majk. The 34th majk was erected to the
north of the empty Hurtz majk on the edge of the ridge. The
35th majk was erected to the north of the border garrison of
Mangutnuk on the top of the crest of the hill. The 36th majk
was established on top of the mound in the spit of land running into the big River Turgin which is to the north of the
empty majk of Kul. To the north of Tosoktoiskij border garrison atop the mound called Tosok was erected the 37th majk.
The 38th majk was erected to the north of the empty majk of
Dzuchinskij on the crest of the mound called Ho. The 39th
majk was erected to the north of the Horin Narasin border
garrison on top of a mound on an outcropping of Horin
Narasin. The 40th majk was erected on a ball-like mountain
north of the empty majk of Sendurt. To the north of the Ubur
Toktor border garrison on the Toktor River, and on top of
the ridge on the left slope of Toktor mound was erected the
41st majk. To the right of the empty majk of Kookoo Ishig
and on top of the northern slope of Chernoj mound was
erected the 42nd majk. The 43rd majk was erected to the
north of the border garrison of Turkijn which is on the
Uboorbirk River and along the northern side of the Turkijn
Range, on top of the mound. The 44th majk was erected on
the high point of the ridge to the north of the left (eastern)
majk of Turkijn. The 45th majk was erected to the north
of the border garrison of Dorolg on the ridge on the right
hand (western) slope of the mound atop Tsagin Nor. The
46th majk was erected away from the empty Imalg majk and
on top of the northern mound of Kookoo Tolog. The 47th
majk was erected to the northeast of the border garrison of
Ulint, on the northern bank of the Imalg River, on the mound
called Hara Tolog. To the north of the empty majk of Irin,
on the northern bank of the Imalg River, on the eastern slope
of the range, on the mound on the outcropping was erected the
48th majk. The 49th majk was erected to the northeast of the

border garrison of Obot, in the steppe, on top of two hillocks. The 50th majk was erected to the north of the empty majk of Nipi, on a mound in the steppe. The 51st majk was erected to the north of the border garrison of Mogidzig, at the end of the range up on top. The 52nd majk was erected to the north of the empty majk of Tsipt on a high spot in the steppe. The 53rd majk was erected on top of the end of the ridge to the north of the border garrison of Dtzerent. The 54th majk was erected on top of a mound to the north of the empty majk of Ink Tolog, in the steppe. The 55th majk was erected in the northern direction from the border garrison of Munk Tolog, in the steppe. The 56th majk was erected in the steppe to the north of the empty majk of Angarhai. The 57th majk was erected in the steppe to the north of the border garrison of Kubeldzik. The 58th majk was erected in the steppe to the north of the empty majk of Tarbagdah. North of the border garrison of Tsagan-Ola, nearer Schar-Ola, was erected the 59th majk. The 60th majk was erected to the north of the empty majk of Tabun Tolog and on top of the nearest mound of Bor Tolog. To the north and near the border garrison of Tsokt, on top of a nearby mound, was erected the 61st majk. The 62nd majk was erected to the north of the empty majk of Irdin Tolog, on top of a nearby high place. The 63rd majk was erected on the right-hand (western) bank of the Argun River, opposite the middle stream of Hylarskij on the spit of land opposite the Abajijgat mound.

Here the new border meets with the old and already established border.

Document 4

BUR TREATY: BOUNDARY PROTOCOL
EXCHANGED ON THE BUR RIVER
ON OCTOBER 27, 1727

(Partial Text)

The agreement was made for Russia by Kolichov and for China by Dariambij Besigoj, Tusulakchij Tushimel Pufui, and Detzergen, and Araptan.

The boundary begins between the Rivers of Kiakhta and Orogioty. To the right of this new marker, on the Orogioty mound have been erected two new markers; from there if you walk along Timek Koodzuin Bichikt Hosheg and as you cross the River Seleng toward Boolait Ola, on the left-hand side two markers were erected; two markers were erected on the southern end of the mound where the south side of the ridge of Kookoochelotooin meets the end of Janhorola; on Hygor two markers were erected; we crossed Bogosunama and on the spit of land, in the Gooizan-Ola range, situated between the southern slope of the Zermlik mound and the northern slope of the Mertzel mound, we set up two markers; we crossed the Ziltoor River between Hootoogajt and Goondzan and on Hootoogajt-Ola, on the left slope, we erected two markers; near the Boorhold River on the top of the rise, on the road, we set up two markers. This place is between the right-hand slope of Hootoogajt-Ola and the left slope of Kookoonarooga. On the road atop Oodin Zoin, which is on the left bank of the Kootzoonrat River, we set up two markers; near the Tzedj River, high up on the road, we have erected two markers; on an elevation near the Modoonkool River, high up on the road, we have set up two markers; along the Boorool River, on top of the road on Bogootadabagaja,

---

From *Treaties, Conventions, etc., Between China and Foreign States*, Vol. I, pp. 25–27. This translation was made from the Russian by Glen G. Alexandrin of Villanova University, Villanova, Pennsylvania.

we have set up two markers; on the left bank of the Keket River, on the road and before reaching Schitdabag, we have erected two markers; on top of the road on Kisiniktdabag, which lies between the right slope of Oodinzon Gurbi and the left bank of the Munkunkiket River, we put up two markers; near the Uri River and on top of Gurbidabag we have put up two markers; high up on the road atop Gurbi and on the right bank of the Hanh River we have set up two markers; on the road atop Nookootdabag near Narinhor we set up two markers; near the left bank of the Tengiss River, on the road atop Ergik Targak Tajga, we have set up two markers; atop the Toros Dabag Road, near the Bedikem River, we have set up two markers; on the right bank of the Uus River, in the Ergik Targak Tajga Range, and on top of the Kinzemed Ridge, we have set up two markers. There we crossed the Uus River and set up two markers. On the road atop Honin Dabag we put up two markers; on the Kem Kemcheek Bom we put up two markers; on top of Shabin Dabag, on the road we put up two markers.

Including the first marker on Kiakhta, there were, altogether, 24 markers erected and these newly erected markers, from Kiakhta to Shabin Dabag, mark the new boundary.

Document 5

KIAKHTA TREATY OF PEACE AND BOUNDARY,
SIGNED AT KIAKHTA ON OCTOBER 27, 1727

(Partial Text)

Article I

The present treaty was signed for the eternal conservation of peace between the two empires. . . .

From Edward Hertslet, *China Treaties,* 3d ed. (London: Harrison and Son, 1908), Vol. I, pp. 439–446. This translation was made from the French by William C. Stallings, Jr.

Article III

The officials of the Chinese Empire and the Illyrian Count Sawa Wladislawitche, ambassador from the Russian Empire, determined that the principal objective of their work was the settlement of the boundaries between the two empires but that governing those boundaries without scrupulous inspection of the terrain would be impossible. Toward this end:

The Illyrian Count Sawa Wladislawitche, ambassador from the Russian Empire, went to the frontier accompanied by Tsereng, adjunct general of the Chinese Empire, Doroi-giyon, viceroy of several Mongolian tribes and son-in-law of the emperor.

Be-szuge, commander of the imperial guard, and Toulichin, vice-president of the ministry of war. They agreed in the following manner on the locations through which the boundary should pass. The land situated between the guardhouse of the Russian Empire, near the stream Kiaktou and the Obo (a pile of stones which serves as a marker) of the Chinese Empire, which is situated at the top of the mountain Orkhoitou, should be equally divided and another Obo should be erected to serve as a marker of the boundary. At the same location, a warehouse of business should be established and commissars should be sent there.

From this location to the east, the border passes through the ridge of Bourgoutei up to the guardhouse of Kiran. Past the guardhouse of Kiran are those of Tsiktei, Arou-Kidoure and Arou-Khandangsou; the boundary runs through these four guardhouses in a straight line along the Tchoukou (Tchikoi) and Arou-Khandangsou rivers toward the location of the Mongolian guardhouse Tsagan-Oola (a white mountain). The desert between the land inhabited by subjects of the Russian Empire, and between the points of the Mongolian guardhouses, will be equally divided as at Kiaktou. Wherever there are, in the neighborhood of the land inhabited by the subjects of the Russian Empire, mountains, summits of mountains, and rivers, these will serve to determine the boundary;

and also wherever there are mountains or rivers in the neighborhood of the Mongolian guardhouses. These will similarly be chosen to determine the boundary. But wherever there are only vast plains without rivers or mountains, these have been equally divided and markers have been erected at the center to determine the boundary which has been settled to be from the marker of the guardhouse of Tsagan-Oola to the banks of the Argun River.

Those sent from the two empires to inspect the areas situated beyond the marker of the Mongolian guardhouse of Tsagan-Oola, agreed to run the boundary from the two markers at the center, erected at Kiaktou and on the mountain Orkhoitou, to the west through the following places: mounts Orkhoitou, Toumen, Koudchoukhoun, Bitsiktou, Kochogo, or Kochonggo.

The center of this equally divided chain of mountains was agreed upon as the boundary. Wherever there are mountains or rivers at the center, these have been equally divided, as they are presently; from the Chabinai-Dabagan to the banks of the Ergoune River, all that which is to the south (of the new boundary) belongs to the Chinese Empire, and all that is to the north to the Russian Empire.

After having finished the division of the land and having printed a description and exact map of it, the two parties reciprocally discussed these descriptions. They were sent to the heads of the two empires. The subjects who were illegally on the other side of the determined border and who had established residence there were sought out and taken back into their own country. The same action was undertaken in regard to vagabonds so that the frontier might be totally rid of them. . . .

Article IV

Now that the boundaries to the frontier of the two empires have been determined and since fugitives can not be ad-

mitted, it is agreed with the Illyrian Count Sawa Wladislawitche, ambassador from the Russian Empire, to establish
a free commerce between the two States.

Article VII

As to the bordering areas situated near the Oud River and
others, they have already been the subject of negotiations between the Head of the Interior, Sounggoutou and Fioo-for
Aliyeksiyei (Feodor Alexiewithcy Golowin). For the present,
these lands will remain undecided between the two parties;
but they will be subsequently determined by ambassadors
or by correspondence. At this time, the following remark was
made to the Illyrian Count Sawa Wladislawitche, ambassador
from the Russian Empire: "Since you have been sent as a
plenipotentiary of your empress to settle all affairs, we ought
to also settle the following. Presently your subjects often
cross the border to go into a country called Khinggan-Tou-
gourik, and if, as a result, a settlement about this is not made
during this negotiation, it is to be feared that this will cause
quarrels between bordering subjects. Since similar quarrels
are prevented in the contents of the Peace Treaty between the
two empires, we ought to settle this matter immediately." The
ambassador from the Russian Empire responded: "My Empress
did not give me the authority to negotiate the lands situated
toward the east. We do not have an exact knowledge of these
lands: it is therefore necessary that everything remain as it
has been settled; but, so as to prevent any of our subjects
from crossing the border, I will forbid it in the future." Our
representatives replied; "If your empress did not give you
the authority to negotiate the lands to the east, we will say
nothing more about it, and we must leave things as they
are. But, after your return, warn your subjects against crossing the border because, if someone entering our territory were
seized, we would punish him. You would therefore not be
able to say that we had violated the Peace Treaty. If, on the

contrary, one of our subjects crosses your border, you will equally have the right to punish him; finally, since nothing has been decided about the River Oud and the cantons which neighbor it, they will remain as before; but your subjects may not settle there any closer than they are at present. . . ."

Document 6

KIAKHTA SUPPLEMENTARY TREATY,
AMENDING ARTICLE X OF THE KIAKHTA TREATY OF 1727,
SIGNED AT KIAKHTA ON OCTOBER 18, 1768

(Partial Text)

Although the eleven Articles of the Peace Treaty [the Treaty of Kiakhta of 1727] were to be maintained as eternally invariable, it has, however, become necessary to move the Russian boundary markers from the area of Mount Bourgoutai to Bitsiktou, Kochou, and other locations to supervise the frontier on the ridge of the mountains; but everything will remain as settled previously near the two commercial warehouses at Kiaktou and Tsourkhaitou where there is no entrance duty. Some errors having gone unnoticed in the Russian and Latin copies, and several essential points having been forgotten, it was thought appropriate to correct and rectify them. Further, the discussions which took place between the two empires previously will be disregarded and the fugitives will not be called back. What was stated in Article X of the preceding Convention [the Treaty of Kiakhta of 1727] concerning the method of preventing robbery and desertion among respective subjects living around the border appeared too equivocal and indeterminate. Article X of the Convention

---

From *Treaties, Conventions, etc., Between China and Foreign States,* Vol. I, pp. 61–63. This translation was made from the French by William C. Stallings, Jr.

was therefore completely rejected; another, in place of the former, was drawn up and put into effect. According to the present Convention, each party must hereafter govern its subjects to prevent similar matters from recurring. If, at the new assembly, which should take place at the frontier, any evidence is discovered or other irregularities are reported, the commanders will be required to examine them without delay and with loyalty. If, on the contrary, they neglect their duty, each party must punish them according to its own laws. As to the search and apprehension of the brigands and the punishment of those who illegally cross the border, the following has been drawn up and agreed upon. . . .

Document 7

AIGUN TREATY OF FRIENDSHIP AND BOUNDARIES, SIGNED AT AIGUN ON MAY 16/28, 1858

(Partial Text)

Article I

The left bank of the Amur River, beginning at the Argun River, to the mouth of the Amur, will belong to the Russian Empire, and its right bank, down to the Ussuri River, will belong to the Chinese Empire; the territories and locations situated between the Ussuri River and the sea will, as they are presently, be commonly owned by the Chinese Empire and the Russian Empire until the boundary between the two States is settled. Navigation on the Amur, the Soungari, and the Ussuri is permitted only to vessels of the Chinese Empire and those of the Russian Empire; Navigation on these rivers

---

From *Treaties, Conventions, etc., Between China and Foreign States,* Vol. I, pp. 81–82. This translation was made from the French by William C. Stallings, Jr.

will be forbidden to vessels of all other States. The Manchu inhabitants settled on the left bank of the Amur, to the Zeya River up to the village of Hormoldzin to the south, will forever retain their former domiciles under the administration of the Manchu Government, and the Russian inhabitants will not be allowed to give them any offense nor cause them any vexation.

Article II

In the interest of satisfactory mutual relations of the respective subjects, the riverside inhabitants of the Ussuri, the Amur, and the Soungari, subjects of both Empires, are permitted to trade among themselves, and on both banks, the authorities must reciprocally protect the traders.

Article III

The stipulations, settled in common consent by the Plenipotentiary of the Russian Empire, the Governor-General Mouraview, and the Commander in Chief on the Amur, the Plenipotentiary of the Chinese Empire, I Chan, will be exactly and inviolably executed forever; to this effect, the Governor-General Mouraview, representing the Russian Empire, placed a copy of the present Treaty, written in the Russian and Manchu languages, in the hands of the Commander in Chief Prince I Chan, representing the Chinese Empire, and the Commander in Chief Prince I Chan gave a copy of the present Treaty, written in the Manchu and Mongolian languages, to the Governor-General Mouraview, representing the Russian Empire. All the stipulations recorded in the present [Treaty] will be published for the information of those inhabitants of both Empires living near the border.

Document 8

TREATY OF TIENTSIN, 1858,
SIGNED AT TIENTSIN ON JUNE 1/13, 1858

(Partial Text)

Article IX

The undetermined areas of the frontier between China and Russia should be examined without delay at these areas themselves.

The two Governments will for this purpose appoint delegates who will determine the line of demarcation and will conclude from their examination with an Agreement, which will be annexed as a Separate Article to the present Treaty.

Maps and detailed descriptions of the frontier will then be drawn up and will serve as incontestable documents for the future.

From *Treaties, Conventions, etc., Between China and Foreign States,* Vol. I, pp. 85–91. This translation was made from the French by William C. Stallings, Jr.

Document 9

PEKING ADDITIONAL TREATY OF COMMERCE,
NAVIGATION AND LIMITS,
SIGNED AT PEKING ON NOVEMBER 2/14, 1860

(Partial Text)

Article I

In order to corroborate and elucidate Article I of the Treaty signed in the city Aigun, May 16, 1858, and in execution of

---

From Edward Hertslet, *China Treaties,* Vol. I, pp. 461–471. This translation was made from the French by William C. Stallings, Jr.

Article IX of the Treaty signed on the first of June of the same year in the city Tientsin, it is stipulated that:

Henceforth the eastern frontier between the two empires shall commence from the juncture of the rivers Shilka and Argun, will follow the course of the River Amur to the junction of the River Ussuri with the latter. The land on the left bank (to the north) of the River Amur belongs to the empire of Russia, and the territory on the right bank (to the south) to the junction of the River Ussuri to the empire of China. Further on, the frontier line between the two empires ascends the rivers Ussuri and Sungacha to where the latter issues from Lake Kinka; it then crosses the lake, and takes the direction of the River Belen-ho or Tur; from the mouth of that river it follows the mountain range to the mouth of the River Huptu (a tributary of the Suifan), and from that point the mountains situated between the River Hun-Chun and the sea, as far as the River Tumen-Kiang. Along this line the territory on the east side belongs to the empire of Russia, and that on the west to the empire of China. The frontier line rests on the River Tumen at twenty li above its mouth into the sea.

Further, in execution on the same Article IX of the Treaty of Tientsin a map was prepared on which, for more clarity, the boundary line is traced in a red line and indicated by letters of the Russian alphabet. This map is signed by the Plenipotentiaries of the two Empires and sealed with their stamps.

If there should exist lands colonized by Chinese subjects (in the above-mentioned areas) the Russian Government promises to allow these inhabitants to remain there and also to permit them to engage, as in the past, in hunting and fishing.

After the frontier boundaries have been settled, the line of demarcation of the frontier ought to remain forever invariable.

Article II

The boundary line to the west, undetermined until now, should henceforth follow the direction of the mountains, the courses of the larger rivers and the presently existing line of Chinese pickets. Beginning at the last lighthouse, called Chabindabaga [in Mongolia] which was established in 1728 after the signing of the Treaty of Kiakhta, the boundary line will run southwest toward the Lake Dsai-sang, and then extends to the mountains called Tengri-chan or Alatau of the Kirghises or Thian-chan-nana-lou (southern branches of the mountains Celestes), which are situated to the south of the Lake Issik Kul, and from this point down to the possessions of Kokand along the above mountains.

Article III

Henceforth all questions regarding the frontiers which could subsequently arise will be settled according to the stipulations of Articles I and II of the present Treaty. For the settlement of the eastern boundary from the Lake Hinkai to the Tumen River and the western boundary from the lighthouse Chabindabaga [in Mongolia] down to the possessions of the Kokand, the Russian and Chinese Governments will appoint Commissars. For the inspection of the eastern frontiers, the Commissars should meet at the junction of the Ussuri River during the month of the next April. For the inspection of the western frontier, the meeting of the Commissars will take place at Tarbagatai, but the date is not set.

As determined in Articles I and II, four maps and detailed descriptions (two in the Russian language and two in the Chinese or Manchu language) will be prepared by the Commissars. These maps and descriptions will be signed and sealed by the Commissars, after which two copies, one in Russian and one in Chinese or Manchu, will be returned to the Russian Government and two similar copies will be returned to the Chinese Government to be kept by them.

For the return of the maps and descriptions of the frontier line, a corroborated protocol will be set up by the signature and the affixing of the seals of the Commissars; this will be considered as an Additional Article to the present Treaty.

Article IV

Over the entire frontier line established by Article I of the present Treaty, commerce free of all duty or restrictions is established between the subjects of the two States. The local chiefs of the frontier should grant particular protection to this commerce and to those who engage in it.

The settlements pertaining to commerce established in Article II of the Treaty of Aigoun are confirmed by the present Treaty.

Article V

In addition to the commerce existing at Kiakhta, the Russian merchants will enjoy their former right of going from Kiakhta to Peking for commercial business.

It is equally permitted for them to trade on the road at Urga and at Kalgan without being still obligated to establish there a wholesale business.

The Russian Government will have the right to install a Consulate at Urga and its staff, and also construct there a building for this function. The Governors of Urga should be consulted about the grant of land for this building, the settlement of its dimensions, and also the grant of land for a pasture.

The Chinese merchants are equally permitted to go into Russia to trade.

Article IX

The extent to which the commercial relations between the subjects of the two Empires have developed and the settlement of the new boundary line henceforth renders inapplicable the former regulations established in the Treaties signed at Nerchionsk and at Kiakhta, as well as by the Conventions which served as supplements to these treaties; the relations between the authorities of the frontiers and the regulations established for the inspection of frontier affairs no longer correspond to the present circumstances. . . .

Document 10

ADDITIONAL ARTICLE TO THE TREATY OF PEKING, SIGNED AT THE MOUTH OF THE BELENKHE ON JUNE 16/28, 1861

(Partial Text)

[The joint border commission created under the Additional Treaty of Peking of 1860] met at the mouth of the Belenkhe (Toure, in Russian) for the purpose of signing and exchanging the maps and detailed descriptions of the frontier, executed according to Articles I and II of the Additional Treaty of Peking.

After definite verification of all copies of the maps and descriptions, these parties found themselves to be in complete agreement.

The Commissars of the Empires of Russia and Manchu China then affixed their signatures and seals to two maps written in the Russian language and in the Manchu language which are an addition to the Treaty of Peking; they did the

From *Treaties, Conventions, etc., Between China and Foreign States*, Vol. I, pp. 123–124. The translation was made from the French by William C. Stallings, Jr.

same to four maps and descriptions of the frontier from the Ussuri River to the sea, two of which were in Russian and two in Chinese.

Then, the first Commissar of the Russian Empire placed in the hands of the first Commissar of the Chinese Empire a copy of the detailed map of the frontier, written in the Russian and Manchu languages, and the first Commissar of the Chinese Empire, having received said map, in turn, gave to the first Commissar of the Russian Empire an analogous map, written in the same languages. In the same manner, the other four maps with descriptions of the Ousouri to the sea were exchanged.

Document 11

PROTOCOL OF CONFERENCE BETWEEN RUSSIA AND CHINA DEFINING THE BOUNDARY BETWEEN THE TWO COUNTRIES, SIGNED AT TCHUGUCHAK [TARBAGATAI] ON SEPTEMBER 25/OCTOBER 7, 1864

In fulfilment of the Treaty of Peking and with the view of strengthening the good relations existing between the two Empires, it was by mutual accord determined in the town of Tarbagatai with respect to the delimitation of the country subject to partition between the two countries, and commencing from Shabin-dabaha to the Tsun-lin range bordering on Kokan territory, to mark the line of frontier along the ridges of mountains, large rivers, and existing Chinese pickets, and having constructed a map of the country adjoining the frontier to indicate on it by a red line the boundary between the two Empires. Wherefore they have drawn up the present Protocol, in which they have set forth the names of the places defining the line of frontier determined at the present Conference, and adopted the rules for defining such frontier, which are embodied in the following Articles:

From Edward Hertslet, *China Treaties,* Vol. I, pp. 472–478.

Article I

Commencing from the boundary mark of Shabin-dabaha the frontier will first run westward, then southward along the Sayan ridge; on reaching the western extremity of the Tannu-ola range, it will turn to the south-west, following the Sailin-gem range, and from the Kuitun mountains it will run westward along the great Altai range. On reaching the mountains situated between the two Kalguty rivers (Kaliutu in Chinese), which flow north of Tzaisan-nor lake, the frontier will turn to the south-west, and following along the above mountains will extend to Tchakilmes mountain, on the north shore of Tzaisan-nor mountains. From hence, making a turn to the south-east, the frontier is to extend along the shore of Tzaisan-nor lake, and along the Black-Irtysh river to Manitugatul Khan picket.

Along this whole extent the watershed is to be adopted as the basis for defining the frontier between the two Empires, in such a manner that all the country along which rivers flow to the eastward and southward is to be apportioned to China, and all the country through which rivers flow to the west and north shall be allotted to Russia.

Article II

From the picket of Manitugatul Khan, in a south-easterly direction, the line of frontier is to abut on the Sauri mountains (Sairi-ola in Chinese); beyond this it will first trend to the south-west, and then west along the Tarbagatai range. On reaching the Khabar-asu pass (Hamar-dabakhan in Chinese) it will turn to the south-west and proceeding along the picket road, the frontier will extend along the pickets Kumur-chi, Karabulak, Boktu, Veitan-tszi (Kok-tuma in Russian), Manitu, Sara-bulak, Chelan-togoi, Ergetu, Barluk, Modo-bar-luk. From hence the frontier is to extend along the valley between the Barluk and Alatau ranges, and beyond, between the Aruzindalan and Kabtagai pickets, the line is to be drawn along the most elevated point of this valley, abutting on the eastern extremity of the Altan-Tebshi mountains. The watershed is to be taken as a basis for the line of demarcation between the two Empires along this whole extent of country, and in such a manner that all country along which waters flow eastward and southward is to be assigned to China, and all country with waters flowing westward is to be allotted to Russia.

Article III

From the western extremity of the Altan-Tebshi mountains the frontier is to run westward along the great range of mountains known under the general name of the Alatau range, namely, along the summits of the Altan-Tebshi, So-Daba, Kuke-tom, Khan-Karchagai, and others. Along this extent all the country through which rivers flow northward is to become Russian territory, and all the country having rivers flowing southward is to be allotted to China.

On reaching the Kongor-obo mountains, which serve as the watershed of the rivers Sarbaktu flowing eastward, the Kok-su (the Kuke-olom of the Chinese) flowing westward, and the Kuitun (the Ussek of the Russians) flowing southward, the boundary is to deflect to the south.

Along this extent all the country through which rivers such as the Kok-su and others flow to the westward is to be assigned to Russia, and all the country along which rivers such as the Sarbaktu and others flow to the eastward is to become Chinese territory.

From hence, proceeding along the summits of the Koitas mountains, situated west of the Kuitun river, and reaching the point at which the river Turgen flowing southward issues out of the mountains, the boundary is to extend along the Turgen river and through the Borohudzir, Kuitun, Tsitsikhan, Horgos pickets, and be carried to the Ili-buraitsikin picket. Here, crossing the Ili river, the line of boundary is to run southward to the Tchun-tszi picket; from thence, turning to the south-east, the boundary shall be extended to the source of the Temurlik river. Thence, deflecting to the eastward, the line of frontier shall proceed along the summits of the Temurlik range, otherwise known under the name of the Nan-Shan range, and skirting the camping-grounds of the Khirghizes and Buruts (Dikkokamenni Khirghizes), the boundary shall turn in a south-westerly direction at the source of the Kegen river (the Gegen of the Chinese).

Along this extent all the country through which rivers run westward of the Kegen and other rivers shall belong to Russia, while all the country through which run rivers east of Undu-bulak and other rivers shall be allotted to China.

Further, proceeding to the south-west, the boundary shall run along the summits of Karatau mountains, and reaching the Birin-bash mountains (Bir-basha of the Chinese), the line of frontier shall extend along the river Daratu, flowing southward toward the Tekes river. The boundary, after crossing the Tekes river, shall extend along the Naryn-Nalga river and then abut on the Tian-Shan range. From hence, proceeding in a south-westerly direction, the frontier shall run along the summits of the Khan-Tengere, Savabsti, Kukustluk (Gunguluk of the Chinese), Kakshal (Kakshan of the Chinese), and other mountains, situated to the southward of Temurtunor lake, and known under the general name of the Tian-Shan range, separating Turkestan from the camping-grounds of the Buruts; and the boundary shall then abut on the Tsun-lin range which extends along the Kokandian frontier.

Article IV

At points occurring along ridges of mountains, large rivers, and permanent picket stations, which, after the present boundary delimitation shall have become Russian territory, and which are consequently situated on the side of the boundary line, there formerly existed Chinese pickets, as in the Ulusutai and Kobdo districts, on the northern side of the great Altai and other ranges; Ukek and other pickets in the Tarbagatai district on the northern side of the Tarbagatai range; Olon-Bulak and other pickets, on the northern side of the Alatau range; Aru-Tsindallan and other pickets in the Ili district; Konur-Olen (Kongoro-olon of the Chinese) and other pickets. Until the boundary marks shall have been placed, the Chinese authorities may, as formerly, send their soldiers to these points for frontier service. With the arrival next year of the Commissioners from both sides for placing the boundary marks, the above-mentioned pickets must be removed to the Chinese side of the boundary in the course of one month, counting from the time of placing the boundary mark at that point from which the picket must be withdrawn.

Article V

The present delimitation of the boundary has been undertaken with a view of consolidating permanently friendly relations between the two Empires; consequently, in order to avoid disputes respecting the inhabitants of the conterminous zone, it is hereby determined to adopt as a basis the day of exchange of this Protocol, i.e., wherever such inhabitants may be seated at that time, there they are peaceably to abide and to remain in enjoyment of the means of existence assigned to them, and to whichever Empire the camping-grounds of these inhabitants may have passed, to such Empire shall such inhabitants and their land belong, and by such Empire shall they be governed. And if, after this, any of them shall remove from their previous place of residence and cross the border, such people shall be sent back, and thus all confusion and uncertainty on the boundary terminated.

Article VI

On the expiration of 240 days after the exchange of this Protocol respecting the boundary now defined, the Commissioners of both sides shall for the purpose of placing the boundary marks meet at appointed places, viz., from the Russian side the Commissioners shall assemble at a place situated between the Aru-Tsindallan and Kaptagai localities and here divide into two parties, one of which, together with the Commissioners from the Ili district, shall, for the purpose of placing the boundary marks, proceed to the southwest along the line of frontier now fixed, and place such marks. The other party, together with the Commissioners from the Tarbagatai district, shall proceed to the north-east, along the line of boundary now determined, and place the boundary marks.

To the Manitugatul Khan picket shall proceed the Commissioner from the Kobdo district for the purpose of placing the boundary marks, and he shall, conjointly with the Russians, place such marks along the boundary line now fixed; to the Sogok picket shall proceed the Commissioner empowered by the Ulusutai district to place the boundary marks, and he shall conjointly with the Russians, place such boundary marks along the line of frontier as far as the Shabin-dabaha picket.

For placing the marks the following rule shall be observed: where the boundary runs along high mountains, the summits of the mountains are there to be taken as the boundary line; and where it runs along large rivers, there the banks of the rivers are to serve as the line of frontier; at places where the boundary runs across mountains and rivers, new boundary marks are to be placed at all such places. In general, along the whole frontier the direction of the course of waters is to be taken into consideration when placing the boundary marks, and these marks are to be erected according to the nature of the locality. If, for instance, there is no pass through the mountains and consequently the placing of boundary marks would at such points be attended with difficulty, then the range of mountains and the course of flowing waters must be taken as the basis for the boundary line. In placing the marks in a valley, 30 fathoms (20 Chinese fathoms) must be left as intermediate ground.

All products of mountains and rivers to the left of the erected boundary marks shall belong to China, and all products of mountains and rivers on the right side of the boundary marks shall belong to Russia.

Article VII

After the boundary marks shall have been placed the Commissioners appointed by both sides for the erection of such marks must, in the following year, draw up a memorandum of the number of boundary marks erected by them, and specify the names of the localities where the marks have been placed by them, and they shall exchange such memoranda.

Article VIII

After the boundary marks shall have been erected by them along the whole line of frontier now determined between the two Empires, should it anywhere appear that the source of a river is situated within Chinese territory, and its course run within the confines of the Russian Empire, in such case the Chinese Empire must not alter the former bed of the river nor dam its course; and so conversely, should the source of the river be situated in Russian territory, and its course run within Chinese limits, the Russian Empire must not alter its former bed or dam its course.

Article IX

Hitherto the Amban rulers of Urga have alone been in communication with the Governor of Kiakhta on public matters, and the Tzian-Tziun of Ili and the Hobei-Amban of Tarbagatai have similarly had relations with the Governor-General of Western Siberia. Now, with the establishment of the present frontier, should any matter arise within the Ulusutai and Kobdo districts necessitating mutual relations, the Tzian-Tziun of Ulusutai and the Hobei-Amban of Kobdo shall in such case enter into communication with the Governor of the Province of Tomsk and with the Governor of the Semipalatinsk region. The correspondence between them may be conducted either in the Manchurian or Mongolian tongue.

Article X

Prior to this, some inhabitants of Tarbagatai had established farms and ploughed up land in five places in the Tarbagatai district, west of Baktu picket, on the river Siao-Shui, and had paid rent for the same to the Government. With the establishment of the present boundary the above localities have become Russian territory; the immediate removal of the above-mentioned agriculturists would, however, be attended with hardship to them. A period, therefore, of ten years shall be allowed them, counting from the time of erection of the boundary marks, and during this term they shall be gradually transferred to the interior parts of China.

In this manner the Commissioners imperially appointed on both sides for the delimitation of the boundary have at their present meeting determined by mutual accord the boundary line, have prepared in quadruplicate a map of the whole frontier as now fixed, and inscribed on this map in the Russian and Manchurian languages the names of the places situated on the boundary, and have affixed their seals and signatures to such maps. They have likewise drawn up this Protocol in the Russian and Manchurian languages and, having prepared four copies in each language, they, the Boundary Delimitation Commissioners of both sides, have attested these documents by affixing their seals and signatures thereto.

When mutually exchanging these documents the Commissioners of both Empires shall retain a copy of the map and a copy of the Protocol for their guidance; the remaining two copies of the map, and two copies of the Protocol, the Commissioners of both Empires shall present to their respective

Ministries of Foreign Affairs for embodiment in the Treaty of Peking, and in supplement thereto.

Document 12

TREATY OF ST. PETERSBURG, SIGNED AT ST. PETERSBURG ON FEBRUARY 12/24, 1881

(Partial Text)

Article I

His Majesty the Emperor of All the Russias consents to the reestablishment of the authority of the Chinese Government in the country of Ili, temporally occupied since 1871 by the Russian armies.

Russia remains in possession of the western part of this country, within the boundaries indicated in Article VII of the present Treaty.

Article II

His Majesty the Emperor of China has undertaken to enact the proper measures to protect the inhabitants of the country of Ili, no matter what their race or religion, from any danger to their property or persons, for acts committed during or after the disturbance which took place in this country. A proclamation to this effect will be prepared by the Chinese authorities, in the name of His Majesty the Emperor of China, to the population of the country of Ili, before the return of this country to the said authorities.

From Edward Hertslet, *China Treaties*, Vol. I, pp. 483–492. This translation was made from the French by William C. Stallings, Jr.

Article III

The inhabitants of the country of Ili will be free to remain on at the place of their present residence as Chinese subjects, or to emigrate to Russia and adopt Russian dependence. They will be called upon to declare themselves on this matter before the reestablishment of the Chinese authority in the country of Ili, and a delay of one year from the day of the return of the Chinese authorities will be granted to those who show the desire to emigrate to Russia. The Chinese authorities will in no way oppose the exportation of their movable property and voluntary emigration.

Article IV

Russian subjects possessing lands in the country of Ili will keep their property rights, even after the reestablishment of the authority of the Chinese Government in this country.

This resolution is not applicable to the inhabitants of the country of Ili who will adopt Russian subjection at the time of the reestablishment of the Chinese authority in this country.

Russian subjects whose lands are situated outside of the sites appropriated at the Russian trading depots, as a result of Article XIII of the Treaty of Kouldja of 1851 will have to pay the same tax and contributions as Chinese subjects.

Article V

The two Governments will delegate to Kouldja Commissars who will proceed with one party's return and the other's withdrawal from the administration of the province of Ili, and who, in general, will be charged with the execution of the stipulations of the present Treaty with regard to the reestablishment of the authority of the Chinese Government in this country.

The said Commissars will discharge their duties, conforming to the agreement which will be established with regard to the withdrawal of one party and the return of the other, of the administration of the country of Ili, under the Governor-General of Turkestan and the Governor-General of the Provinces of Chan-si and of Kan-sou, charged by the two Governments with the direction of this affair.

The withdrawal of the administration of the country of Ili will be completed within three months, or as soon as possible, from the date of the arrival at Tashkend of the officer, who will be delegated by the Governor-General of Chan-si and of Kan-sou in conjunction with the Governor-General of Turkestan, to notify it of the ratification and promulgation of the present Treaty by His Majesty the Emperor of China.

Article VI

The Government of His Majesty the Emperor of China will pay the Russian Government the sum of 9,000,000 metal roubles, to cover the expenses occasioned by the occupation of the country of Ili by the Russian troops since 1871 to satisfy all the pecuniary demands given rise to, up to this time, by the loss of goods, pillaged of Chinese territory, that the Russian subjects have sustained, and to furnish aid to the families of the Russian subjects killed in the armed attacks in which they were victims on Chinese territory.

The above-mentioned sum of 9,000,000 metal roubles will be discharged, within a two-year term from the day of the exchange of the ratifications of the present Treaty, according to the order and the conditions agreed upon by the two governments in the special Protocol annexed to the present Treaty.

Article VII

The western part of the country of Ili is incorporated with Russia to serve as a place of settlement for inhabitants of the country who will adopt Russian dependence, and who, by that fact, will have to abandon the lands they hold.

The frontier between the Russian possessions and the Chinese province of Ili will run, from the Bedjin-Taou Mountains, along the course of the Khorgos River, to the point where it meets the Ili River, and crossing the latter, will run southward, to the Ouzontaou mountains, with the village of Koldjat to the west. From this point it will follow, running southward, the line fixed by the Protocol signed at Tchougoutchak in 1864 (No. 83).

Article VIII

One segment of the boundary line, settled by the Protocol signed at Tchougoutchak in 1864 to the east of Lake Zai Pan, having been found defective, the two governments will appoint Commissars who, by common agreement, will modify the former line so as to eliminate these flaws, and to establish an efficient separation between the Kirghise tribes under the two Empires.

The new line will be, as much as possible, in an intermediary direction between the former boundary and a straight line running from the Kouitoun Mountains to the Saour Mountains crossing the Tcherny-Irtych.

Article IX

Commissars will be appointed by the two Contracting Parties to provide with the planning of the demarcation stakes on with the line determined in the preceding Articles VII and VIII and those areas not yet staked. The time and place of the meeting of the Commissars will be settled by an agreement between the two Governments.

The two Governments will similarly appoint Commissars to examine the frontier and to install the demarcation stakes between the Russian Province of Ferganah and the western

part of the Chinese Province of Kachgar. These Commissars
will use the existing boundary as the basis for their work.

Article XVIII

The stipulations of the Treaty concluded at Aigoun, May
16, 1858 (No. 80), concerning the rights of the subjects of the
two Empires to navigate the Amur, the Soungari, and the
Oussouri and to trade with the people of the riverside localities are and remain confirmed.

The two Governments will proceed to establish an agreement concerning the method of administering the said stipulations.

Article XIX

The provisions of the former Treaties between Russia and
China not modified by the present Treaty remain in full force.

Document 13

TSITSIHAR TREATY: DELIMITATION OF FRONTIER,
RIVER ARGUN AND RIVER AMUR,
SIGNED AT TSITSIHAR ON DECEMBER 7/20, 1911

Article 1. The land frontier between the Russian and Chinese Empires in the section from the frontier point No. 58,
Tarbaga-Dakhu, to the frontier point No. 63, Abagaitu, as
indicated in the Protocol of the second Agreement, signed in
the town of Tsitsihar, 25th November (8th December), 1911,
Russian style, and the 18th of the 10th month of the 3rd year
of the Administration of Suan-Tun, Chinese style, and the
maps exchanged which were attached to it, in the future to be

From British Foreign Office, *British and Foreign State Papers* (London, no
date), Vol. 104, pp. 883–889.

the line running straight through the frontier points specified below, with the names corresponding to the points specified in the Abagaitu letter of the year 1727, Russian style, and the 5th year of the Administration of Un-Chjen, Chinese style.

This frontier line is marked by the red line which is drawn on the maps exchanged, referred to above, from the frontier point No. 58 to the frontier point No. 63, and further along the Mutny tributary up to the River Argun.

The Frontier Points

(a) Tarbaga-Dakhu, the 58th frontier point, is on the Steppe, 6 Russian versts and 312 sajenes, or 12.64 Chinese li (7,220.16 metres) directly to the south from the summit of the mountain of Tarbaga-Dakhu.

(b) Tsagan-Ola, the 59th frontier point, is situated on a height 7 Russian versts and 60 sajenes, or 13.5 Chinese li (7,760.8 metres) towards the north-west from the northern shore of Lake Khara-Nor.

(c) Tabun-Tologoi, the 60th frontier point, is situated at the frontier fortification of the beginning of the Tszin Dynasty, or Chingiskhan fort, 4 Russian versts or 7.4 Chinese li (4,360 metres) to the north-west from the northern shore of Lake Tsagan-Nor.

(d) Soktu, the 61st frontier point, is situated 4 Russian versts and 450 sajenes or 9 Chinese li (5,341 metres) from the station building of "Manchuria" of the Chinese Eastern Railway to the north-east, on a height, and 400 Russian sajenes or 1.5 Chinese li (872 metres) from the frontier fortification of the Tszin Dynasty, or Chingiskhan fort, towards the south.

(e) Erdyni-Tologoi, the 62nd frontier point, is situated on the northern slope of a mountain with four summits, and is 12 Russian versts, 400 sajenes, or 24.4 Chinese li (13,952 metres) to the south-east of Soktu, the 61st frontier point.

(f) Abagaitu, the 63rd frontier point, is situated on the western bank of the River Dalan Olom, or Mutny tributary, and is

6 Russian versts and 300 sajenes, or 12.2 Chinese li (7,194 metres) to the south-west from the Russian settlement of Abagaitu, and 3 versts, 250 sajenes, or 6.5 Chinese li (3,715 metres) to the south-west of the Krestovoi Mountain, as it is called in Russia, and Abagaitu, as it is named in Chinese.

[Article] 2. The water frontier between the Russian and Chinese Empires, from the mouth of the River Argun, that is, from the point of its junction with the River Amur (Kheiluntszian), up to the 63rd frontier point, Abagaitu, in accordance with the Treaty of Nerchinsk of 1689, Russian style, and the 28th year of the Administration of Kan-Si, Chinese style, and the Protocols 1 and 3 of the Agreements of 1911, by Russian style, and the 3rd year of the Administration of Suan-Tun, Chinese style, shall be as formerly determined by the course of the River Argun.

The ownership of the islands in the River Argun, in accordance with Protocols 1 and 3 of the Agreements, has been amicably apportioned as follows:

(a) Islands indicated on the maps exchanged as Nos. 1, 2, 3, 4, 5, 7, 8, 11, 12, 13, 14, 15, 16, 17, 18, 19, 21, 23, 26, 28, 29, 32, 34, 35, 36, 38, 43, 44, 45, 46, 47, 48, 49, 51, 55, 59, 60, 61, 62, 63, 64, 65, 66, 67, 69, 70, 71, 73, 75, 76, 77, 80, 83, 84, 86, 87, 88, 90, 92, 93, 94, 101, 102, 104, 106, 107, 108, 109, 111, 112, 113, 114, 115, 116, 117, 118, 119, 120, 127, 128, 129, 130, 132, 136, 137, 139, 142, 143, 146, 151, 152, 156, 157, 158, 160, 161, 162, 165, 166, 169, 170, 171, 174, 176, 177, 178, 180, 182, 193, 194, 197, 200, 202, 203, 206, 209, 211, 212, 214, 215, 216, 218, 219, 221, 223, 224, 226, 227, 228, 230, 231, 232, 235, 237, 238, 239, 243, 244, 245, 247, 248, 251, 252, 255, 256, 258, 262, 267, 268, 269, 270, 271, 272, 273, 274, 275, 276, 278, 279, and 280 belong to Russia.

(b) Islands indicated on the maps exchanged as Nos. 6, 9, 10, 20, 22, 24, 25, 27, 30, 31, 33, 37, 39, 40, 41, 42, 50, 52, 53, 54, 56, 57, 58, 68, 72, 74, 78, 79, 81, 82, 85, 89, 91, 95, 96, 97, 98, 99, 100, 103, 105, 110, 121, 122, 123, 124, 125, 126, 131, 133, 134, 135, 138, 140, 141, 144, 145, 147, 148, 149, 150, 153,

154, 155, 159, 163, 164, 167, 168, 172, 173, 175, 179, 181, 183, 184, 185, 186, 187, 188, 189, 190, 191, 192, 195, 196, 198, 199, 201, 204, 205, 207, 208, 210, 213, 217, 220, 222, 225, 229, 233, 234, 236, 240, 241, 242, 246, 249, 250, 253, 254, 257, 259, 260, 261, 263, 264, 265, 266 and 277 belong to China.

The remaining details in the question of the State frontier from Nos. 58 to 63 frontier points and from the mouth of the River Argun to the same No. 63 frontier point are set forth in Protocols Nos. 1, 2, and 3 of the Agreements with the maps exchanged and the tables of islands attached to them bearing the signatures and seals of both Commissioners. These protocols, maps, and tables of islands have equal force with this present Act and must be mutually observed.

Done at the town of Tsitsihar, 7th (20th) December, 1911, according to Russian style, and the 1st of the 11th moon of the 3rd year of the Administration of Suan-Tun, according to Chinese style, in the Russian and Chinese languages, in duplicate in each language, which, upon being signed and having their seals attached, both Commissioners finally exchanged so that each party has originals in Russian and Chinese.

The original bears the signatures and seals of the Plenipotentiary and Commissioner of the Great Russian State, Major-General Putilov, dispatched by Imperial command, and the Plenipotentiary of the Great Daitsin State, the State official appointed by Imperial command for the delimitation of the frontier, Chjou, the Governor of the Province Kheiluntszian.

PROTOCOL OF AGREEMENT No. 1
October 18 (31), 1911

On the basis of the reports made by the assistants of the presidents of the Russian and Chinese Delimitation Commissions, Messrs. Jdanov and Sun, respecting the section of the river frontier of the States from the mouth of the River Argun to the Argun station and higher, the presidents of the Russian and Chinese Commissions, having verified these reports, have enacted that the islands indicated on the map under Nos. 1, 2,

3, 4, 5, 7, 8, 11, 12, 13, 14, 15, 16, 17, 18, 19, 21, 23, 26, 28, 29, 32, 34, 35, 36, 38, 43, 44, 45, 46, 47, 48, 49, 51, 55, 59, 60, 61, 62, 63, 64, 65, 66, 67, 69, 70, 71, 73, 75, 76, 77, 80, 83, 84, 86, and 87 shall belong to Russia; and the islands indicated under Nos. 6, 9, 10, 20, 22, 24, 25, 27, 30, 31, 33, 37, 39, 40, 41, 42, 50, 52, 53, 54, 56, 57, 58, 68, 72, 74, 78, 81, 82, and 85 shall be regarded as belonging to China.

In view of the fact that the numbers of the islands indicated in accordance with the maps certified by the seals of the presidents of the preparatory Commissions and exchanged at the station "Manchuria" do not agree with the numbers in the Protocols of the revision by the members of the preparatory Commissions; and that Nos. 85, 86, and 87 do not appear at all on the maps exchanged at the station "Manchuria"; and that, moreover, these three numbers in the Protocols of the revision by the members of the two preparatory Commissions also differ with the numbers of the joint revision carried out by M. Usat, member of the Russian Frontier Commission, and Mr. Sun-siaolian, president of the Chinese Frontier Commission. These numbers are arranged in a special comparative table, and a special detailed map has been compiled showing the numbers in accordance with the Protocol of this Agreement, signed, printed, and exchanged and attached to this Protocol in order to avoid misunderstanding. The small maps which were exchanged originally and the maps exchanged at the station "Manchuria" have been returned by each party.

PROTOCOL OF AGREEMENT No. 2
November 25 (December 8), 1911

The Russian and Chinese Frontier Delimitation Commissions at Tsitsihar, by mutual agreement, have jointly recognized that the line of land frontier between Russia and China in the section from the frontier point, Tarbaga-Dakhu, No. 58, to the frontier point, Abagaitu, No. 63, passes directly through the following points with names corresponding to those names given to the frontier points in the Treaty:

1. Tarbaga-Dakhu, the 58th frontier point, is on the Steppe, 6 Russian versts and 312 sajenes, or 12.64 Chinese li (7,220.16 metres) directly to the south from the summit of the mountain of Tarbaga-Dakhu.

2. Tsagan-Ola, the 59th frontier point, is situated on a height 7 Russian versts and 60 sajenes, or 13.5 Chinese li (7,760.8 metres) towards the north-west from the northern shore of Lake Khara-Nor.

3. Tabun-Tologoi, the 60th frontier point, is situated at the frontier fortification of the beginning of the Tszin Dynasty, or Chingiskhan fort, 4 Russian versts, or 7.4 Chinese li (4,360 metres) to the north-west from the northern shore of Lake Tsagan-Nor.

4. Soktu, the 61st frontier point, is situated 4 Russian versts and 450 sajenes, or 9 Chinese li (5,341 metres) from the station building of "Manchuria" of the Chinese Eastern Railway to the north-east, on a height, and 400 Russian sajenes, or 1.5 Chinese li (872 metres) from the frontier fortification of the Tszin Dynasty, or Chingiskhan fort, towards the south.

5. Erdyni-Tologoi, the 62nd frontier point, is situated on the northern slope of a mountain with four summits, and is 12 Russian versts, 400 sajenes, or 24.4 Chinese li (13,952 metres) to the south-west of Soktu, the 61st frontier point.

6. Abagaitu, the 63rd frontier point, is situated on the western bank of the River Dalan-Olom or Mutny tributary, and is 6 Russian versts, 300 sajenes, or 12.2 Chinese li (7,194 metres) to the south-west from the Russian settlement of Abagaitu, and 3 versts, 250 sajenes, or 6.5 Chinese li (3,715 metres) to the south-west of the Krestovoi Mountain, as it is called in Russian, and Abagaitu, as it is named in Chinese.

An exchange of the present Protocol of Agreement, with the map attached to it, both duly signed and sealed by the two presidents, took place, upon the completion of all negotiations, between the two frontier Commissions in the town of Tsitsihar. Subsequently, representatives of each party will be dispatched to proper places to make measurements in the actual locality in accordance with the direction and distances indicated in the Protocol of this Agreement and the map attached to it, and to mark the frontier points. Should the map exchanged prove to be inaccurately drawn up, such inaccuracies must be corrected in loco by mutual agreement of the two representatives.

This year, temporary mounds of stones as marks will be erected on the frontier points, and in the spring of next year, at a duly appointed time and in accordance with a joint determination of the latitude and longitude of these points, frontier marks will be erected on which there will be cut in the Russian and Chinese languages the name of the frontier point with its latitude and longitude. A trench must be dug along the whole line of the frontier.

A Supplementary Act, which will be conjointly drawn up by the two representatives after completion of the delimitation of the frontier in situ, will be exchanged by them and attached as a document to the Protocol of the present Agreement.

PROTOCOL OF AGREEMENT NO. 3
November 25 (December 8), 1911

Having verified the reports made by the assistants of the presidents of the Russian and Chinese Frontier Delimitation Commissions, Messrs. Jdanov and Sun, respecting the river section of the frontier of the two States from the island marked No. 87 on the map exchanged, and attached to the Protocol of the Agreement No. 1, to the frontier point marked No. 63 (Abagaitu) on the map exchanged, and attached to the Protocol of the Agreement No. 2, the presidents of the Russian and Chinese Commissions have enacted that:

1. The State frontier between Russia and China from the mouth of the River Argun to the frontier point No. 63, Abagaitu, shall be the course of the River Argun, in accordance with the former Treaty of 1689, or the 28th year of the Administration of Kan Si.

2. The islands indicated on the map exchanged under Nos. 89, 91, 95, 96, 97, 98, 99, 100, 103, 105, 110, 121, 122, 123, 124, 125, 126, 131, 133, 134, 135, 138, 140, 141, 144, 145, 147, 148, 149, 150, 153, 154, 155, 159, 163, 164, 167, 168, 172, 173, 175, 179, 181, 183, 184, 185, 186, 187, 188, 189, 190, 191, 192, 195, 196, 198, 199, 201, 204, 205, 207, 208, 210, 213, 217, 220, 222, 225, 229, 233, 234, 236, 240, 241, 242, 246, 249, 250, 253, 254, 257, 259, 260, 261, 263, 264, 265, 266, and 277 shall be regarded as belonging to China.

3. The islands indicated on the map exchanged under Nos. 88, 90, 92, 93, 94, 101, 102, 104, 106, 107, 108, 109, 113, 114, 116, 118, 119, 127, 128, 129, 130, 132, 136, 137, 139, 142, 143, 146, 151, 152, 156, 157, 158, 160, 161, 162, 165, 166, 169, 170, 171, 174, 176, 177, 178, 180, 182, 193, 194, 197, 200, 202, 203, 206, 209, 212, 214, 215, 216, 218, 219, 221, 223, 224, 228, 230, 231, 232, 235, 237, 238, 239, 243, 244, 245, 247, 248, 251, 252, 255, 256, 258, 262, 275, 276, and 278 shall be regarded as belonging to Russia.

4. The islands indicated on the map exchanged under Nos. 111, 112, 115, 117, 120, 211, 226, 227, 267, 270, 272, 273, 274, 279, and 280 as having been formed between the old channel of the Argun, the former State frontier, and the modern Argun, which in the course of time has gradually moved westward, shall remain in the possession of Russia. And the State frontier between Russia and China shall be the modern course of the River Argun.

On the banks of the old and modern Argun, opposite the islands Nos. 227, 269, 273, 279, and 280, representatives, who will be dispatched from both parties in the spring of next year at an appointed time, shall erect stone marks on which shall be cut in Russian and in Chinese the areas of these islands in versts or "dessiatines"; the distance from these marks to the banks of the old and new channel of the Argun in accordance with the map exchanged; and the latitude and longitude of the site of the marks as conjointly determined. Preliminary to this work, temporary marks shall be placed as agreed to with reference to the land frontier in the Protocol of the Agreement No. 2.

For the remaining small islands, the maps sealed and signed which have been exchanged shall serve as proof.

5. The maps and the explanatory table of islands signed, sealed, exchanged by the two presidents of the Commissions, and attached to this Protocol shall serve as a guide in the future.

The maps exchanged by the preparatory Commissions shall be respectively returned by each party.

Document 14

PROTOCOL OF DELIMITATION
ALONG THE HORGOS [KHORGOS] RIVER,
SIGNED ON MAY 30/JUNE 12, 1915

We, the delegates of the mixed Russo-Chinese commission, comprising, from the Imperial Russian Government Collegiate Assessor Biseroff, acting Chief Official for Special Service, attached to the Military Governor of Semiretchensk Province, Collegiate Secretary Mochoff, Surveyor to the Provincial Administration of Semiretchensk, and Yunicheff, Aksakal of the Consulate in Kuldja; and from the Chinese Republic, the Solon Amban Fushan, the Acting Magistrate Hwang Sheng of the Horgos District, and Hsu Chi Hsien, Official on Special Service, in the presence of the Imperial Russian Consul in Kuldja, Brodianski, Messrs. Chen Show Hsi, Yen Fei Hsiang, and Taoyin Hsu Chin have agreed:

To commence the erection of temporary survey marks along the course of the River Horgos upwards from the point where the bed, issuing from the mountains, splits up into several branches (above the height of the Horgos), to the disputed

From John Van Antwerp MacMurray, *Treaties and Agreements With and Concerning China* (Oxford University Press, 1921), Vol. II, p. 1245.

island—this latter to be divided into two halves from north to south, the eastern side going to China and the western to Russia—up to the junction of the two rivulets issuing from their sources (the Karasuk rivulets) farther on forming the channel of the River Horgos along which the frontier continues to the River Ili. The use of the water of the River Horgos to be fixed thus: the mountain water of the River Horgos to be left for the use of both states at that part at which, at the present time, irrigation canals lead off water; on both sides of the River Horgos belonging to China and Russia the water from the source (Karasuk) below the island (with the exception of the irrigation canal carrying water in Russian territory from the rivulet of origin at a point above the junction of the rivulets from source) to be equally divided. Into the dry channel, the head of which is above the Chinese post of Fulgen-Alinn, the Chinese bind themselves to let in water only in such quantities as are required for the above-mentioned post. The present protocol is written in Russian and Chinese in two copies and signed by the delegates of Russia and China in the town of Kure.

Notes

INTRODUCTION

1. See also W. A. Douglas Jackson, *The Russo-Chinese Borderlands* (D. Van Nostrand Co., 1962), pp. 1–18.

2. See "A Comment on the Statement of the Communist Party of the United States of America," an editorial in *Jen-min Jih-pao* ("People's Daily," cited hereafter as *JMJP*), March 8, 1963.

3. *Ibid.*

4. *Ibid.*

5. V. M. Khuostov, "The Chinese 'Account' and Historical Truth," *Mezhdunarodnaya Zhizn* ("International Life"), No. 10, Oct. 1964, cited in John Gittings, *Survey of the Sino-Soviet Dispute* (Oxford University Press, 1968), pp. 164–166; the Statement of the Government of the People's Republic of China, May 24, 1969, in *Peking Review,* May 30, 1969, pp. 3–9; and the Document of the Ministry of Foreign Affairs of the People's Republic of China, Oct. 8, 1969, *ibid.,* Oct. 10, 1969, pp. 8–15.

6. *Ibid.* See also the Letter of the Central Committee of the Chinese Communist Party of Feb. 29, 1964, to the Central Committee of the Communist Party of the Soviet Union, in *Peking Review,* May 8, 1964, pp. 12–18.

7. *Pravda,* Sept. 2, 1964, in *Current Digest of the Soviet Press*

(cited hereafter as *CDSP*), Vol. XVI, No. 34, Sept. 16, 1964, pp. 3–7; and *Pravda*, Sept. 20, 1964, in *CDSP*, Vol. XVI, No. 38, Oct. 14, 1964, pp. 3–6.

8. *Ibid.*

9. See the Letter of the Central Committee of the Communist Party of the Soviet Union of Nov. 29, 1963, to the Central Committee of the Chinese Communist Party, in *JMJP*, May 9, 1964.

10. *Hung Ch'i* ("Red Flag") and *JMJP*, Sept. 6, 1963. The Chinese charge of Soviet intrusion in Sinkiang was made twice in 1964. See Hsinhua ("New China") News Agency dispatch, April 28, 1964; and *Peking Review*, Sept. 11, 1965, pp. 5, 26.

11. *Pravda*, Sept. 23, 1963, in *CDSP*, Vol. XV, No. 38, Oct. 16, 1963, p. 16.

12. See Hsinhua News Agency dispatch, July 10, 1966; *U.S. News & World Report*, Dec. 6, 1965, p. 44; *The Military Balance 1969–70* (London: The International Institute for Strategic Studies, 1969); *The Washington Post*, Aug. 3, 1966, p. 14; and Jan. 4, 1967, p. 10; and *The New York Times*, May 31, 1964, p. 9; Aug. 17, 1966, p. 4; and March 3, 1969, p. 1.

13. It is reported that in 1964 Soviet infantry troops in the Vladivostok area conducted military maneuvers that assumed a nonnuclear Chinese Communist invasion of the Soviet Maritime Province. J. Malcolm Mackintosh, "The Soviet Generals' View of China in the 1960's," in Raymond L. Garthoff (ed.), *Sino-Soviet Military Relations* (Frederick A. Praeger, Inc., Publishers, 1966), p. 187.

14. For the buildup of Soviet military power in Outer Mongolia since the middle of the 1960's, see *The New York Times*, March 16, 1966, p. 8; and Tsao Chih-ching, "Peiping-Soviet Border Clashes," *Issues and Studies* (Taipei), May 1969, p. 10. It is to be noted that the Soviet Union and Outer Mongolia signed a twenty-year Treaty of Friendship, Cooperation, and Mutual Assistance in January 1966. See *Pravda*, Jan. 18, 1966, in *CDSP*, Vol. XVIII, No. 3, Feb. 9, 1966, pp. 7–8.

15. See, for example, *Izvestia*, March 4, 1969, in *CDSP*, Vol. XXI, No. 9, March 19, 1969, p. 17; *Pravda*, March 8, 1969, in *CDSP*, Vol. XXI, No. 10, March 26, 1969, pp. 3–5; and *Peking Review*, March 7, 1969, pp. 5–7; and March 14, 1969, pp. 3–5, 14–15.

16. *Ibid.*

17. "Amur" is the Russian name. The Chinese call it Hei-lung Chiang ("the River of the Black Dragon"). The river is some 1,240 miles long and flows north. The Ussuri also flows north.

18. See *Peking Review,* June 13, 1969, pp. 4–5; July 11, 1969, pp. 6–7; and Aug. 15, 1969, p. 13; *Pravda,* Aug. 15, 1969, in *CDSP,* Vol. XXI, No. 33, Sept. 10, 1969, pp. 3–5; and *The New York Times,* Aug. 15, 1969, pp. 1, 4; and Aug. 16, 1969, p. 4.

19. The term "social imperialism" was originally invented by Lenin when he denounced the activities of his Social Democratic foes (the Second International) as "socialism in words, imperialism in deeds, the growth of opportunism into imperialism." Vladimir Lenin, "The Tasks of the Third International" (July 14, 1919), *Selected Works* (International Publishers Co., Inc., 1943), Vol. X, p. 42. The term is now used by the Chinese Communists as a derogatory label for the Soviet Union. Simple "imperialism" denotes the United States in Chinese Communist statements.

20. *Peking Review,* March 14, 1969, p. 5; March 7, 1969, pp. 6–7; March 14, 1969, pp. 3–4; and "Leninism or Social Imperialism?" a joint editorial of *JMJP, Hung Ch'i,* and *Chieh-fang Chün-pao* ("Liberation Army Daily"), April 22, 1970.

21. See *Sekai Shuho* ("World Weekly," Tokyo), Aug. 11, 1964.

22. Cited in *The Washington Post,* March 24, 1969, p. 20.

23. *Ibid.*

24. See *Pravda,* March 8, 1969, in *CDSP,* Vol. XXI, No. 10, March 26, 1969, pp. 6–7; and March 9, 1969, in *ibid.,* p. 7.

25. A full English translation of Yevtushenko's poem called "On the Red Snow of the Ussuri" was published in *The Washington Post,* April 13, 1969, Sunday Outlook Section, p. 1.

26. Cited in *The New York Times,* March 21, 1969, p. 3.

27. For a detailed discussion of Soviet threat of a preemptive nuclear strike against Communist China, see Chapter 3 of this book.

28. *Newsweek,* March 31, 1969, p. 33.

29. Hsinhua News Agency dispatch, Aug. 15, 1969. See also *Peking Review,* Special Issue, April 28, 1969, p. 29.

30. See, for example, *Strategic Survey 1970* (London: Inter-

national Institute of Strategic Studies, 1970); *The New York Times,* Aug. 31, 1969, p. 4; Nov. 19, 1969, p. 11; May 19, 1970, p. 14; July 5, 1970, p. 2; July 22, 1970, p. 5; and *The Sun* (Baltimore), July 30, 1971, pp. 1–2.

31. See, for example, *Pravda,* Jan. 21, 1970, in *CDSP,* Vol. XXII, No. 10, April 7, 1970, pp. 13–14; *Pravda,* Feb. 18, 1970, in *CDSP,* Vol. XXII, No. 7, March 7, 1970, p. 9; *Pravda,* Jan. 10, 1970, in *CDSP,* Vol. XXII, No. 2, Feb. 11, 1970, pp. 20–21; Hsinhua News Agency dispatch, July 9, 1969; Aug. 15, 1969; and Jan. 4, 1970; and *JMJP,* Sept. 30, 1969.

32. Stanley Karnow's dispatch from Khabarovsk, in *The Washington Post,* Aug. 15, 1970, p. 15.

33. For a detailed discussion of the classic Maoist strategy of a protracted war, see Chapter 4 of this book.

34. *Pravda,* Aug. 28, 1969, in *CDSP,* Vol. XXI, No. 35, Sept. 24, 1969, pp. 3–4.

35. *Pravda,* Aug. 14, 1969, in *CDSP,* Vol. XXI, No. 33, Sept. 10, 1969, pp. 6–7.

36. See, for example, *JMJP,* Sept. 14, 1969; and Sept. 17, 1969; *JMJP, Hung Ch'i,* and *Chieh-fang Chün-pao,* Jan. 1, 1970; and Aug. 1, 1969; and *The New York Times,* Aug. 30, 1969, pp. 1, 5; and Dec. 28, 1969, p. 7.

37. *Peking Review,* Oct. 24, 1969, pp. 7–13.

38. *The New York Times,* June 5, 1971, p. 2; Aug. 10, 1971, p. 15; and *Der Spiegel* (Hamburg, West Germany), Feb. 2, 1970, p. 100.

39. *Forces Aériennes Françaises,* Feb. 1970, pp. 171–189; *The New York Times,* Sept. 12, 1969, p. 5; Sept. 13, 1969, p. 1; and *The Washington Post,* Sept. 13, 1969, p. 16.

40. See, for example, *The New York Times,* June 11, 1970, p. 1; and Edgar Snow, "Talks with Chou En-lai: The Open Door," *The New Republic,* March 29, 1971, p. 23.

Chapter 1. THE HISTORICAL BACKGROUND
OF THE SINO-SOVIET TERRITORIAL DISPUTE

1. C. P. Fitzgerald, "Tension on the Sino-Soviet Border," *Foreign Affairs,* July 1967, p. 683.

2. *JMJP,* March 8, 1963.

3. In many of the outlying Manchurian areas of the old Middle Kingdom, for example, the Ming Dynasty relied on the troops of native chieftains, since the region of Chinese settlement actually extended only as far as the Liao valley (including the Liaotung Peninsula). The native chieftains and their garrisons were all under the direct control of Chinese commanders during the first part of the Ming rule. However, in the latter half of the dynasty, areas outside of Kirin and southeastern Heilungkiang were not under their direct supervision and were only paying tributes to the Chinese emperors. Li Chi, *Manchuria in History* (Peking: Peking Union Bookstore, 1932), pp. 13–16.

4. Yakutsk was founded by Russians in 1632.

5. Ernest G. Ravenstein, *The Russians on the Amur* (London: Trübner and Co., 1861), pp. 9–13.

6. *Ibid.*, pp. 12–13.

7. George R. Wright, *Asiatic Russia* (McClure, Philips and Co., 1902), Vol. I, pp. 167–173.

8. Ai-chen K. Wu, *China and the Soviet Union: A Study of Sino-Soviet Relations* (John Day Co., Inc., 1950), pp. 55–56.

9. Nerchinsk was founded by Russians in 1655 at the junction of the Nercha and the Shilka. At first it was called Nelyudskoi, which means "without people."

10. Ravenstein, *op. cit.*, pp. 38–40.

11. Vladimir (pseudonym of Zenone Volpicelli), *Russia on the Pacific and the Siberian Railway* (London: S. Low, Marston and Co., 1899), p. 134.

12. Victor A. Yakhontoff, *Russia and the Soviet Union in the Far East* (Coward-McCann, Inc., 1931), pp. 10–12.

13. Vladimir, *op. cit.*, p. 164.

14. The Chinese had traditionally been trained and accustomed to the idea that the Middle Kingdom was the center of world civilization and the only true power on the earth. Accordingly, they had conceived international relations as an affair between the center (China) and its tributaries and "barbarian" neighbors paying homage to the Chinese emperors.

15. Both Russia and China negotiated in Latin. The Russians had a German interpreter who knew Latin, and the Chinese were helped by two Jesuits, a Portuguese named Pereira and a Frenchman named Gerbillon.

16. The Russian-Chinese agreement in Peking on April 1, 1727, specified that the boundary through the Ud valley region would remain undefined as in the Treaty of Nerchinsk, because of the lack of precise geographical data concerning the region. See International Boundary Study No. 64, Feb. 14, 1966, *China-USSR Boundary* (Issued by the Geographer. Office of Research in Economics and Science, Bureau of Intelligence and Research, United States Department of State, Washington, D.C.), p. 8.

17. Gaston Cahen, *Some Early Russo-Chinese Relations,* tr. and ed. by W. Sheldon Ridge (Shanghai: "The National Review" Office, 1914), pp. 87–88.

18. The Bur Treaty of August 20, 1727, which the two empires exchanged on the Bur River near Kiakhta (or Kyakhta), delimited the Chinese-Russian boundary between present-day Mongolia and the upper Argun rather vaguely. (For the text of the Bur Treaty of August 20, 1727, see *Treaties, Conventions, etc., Between China and Foreign States,* 2d ed., Shanghai: Statistical Department of the Inspectorate General of Customs, 1917, pp. 14–17.) This treaty was immediately replaced by two boundary protocols, the first exchanged at Abagatuy on October 12, 1727 (see note 19 and *Document 3*), and the second exchanged on the Bur River on October 27, 1727 (see *Document 4*).

19. This protocol of October 12, 1727, is also referred to as the Abagatuy Treaty (see *Document 3*). The protocol delimited the boundary east of Kiakhta by a description of sixty-three markers forming the frontier east of Kiakhta to the headwaters of the Argun River.

20. This protocol of October 27, 1727 (see *Document 4*) delimited the boundary of the August 20, 1727, Bur Treaty for the area west of Kiakhta. (On the Bur Treaty, see note 18 of this chapter.) Twenty-four points were identified.

21. The actual date of signing of the Treaty of Kiakhta (see *Document 5*) is not clear, but October 27 seems to be logical and correct.

22. See note 16 of this chapter.

23. This border section was more precisely defined by the Treaty of Tsitsihar of December 7/20, 1911 (see *Document*

13). See also John Van Antwerp MacMurray, *Treaties and Agreements With and Concerning China, 1894–1919* (Oxford University Press, 1921), Vol. I, p. 919.

24. Until 1921, Tannu Tuva was known internationally as Uriankhai and in China as Tannu Uriankhai. It is a region located northwest of Outer Mongolia and embraces an area of about 65,000 square miles. It is famous for its scenic beauty, and also rich in natural resources, including uranium.

25. The Treaty of Kiakhta permitted Russian traders to cross Mongolia. From 1727 to 1850, however, there was little trade between China and Russia across Mongolia.

26. Article 10 of the Kiakhta Treaty of 1727 (see *Document 5*) dealt with frontier traffic between China and Russia. This article was amended by the Kiakhta Supplementary Treaty (see *Document 6*), signed on October 18, 1768. The latter treaty also made minor modifications in the boundary posts in the vicinity of "Mount Bourgoutei" so that the border would pass on the reverse side of the mountain.

27. Vladimir, *op. cit.*, pp. 173–175.

28. *Ibid.*, pp. 179–193.

29. In 1673, the Manchu court closed up the outlying regions of Manchuria (with the exception of the old Chinese settlement in the Liaotung region) to Chinese immigration partly to preserve its patrimony and partly to enjoy a monopoly of Manchurian trade in fur, ginseng, and pearl, and Heilungkiang and part of Kirin were made royal parks. The limit of permitted Chinese settlement in the Liaotung region was marked off, and in the east the Koreans were forbidden to cross the Manchurian border. Between the Yalu River, the boundary of Korea, and this delimited region, there was a no-man's-land or neutral zone approximately fifty miles wide. See Peter S. H. Tang, *Russian and Soviet Policy in Manchuria and Outer Mongolia 1911–1931* (Duke University Press, 1959), pp. 16–17; Alexander Hosie, *Manchuria, Its People, Resources, and Recent History* (J. B. Millet Co., 1910), p. 17; Owen Lattimore, *Manchuria, Cradle of Conflict* (The Macmillan Company, 1932), pp. 32–33; and William W. Rockhill, *China's Intercourse with Korea from XVth Century to 1895* (London: Luzac & Co., 1905), p. 29.

30. Peter S. H. Tang, *op. cit.,* p. 17.

31. Wright, *op. cit.,* pp. 203–204.

32. Vladimir, *op. cit.,* pp. 236–239.

33. In 1858, Ust-Zeiski was rechristened with the name Blagoveshchensk ("the Annunciation").

34. Ravenstein, *op. cit.,* pp. 143–144.

35. *Ibid.,* pp. 253–254.

36. Two weeks after the Treaty of Aigun was signed (June 1/13—see *Document 7*), both Russia and China signed the Tientsin Treaty of Peace, Amity, Commerce, and Navigation (see *Document 8*). While this treaty was mainly commercial, it did include a brief section on boundaries. It stipulated that the frontiers between the two empires not yet delimited were to be surveyed. Actually, however, this clause was redundant because the Treaty of Aigun covered this point. This redundant provision was included by negotiators in Tientsin because they were unaware at that time that the Treaty of Aigun had already been signed.

37. See Peter S. H. Tang, *op. cit.,* pp. 4–5. This enclave stretched for some fifteen miles down the Amur River from the mouth of the Zeya River and was situated only a short distance from the city of Blagoveshchensk.

38. This area is known today as the Soviet Maritime Province, with Vladivostok as its capital. Vladivostok ("Ruler of the East") was opened in 1860.

39. In 1886 the Chinese protested to the Russians that the boundary markers on the Tumen River had been removed. (It is also possible that some of these border markers might have rotted away.) Border commissioners from both countries met in May 1886. The Treaty of Peking of 1860 had stated that the boundary met the river 20 *li* from the sea, but there was some dispute as to where the mouth of the river actually began. The Russians felt that the border lay an additional 20 *li* inland from the point where the Chinese thought that it was. The end result was a compromise. The boundary was established halfway between these points, or, as the Chinese had calculated it, 30 *li* (10.4 miles) from the river mouth. See S. McCune, "Physical Basis for Korean Boundaries," *The Far Eastern Quarterly,* May 1946, p. 280.

40. The area that was surrendered covered the khanates of western Turkestan, Andijan, Kokand, Bokhara, Tajik, and Samarkand, and later became Russian Turkestan, as distinguished from Chinese Turkestan.

41. Jackson, *op. cit.,* pp. 116–117; and International Boundary Study No. 64, *China-USSR Boundary,* p. 11.

42. *Ibid.*

43. The 1864 Moslem revolts were preceded by the Moslem armed insurrections of 1825–1826, 1827, 1830, and 1857.

44. See Owen Lattimore, *Pivot of Asia: Sinkiang and the Inner Asian Frontiers of China and Russia* (Little, Brown & Company, 1950), pp. 32–35; and T. D. Forsyth, *Reports of a Mission to Yarkand in 1873* (Calcutta: The Foreign Department Press, 1875), pp. 98, 204–213.

45. Yakub Beg was killed in 1877.

46. See Richard A. Pierce, *Russian Central Asia, 1867–1917* (University of California Press, 1960), p. 34.

47. For a detailed geographical description of the Ili valley in Sinkiang, see Harold J. Wiens, "The Ili Valley as a Geographic Region of Hsin-Chiang," *Current Scene,* Aug. 1, 1969, pp. 1–13.

48. See Jack A. Dabbs, *History of the Discovery and Exploration of Chinese Turkestan* (The Hague: Mouton and Co., N.V., Publishers, 1963), p. 64; and Owen Lattimore, *Inner Asian Frontiers of China* (Capitol Publishing Company, 1951), pp. 186–187.

49. See Immanuel C. Y. Hsü, *The Ili Crisis: A Study of Sino-Russian Diplomacy, 1871–1881* (Oxford University Press, 1965), pp. 47–58.

50. *Ibid.,* p. 57; and David J. Dallin, *The Rise of Russia in Asia* (Yale University Press, 1949), p. 32.

51. Dabbs, *op. cit.,* p. 65; and Hsü, *op. cit.,* p. 57.

52. Hsü, *op. cit.,* pp. 59–77.

53. Tseng Chi-tse, Chinese minister in London and Paris, negotiated and signed the Treaty of St. Petersburg for the Manchu court.

54. The Chinese-Russian boundary protocol of May 30/ June 12, 1915, also delimited the Khorgos River as the boundary north of the Ili to the Ala Tau. See *Document 14.*

55. International Boundary Study No. 64, *China-USSR Boundary*, pp. 11–12.

56. *Ibid.*, p. 12; and Jackson, *op. cit.*, p. 117.

57. International Boundary Study No. 64, *China-USSR Boundary*, pp. 12–13; and Jackson, *op. cit.*, pp. 118–119.

58. Nationalist China never recognized the Wakhan Corridor. Communist China, on its official maps published in the mid-1950's, conceded the existence of this corridor after several years of claiming virtually the whole of the Pamir mountain region. On November 22, 1963, Communist China and Afghanistan signed a boundary agreement. This Chinese-Afghan border agreement was significant in two respects: first, it made Peking's recognition of the Wakhan Corridor formal, and, secondly, Povalo Shveikovski (Kokrash Kol) was utilized as the northernmost point on their common boundary. See Harold C. Hinton, *Communist China in World Politics* (Houghton Mifflin Company, 1966), p. 320; and Hsinhua News Agency dispatch, Nov. 22, 1963.

59. The Chinese-Russian alliance was signed on May 22/June 3, 1896, in Moscow. For the English text of the treaty, see MacMurray, *op. cit.*, Vol. I, p. 81.

60. See the English text of the Contract for Construction and Operation of the Chinese Eastern Railway, signed in Berlin on August 27/September 8, 1896, in MacMurray, *op. cit.*, Vol. I, pp. 74–77. Forming a link with the Trans-Siberian Railway and traversing all of Manchuria to Vladivostok, this Manchurian railway cut 340 miles off the route over all-Russian land.

61. This agreement was signed on June 25/July 6, 1898. For its English text, see MacMurray, *op. cit.*, Vol. I, pp. 154–156. This new railway line was called the South Manchurian Branch of the Chinese Eastern Railway.

62. A Chinese-Russian convention for a lease in the Liaotung Peninsula was signed on March 15/27, 1898. For its English text, see MacMurray, *op. cit.*, Vol. I, pp. 119–121.

63. *Ibid.*, pp. 522–526.

64. See Peter S. H. Tang, *op. cit.*, pp. 299–310; Gerald Friters, "The Prelude to Outer Mongolian Independence," *Pacific Affairs*, June 1937, p. 168; and Leo Pasvolsky, *Russia in the Far East* (The Macmillan Company, 1922), p. 55.

65. See *Encyclopaedia Britannica,* 1967, Vol. XV, p. 735; and *The China Year Book,* 1919, ed. by H. T. M. Bell and H. G. W. Woodhead (E. P. Dutton & Co., 1920), pp. 589–590.

66. For the full English text of this agreement, see Mac-Murray, *op. cit.,* Vol. II, pp. 922 ff. See also: Great Britain, Historical Section of the Foreign Office, *Mongolia* (London, H.M. Stationery Office, 1920), pp. 17–20.

67. See Peter S. H. Tang, *op. cit.,* pp. 317–323.

68. See Peter S. H. Tang, *op. cit.,* pp. 399–425; Dallin, *The Rise of Russia in Asia,* pp. 137–143; and Gerard M. Friters, *Outer Mongolia and Its International Position,* ed. by Eleanor Lattimore (The Johns Hopkins University Press, 1949), pp. 130–132.

69. For the full English text of this agreement, see Mac-Murray, *op. cit.,* Vol. II, p. 1066.

70. For the full English text of this tripartite agreement, see MacMurray, *op. cit.,* Vol. II, pp. 1239–1244.

71. See *Document 9.*

72. International Boundary Study No. 64, *China-USSR Boundary,* p. 13.

73. *Ibid.*

74. Neither Nationalist China nor Communist China has recognized the validity of the Tsitsihar Treaty of 1911. Accordingly, the validity of this treaty is in dispute.

75. For the full English text of the Karakhan Declaration, see *The China Year Book,* 1924, ed. by H. G. W. Woodhead (Peking and Tientsin, 1924), pp. 868–870.

76. It must be noted that immediately after the collapse of the Manchu Dynasty and the establishment of the Republic of China in 1911, Chinese nationalists demanded the abrogation of all "unequal" treaties, together with the restoration of China's "traditional" frontiers.

77. For the full English text of the Karakhan Manifesto, see *The China Year Book,* 1924, pp. 870–872.

78. For the details, see Edmund Clubb, "Armed Conflict in the Chinese Borderlands, 1917–1950," in Garthoff (ed.), *Sino-Soviet Military Relations,* pp. 10–19; and George G. S. Murphy, *Soviet Mongolia: A Study of the Oldest Political Satellite* (University of California Press, 1966), pp. 1–28.

79. On November 5, 1921, the Soviet Union and Outer

Mongolia signed a Soviet-Mongolian treaty of friendship in Moscow. This recognized Outer Mongolia as an independent state and made no reference at all to the suzerainty of China over it. At the same time, a northwestern corner of Outer Mongolia, Uriankhai, was proclaimed the "independent" republic of Tannu Tuva under Soviet protection. For the English text of the treaty, see Leonard Shapiro (ed.), *Soviet Treaty Series*, Vol. I, 1917–1928 (Georgetown University Press, 1950), pp. 137–138; and *The China Year Book, 1923*, ed. by H. G. W. Woodhead (E. P. Dutton & Co.), p. 677.

80. See note 24 of this chapter.

81. For the full English text of the Sun-Joffe Declaration, see *The China Year Book*, 1924, p. 863; and T'ang Leang-li, *Foundations of Modern China* (London: Noel Douglas, 1928), p. 167.

82. See Conrad Brandt, *Stalin's Failure in China, 1924–1927* (Harvard University Press, 1959); and Allen S. Whiting, *Soviet Policies in China, 1917–1924* (Columbia University Press, 1954).

83. For the full English text of this agreement, see Shapiro, *op. cit.*, Vol. I, pp. 242–244; and *The China Year Book*, 1924, pp. 1192–1200.

84. For the full English text of the Mukden agreement, see Shapiro, *op. cit.*, Vol. I, pp. 279–281.

85. Peter S. H. Tang, *op. cit.*, p. 153.

86. For the details, see Martin R. Norins, *Gateway to Asia: Sinkiang, Frontier of the Chinese Far West* (John Day Co., Inc., 1944); Allen S. Whiting and Sheng Shih-ts'ai, *Sinkiang: Pawn or Pivot?* (Michigan State University Press, 1958); Allen S. Whiting, "Sinkiang and Sino-Soviet Relations," *The China Quarterly*, July–Sept. 1960, pp. 32–41; and Geoffrey Wheeler, "Sinkiang and the Soviet Union," *ibid.*, Oct.–Dec. 1963, pp. 56–60. The discussion of the Soviet Union's repenetration into Sinkiang during the 1930's and 1940's in this chapter is based on the above source materials, unless another source has been indicated.

87. See George Moseley, *A Sino-Soviet Cultural Frontier: The Ili Kazakh Autonomous Chou* (Harvard University Press, 1966), p. 11.

88. Sheng Shih-ts'ai was replaced in 1944 by Wa Chang-hsin,

who, in turn, was succeeded in 1945 by Chang Chih-chung. In the summer of 1947 Masud Sabri (a Uighur) became Sinkiang's governor. The last governor of the province right before the Chinese Communist victory was Burhan Shahidi.

89. See United States Department of State, *Foreign Relations of the United States: The Conferences at Malta and Yalta, 1945* (Washington, D.C.: Government Printing Office, 1955), p. 984; and Tang Tsou, *America's Failure in China 1941–50* (The University of Chicago Press, 1963), p. 250.

90. For the full English text of this treaty, see Ai-chen Wu, *op. cit.,* pp. 407–411.

91. Friters, *op. cit.,* pp. 212–214.

92. For the full English text of this alliance pact, see *Soviet News* (London), March 1, 1946, p. 1.

93. For the details, see Raymond L. Garthoff, "The Soviet Intervention in Manchuria, 1945–46," in Garthoff (ed.), *Sino-Soviet Military Relations,* pp. 57–81.

94. See Chapter 2.

95. See Ch'eng T'ien-fang, *History of Sino-Soviet Relations* (Public Affairs Press, 1957), pp. 274–275.

96. See note 93 of this chapter.

97. Quoted from Garthoff, *loc. cit.,* pp. 82–83.

Chapter 2. THE TERRITORIAL DISPUTE
          BEFORE THE USSURI BORDER CLASHES
          OF MARCH 1969

1. Quoted from A. Doak Barnett, *Communist China and Asia: Challenge to American Policy* (Harper & Brothers, 1960), p. 67.

2. Mao Tse-tung's speech, September 21, 1949, to the People's Political Consultative Conference, *China Digest* (Peking), Vol. VII, No. 1, Oct. 5, 1949, p. 4.

3. Sun Yat-sen, *San Min Chu I, The Three Principles of the People,* tr. by Frank W. Price (Shanghai: China Committee of the Institute of Pacific Relations, 1927), pp. 91–93.

4. *Ibid.,* pp. 93, 94, 98, and 99.

5. Chiang Kai-shek, *China's Destiny,* tr. by Wang Chung-hui (The Macmillan Company, 1947), p. 242.

6. Hou Ming-chiu, Chen Erh-shiu, and Lu Chen, *General*

Geography of China (in Chinese) (1946), Ch. 1, cited in George B. Cressey, *Land of the 500 Million: A Geography of China* (McGraw-Hill Book Co., Inc., 1955), p. 39.

7. Mao Tse-tung, *Selected Works* (London: Lawrence and Wishart, Ltd., 1954–   ), Vol. II, pp. 259–260. For a statement similar to this, see Mao Tse-tung, *Hsin-min-chu-i* ("On New Democracy") (Yenan: Chieh-fang-she, 1944), pp. 4–5.

8. Edgar Snow, *Red Star Over China* (Grove Press, Inc., 1961), p. 96.

9. C. P. Fitzgerald, *op. cit.*, p. 688. For a study of the Chinese minority in the Soviet Far East, see Walter Kolarz, *The Peoples of the Soviet Far East* (Frederick A. Praeger, Inc., Publishers, 1954), pp. 42–49.

10. See *United States Relations with China* (Washington, D.C.: Government Printing Office, 1949), pp. 596–604; *The New York Times,* Dec. 14, 1949, p. 1; George Moorad, *Lost Peace in China* (E. P. Dutton & Co., Inc., 1949), pp. 162–165, 167; Tsou, *op. cit.*, pp. 335–337; and Max Beloff, *Soviet Policy in the Far East, 1944–1951* (Oxford University Press, 1953), pp. 38–41.

11. *Ibid.*

12. For the Soviet Union's proposal for the joint Sino-Soviet administration of the major industries and mines of Manchuria for thirty years, see United Nations, General Assembly, Fourth Session, *Summary Records of the First Committee* (Lake Success, N.Y., Sept. 20–Dec. 6, 1949), pp. 344–355; *United States Relations with China,* pp. 597–598; Chiang Kai-shek, *Soviet Russia in China: A Summing-up at 70* (Farrar, Straus and Cudahy, 1957), p. 169; and *The New York Times,* March 15, 1946, p. 5.

13. Herbert Feis, *The China Tangle: The American Effort in China from Pearl Harbor to the Marshall Mission* (Princeton University Press, 1953), p. 140.

14. James F. Byrnes, *Speaking Frankly* (Harper & Brothers, 1947), p. 228.

15. Cited from Herbert Feis, *Churchill, Roosevelt, Stalin: The War They Waged and the Peace They Sought* (Princeton University Press, 1957), pp. 408–409.

16. See Vladimir Dedijer, *Tito* (Simon and Schuster Inc.,

1953), p. 322; and Milovan Djilas, *Conversations with Stalin,* tr. by Michael B. Petrovich (Harcourt, Brace and World, Inc., 1962), p. 182.

17. This quotation was taken from a dispatch from the Japanese correspondent Takeda in Peking, in *Mainichi Shimbun,* March 9, 1967. Takeda obtained this text of Mao's speech from a Peking wall poster that appeared on March 8, 1967, during the height of the Cultural Revolution.

18. See Allen S. Whiting, "Mao's First Bid to Washington Rebuffed—in 1945," *The Washington Post,* July 1, 1971, p. 22; and Murrey Marder, "Chou, Mao and the U.S.—Lost Chance in '45?" *ibid.,* July 26, 1971, pp. 1, 8.

19. For the details, see *JMJP,* Feb. 15, 1950; Hsinhua News Agency dispatch, Feb. 16, 1950; *The New York Times,* Feb. 15, 1950, p. 11; Robert C. North, "The Sino-Soviet Agreements of 1950," *Far Eastern Survey,* July 12, 1950, pp. 125–130; and Garthoff (ed.), *Sino-Soviet Military Relations,* pp. 214–218.

20. *JMJP,* Sept. 16, 1950. See also *ibid.,* Jan. 2, 1953.

21. *JMJP,* Sept. 16, 1952.

22. Douglas M. Johnston and Hungdah Chiu, *Agreements of the People's Republic of China 1949–1967: A Calendar* (Harvard University Press, 1968), pp. 30, 34; and *JMJP,* May 26, 1955.

23. *JMJP,* Feb. 15, 1950.

24. *JMJP,* March 29, 1950; and April 2, 1950.

25. Quoted from Harrison E. Salisbury, *War Between Russia and China* (W. W. Norton & Company, Inc., 1969), p. 43.

26. *The New York Times,* June 6, 1956, pp. 1, 3.

27. *Ibid.*

28. *Ibid.*

29. See note 17 of this chapter.

30. For Peking's official complaint that Soviet military aid to Communist China during the Korean War was not given "gratis," but was subject to the repayment of every penny, see *Peking Review,* May 8, 1964, pp. 12–18. The Soviet Union claimed in 1964 that the total figure of Soviet military assistance to Communist China during the Korean conflict amounted to $1.35 billion. See *Soviet News* (London), Aug. 14, 1964, pp. 74–75; and Aug. 17, 1964, pp. 79–80.

31. Johnston and Chiu, *op. cit.*, p. 5.

32. *Ibid.*, p. 57.

33. *JMJP,* Dec. 23, 1957; and Harald Munthe-Kaas, "Amur Amendments," *Far Eastern Economic Review,* May 26, 1966, pp. 355–356.

34. *Ibid.*

35. Harald Munthe-Kaas, *op. cit.*, p. 356.

36. *Ibid.*

37. Theodore Shabad, *China's Changing Map: A Political and Economic Geography of the Chinese People's Republic* (Frederick A. Praeger, Inc., 1956), p. 5.

38. The title of this textbook was "A Short History of Modern China." For a detailed discussion of the 1954 map, see Jacquet-Francillon, "The Borders of China," *The New Republic,* April 20, 1963, pp. 18–22; and Hinton, *op. cit.*, pp. 332–333.

39. *Sekai Shuho,* Aug. 11, 1964.

40. *Asahi Shimbun* (Tokyo), Aug. 1, 1964.

41. See *Documents on International Affairs,* 1954. Issued Under the Auspices of the Royal Institute of International Affairs (London: Oxford University Press), p. 325; Johnston and Chiu, *op. cit.*, p. 34; and *JMJP,* May 26, 1955.

42. Henry Schwarz, "Chinese Migration to North-West China and Inner Mongolia, 1949–59," *The China Quarterly,* Oct.–Dec. 1963, pp. 62–74. In 1962 the Peking regime closed the two remaining Soviet consulates in China.

43. It must be noted that Kao Kang, Manchuria's powerful Communist Party leader, was purged in February 1954 on the charge that he had attempted to build an "independent kingdom" in the region. See Hsinhua News Agency dispatch, Feb. 18, 1954.

44. By the end of the nineteenth century the population of Manchuria was about 14,000,000, of which 80 percent were Chinese. By 1940 the total population of Manchuria was around 44,570,000. Of this total, about 90 percent were ethnically Chinese, despite Japanese restrictions on Chinese immigration. Today pure Manchu groups, whose forefathers were rulers of the Manchu, or Ch'ing, Dynasty, and who are not yet Sinicized, remain only in northern Manchuria, chiefly in

the Aigun district. See *Encyclopaedia Britannica,* Vol. XIV, 1967, p. 760.

45. *Ibid.*

46. *Ibid.*

47. *Ibid.*

48. *China News Analysis* (Hong Kong), March 8, 1957, p. 3.

49. The Editor, "China's Taching Oilfield: Eclipse of an Industrial Model," *Current Scene,* Sept. 17, 1968, p. 3.

50. Hsinhua News Agency dispatch, Aug. 1, 1963.

51. The "autonomous region" concept has been used by Communist China for minority administration. There are five provincial-level "autonomous regions" in China today: the Inner Mongolian Autonomous Region, the Sinkiang-Uighur Autonomous Region, the Ninghsia-Hui Autonomous Region, the Tibetan Autonomous Region, and the Kwangsi-Chuang Autonomous Region. These areas do not enjoy the right to self-determination, but a purely nominal degree of administrative autonomy is granted. According to the Peking *Ta Kung Pao* of Sept. 29, 1962, the Han Chinese constituted about 95 percent of the Chinese mainland's population, and there were 52 minority nationalities totaling around 38 million. The Chinese Communist regime officially condemns any national movement by non-Han minority nationalities that seeks separation from the Chinese People's Republic for independence as "reactionary, bourgeois, and un-Socialist." See *JMJP,* Oct. 2, 1951; June 27, 1958; Article II of the General Program for the Implementation of Nationality Regional Autonomy, Aug. 8, 1952; Hsinhua News Agency dispatch, April 5, 1960; and *Min-tsu T'uan-chieh* ("Nationalities Solidarity," Peking), Nov. 1957, p. 15.

52. *Ibid.*

53. According to the 1953 census, the total population of Inner Mongolia was 6,100,000, and the Mongols and other non-Han minorities represented about 20 percent of it. See Hsinhua News Agency dispatch, Nov. 1, 1954. According to *JMJP,* Dec. 27, 1961, the total population of Inner Mongolia in 1961 was 9,200,000, and the Mongols numbered only 1,200,-000.

54. On the Russian side of Turkestan are the Kirghiz and

Kazakh Soviet Socialist Republics. In Soviet Central Asia there are now 12 million European Russians and 17 million of the local Moslem peoples—Uighurs, Kazakhs, and Kirghizes.

55. The population of Sinkiang includes 14 non-Chinese minority nationalities, such as Uighurs, Kazakhs, Huis, Mongols, Kirghizes, Manchus, Sibos, Tadzhiks, Uzbeks, Tartars, and Russians. In 1953 about 13,000 Russians lived in Sinkiang. For detailed studies on Sinkiang's population, see Hsinhua News Agency dispatch, Nov. 1, 1954; June 28, 1964; Daniel Tretiak, "Peking's Policy Toward Sinkiang," *Current Scene*, Nov. 15, 1963; and Amrit Lal, "Sinification of Ethnic Minorities in China," *ibid.*, Feb. 15, 1970, pp. 11–17.

56. *Ibid.*

57. In 1963, the Chinese, with 300,000, were no. 3 on the population rolls of Sinkiang, being outnumbered both by the Uighurs with 3,640,000 and by the Kazakhs with 475,000. In 1965, the Chinese, with 3,000,000, were outnumbered only by the Uighurs.

58. Whiting, "Sinkiang and Sino-Soviet Relations," pp. 36–37.

59. According to official claims made by Sinkiang Communist authorities in January 1960, 96.6 percent of the population of Sinkiang was collectivized into 451 communes with some 30,000 public dining halls, and half of the area's nomadic herdsmen had settled down in fixed sedentary encampments. *Ibid.*, p. 40.

60. Allen S. Whiting, "Nationality Tensions in Sinkiang," *Far Eastern Survey*, Jan. 1956, pp. 8–13.

61. See Roderick MacFarquhar, *The Hundred Flowers Campaign and the Chinese Intellectuals* (Frederick A. Praeger, Inc., 1960), pp. 8–13.

62. See, for example, Zunun Taipov, "Maoist Outrages on Uighur Soil," *New Times*, Moscow, July 9, 1969, pp. 11–12.

63. Whiting, "Sinkiang and Sino-Soviet Relations," pp. 34, 40; Wheeler, *loc. cit.*, p. 59; and June Dreyer, "China's Minority Nationalities in the Cultural Revolution," *The China Quarterly*, July–Sept. 1968, pp. 100–101.

64. *JMJP* and *Hung Ch'i*, Sept. 6, 1963.

65. See *The Evening Bulletin* (Philadelphia), Jan. 31, 1967,

p. 2; Zunun Taipov, "On the Other Side of the Barricade," *Kazakhstanskaya Pravda*, Sept. 29, 1963; Usman Mametov, "I Can't Be Silent," *ibid.*, Sept. 29, 1963; and O. Matskevich, "Along the Border," *ibid.*, Sept. 24, 1963; the last three articles are translated into English in *CDSP*, Vol. XV, No. 38, Oct. 6, 1963, pp. 16–17, 24.

66. *Ibid.*

67. See Daniel Tretiak, "Peking's Policy Toward Sinkiang: Trouble on the 'New Frontier,' " *Current Scene*, Nov. 15, 1963, p. 11.

68. *JMJP*, October 24, 1962; Oct. 31, 1962; Nov. 15, 1962; and Dec. 15, 1962; and *Hung Ch'i*, Nov. 16, 1962.

69. *JMJP*, Dec. 31, 1962.

70. For the full English text of Khrushchev's speech to the Supreme Soviet, see *The Daily Worker* (New York), Dec. 23, 1962, Supplement, pp. 1–3.

71. *Ibid.*

72. *The Daily Worker*, Jan. 13, 1963, p. 3.

73. Editorial, "Comments on the Statement Made by the Communist Party of the United States of America," *JMJP*, March 8, 1963.

74. *Ibid.*

75. *Ibid.*

76. See note 5 of Introduction.

77. See note 6 of Introduction.

78. See note 9 of Introduction. See also *Izvestia*, Sept. 21, 1963. (English text in *The New York Times*, Sept. 23, 1963.)

79. *Ibid.*

80. *JMJP*, and *Hung Ch'i*, Sept. 3, 1963; and *Peking Review*, Sept. 13, 1963, pp. 6–23.

81. *Pravda*, September 23, 1963, in *CDSP*, Vol. XV, No. 38, Oct. 16, 1963, p. 16.

82. *Ibid.*

83. *Ibid.*

84. See note 63 of this chapter. See also "Former Youth Leader Tells Why He Fled from China," *Soviet News*, Sept. 27, 1963; and *Literaturnaya Gazeta*, Jan. 1967, cited in John Gittings, *op. cit.*, p. 160.

85. See Harrison E. Salisbury, "A 'Free Sinkiang' Held Soviet Aim," *The New York Times*, March 2, 1970, p. 7.

86. See *The Evening Bulletin* (Philadelphia), Jan. 13, 1967, p. 2.

87. *Ibid*. See also note 85 of this chapter.

88. Hsinhua News Agency dispatch, April 28, 1964; Sept. 28, 1965; and *Peking Review*, Sept. 11, 1964, pp. 5, 26; and Oct. 8, 1965, p. 23.

89. Japan and the Soviet Union have a territorial dispute over the Kurile Islands, a group of islands off the eastern tip of Hokkaido. The Japanese claim Kunashiri, Etorofu, Shikotan and the Habomai Islands as their own inherent territory. The Soviet Union, which occupied the islands as a result of the Second World War, has indicated that it would give up two small islands—Shikotan and the Habomai group—if Japan would accept this as a final settlement. Concerning the other islands it says that boundaries changed by one war cannot be changed without another war.

Until the Soviet Union and West Germany signed a no-war pact in August 1970, the Polish-German frontier—the Oder-Neisse line—was one of the most critical and sensitive issues in Europe. The Oder-Neisse line was imposed upon Germany right after the Second World War. Poland and East Germany today recognize the Oder-Neisse line as the permanent boundary line dividing German and Polish territories. West Germany had refused to recognize the line as such until August 1970.

In September 1939, Nazi Germany and the Soviet Union formally partitioned Poland, and Moscow later annexed the eastern part of Poland into its own territory.

In addition to Bucharest's attempt to assert its political and economic independence from Moscow, there is friction between the Soviet Union and Rumania over Bessarabia, a chunk of Rumanian territory seized by the Soviets in the Second World War. See Victor Zorza, "Lost Territory Eyed by Rumania," *The Washington Post*, May 1, 1966, p. 4 (M).

In the famous "winter war," Finland was defeated by the Soviet Union. She lost about 10 percent of her territory to the Soviet Union, including the Karelian Isthmus. When Germany attacked the Soviet Union in 1941, the Finns were again at war with Moscow as "co-belligerent," but not as "ally," along with the Germans. With the German defeat in 1945, Finland lost more of its territory to Moscow. Finland today has 130,119 square miles.

90. See Dennis J. Doolin, *Territorial Claims in the Sino-Soviet Conflict: Documents and Analysis* (Hoover Institution on War, Revolution, and Peace, Stanford University, 1965), p. 22.

91. Doolin, *op. cit.,* pp. 33–36. On September 22, 1964, Soviet Foreign Minister Gromyko submitted to U.N. Secretary-General U Thant a proposal for the peaceful settlement of territorial and frontier issues. *Pravda,* Sept. 24, 1964, in *CDSP,* Vol. XVI, No. 39, Oct. 21, 1964, p. 25.

92. *The New York Times,* Feb. 3, 1964, p. 3.

93. *Peking Review,* May 8, 1964, pp. 12–18.

94. *Ibid.*

95. See *JMJP,* Feb. 1, 1960; and W. Whittan, "The Sino-Burmese Boundary Treaty," *Pacific Affairs,* Summer 1961, pp. 174–183.

96. Hsinhua News Agency dispatch, March 26, 1963; Guy Searls, "Communist China's Border Policy: Dragon Throne Imperialism?" *Current Scene,* April 15, 1962, pp. 16–17; and Hinton, *op. cit.,* pp. 329–330.

97. *The New York Times,* March 22, 1960, pp. 1, 14; May 1, 1960, p. 24; May 14, 1961, p. 4; Hsinhua News Agency dispatch, Oct. 13, 1961; and *New Developments in Friendly Relations Between China and Nepal* (Peking: Foreign Languages Press, 1960), pp. 21–24.

98. Hsinhua News Agency dispatch, March 2, 1963; *The Christian Science Monitor,* March 5, 1963, p. 1; and *Sino-Pakistan "Agreements," March 2, 1963: Some Facts* (New Delhi: Ministry of External Affairs, 1963), pp. 24–28.

99. Hsinhua News Agency dispatch, Nov. 22, 1963.

100. See *Peking Review,* March 14, 1969, pp. 14–15; and *Pravda,* March 30, 1969, in *CDSP,* Vol. XXI, No. 13, April 10, 1969, pp. 4–5.

101. *Pravda,* April 3, 1964, in *CDSP,* Vol. XVI, No. 14, April 29, 1969, p. 5.

102. *Sekai Shuho,* Aug. 11, 1964.

103. *Asahi Shimbun,* Aug. 1, 1964.

104. *Pravda,* Sept. 2, 1964, in *CDSP,* Vol. XVI, No. 34, Sept. 16, 1964, pp. 3–7; and *Pravda,* Sept. 20, 1964, in *CDSP,* Vol. XVI, No. 38, Oct. 14, 1964, pp. 3–6.

105. *Ibid.*

106. Doolin, *op. cit.,* pp. 61–65.

107. *Pravda,* Sept. 26, 1964, in *CDSP,* Vol. XVI, No. 38, Oct. 14, 1964, pp. 3–6.

108. See, for example, *JMJP,* Jan. 15, 1968; and June Dryer, "Inner Mongolia: The Purge of Ulanfu," *Current Scene,* Nov. 15, 1968, pp. 1–13.

109. Harald Munthe-Kaas, "Amur Amendments," *Far Eastern Economic Review,* May 26, 1966, pp. 355–358.

110. *Ibid.*

111. *Ibid.* See also *JMJP,* April 20, 1966; and Hsinhua News Agency dispatch, May 5, 1965.

112. *The Washington Post,* Nov. 10, 1966, p. 4.

113. *The New York Times,* Nov. 22, 1966, p. 12.

114. *The Washington Post,* Jan. 6, 1967, p. 9.

115. *The New York Times,* Nov. 22, 1966, p. 12.

116. *Ibid.*

117. *Ibid.,* June 2, 1966, p. 6.

118. *The Evening Bulletin* (Philadelphia), Jan. 31, 1967, p. 16.

119. *Ibid.,* p. 2.

120. *The Washington Post,* Oct. 30, 1966, p. 1 (D).

121. *The New York Times,* Dec. 16, 1966, p. 1.

122. *The Washington Post,* May 26, 1967, p. 18; and Oct. 11, 1967, p. 26.

123. *Ibid.,* Oct. 11, 1967, p. 26.

124. *Ibid.*

125. *Ibid.*

126. Cited in Anthony Astrachan's dispatch from Moscow, *The Washington Post,* Jan. 29, 1970, p. 18.

127. *Ibid.*

128. See David I. Hitchcock, Jr., "Joint Development of Siberia: Decision-Making in Japanese-Soviet Relations," *Asian Survey,* March 1971, pp. 279–300.

129. See *Mainichi Daily News,* Monthly International Edition, Sept. 1, 1969, p. 9.

130. Hsinhua News Agency dispatch, Dec. 14, 1968; and March 6, 1969. See also "Leninism or Social Imperialism?" a joint editorial of *JMJP, Hung Ch'i,* and *Chieh-fang Chün-pao,* April 22, 1970.

131. *Ibid.*

132. The Brezhnev Doctrine was first formulated in a *Pravda* commentary on Sept. 26, 1968. For its English translation, see *Problems of Communism,* Nov.–Dec. 1968, p. 25.

133. See, for example, *The New York Times,* Jan. 10, 1967, p. 6; and *The Washington Post,* Jan. 10, 1967, p. 11; Jan. 13, 1967, p. 12; and Jan. 15, 1967, p. 23.

134. *The New York Times,* Dec. 6, 1966, p. 1; and *The Washington Post,* Jan. 16, 1967, p. 16.

Chapter 3. THE USSURI BORDER CLASHES OF MARCH 1969
AND THEREAFTER

1. See Tass International Service (Moscow), March 3, 1969, reprinted in *The New York Times,* March 4, 1969, p. 12; *Pravda,* March 8, 1969, in *CDSP,* Vol. XXI, No. 10, March 26, 1969, pp. 3–4; Tass International Service, March 7, 1969, reprinted in *The New York Times,* March 8, 1969, p. 3; *The New York Times,* March 16, 1969, p. 10; and *Pravda,* March 17, 1969, in *CDSP,* Vol. XXI, No. 11, April 2, 1969, p. 5.

2. *Ibid.*

3. *Peking Review,* March 8, 1969, pp. 12–18; March 7, 1969, pp. 5–7; March 14, 1969, pp. 5, 14–15; March 15, 1969, p. 8; March 21, 1969, pp. 7–9; and *JMJP,* March 11, 1969.

4. See Chinese Foreign Ministry's statement on the border dispute with Moscow, March 10, 1969, in *Peking Review,* March 14, 1969, pp. 14–15.

5. For the derivation of the term *thalweg,* see John Westlake, *International Law,* 2d ed. (Cambridge: Cambridge University Press, 1910–1913), Vol. I, p. 144. The doctrine of the *thalweg* may be regarded as a prescriptive or customary law of the subject holding good in the absence of treaty stipulations. The older rule of international law concerning the delimitation of the dividing line formed by a boundary river was that the line followed the middle of the stream. This old rule was laid down by Grotius and endorsed by Vattel. This

rule was modified in the nineteenth century by specifying that in the case of navigable rivers the dividing line would follow the middle of the main channel, technically known as the *thalweg*. (The doctrine of the *thalweg* is also applied to other water boundaries, such as lakes and straits.) According to Charles G. Fenwick, the advantage of the *thalweg* is that when the boundary line follows more closely the chief thoroughfare of commerce it is less subject to change than the middle line between banks. See Charles G. Fenwick, *International Law*, 4th ed. (Appleton-Century-Crofts, 1965), pp. 438–439.

6. *Peking Review*, March 14, 1969, pp. 14–15; and Tass International Service, in *The New York Times*, March 31, 1969, p. 16.

7. On March 25, 1969, for example, Pyotr Y. Shelest, a member of the ruling Soviet Communist Party's Politburo and also chief of the Soviet Ukraine Communist Party, said in Kiev that "the recent events on the Sino-Soviet frontier around the Ussuri occurred at the moment when the problem of West Berlin was growing more acute. This is, as correctly described by many fraternal parties, a stab in the back of the Soviet Union by the Mao clique." *The New York Times*, March 26, 1969, p. 8.

8. Chinese-American collusion has been one of the main propaganda themes of the Soviet Union in recent years. See, for example, *Izvestia*, Oct. 28, 1966, in *CDSP*, Nov. 16, 1966, p. 7; and *Pravda*, Feb. 15, 1967; in *CDSP*, March 8, 1967, p. 9.

9. See, for example, *The New York Times*, March 4, 1969, p. 12. According to *The New York Times*, highly placed European sources recently disclosed that opposition had developed in the Soviet Communist Party to the leadership of Leonid I. Brezhnev. *Ibid.*, May 1, 1969, p. 10.

10. *The New York Times*, March 12, 1969, p. 16; March 13, 1969, p. 3; and *The Washington Post*, March 12, 1969, p. 23.

11. For a detailed study of the conflict between Mao and the professionally-minded army officers, see Tai Sung An, "Chairman Mao Purges Military Professionalism," *Military Review*, Aug. 1968, pp. 88–98.

12. See Introduction of this book.

13. *Pravda*, March 30, 1969, in *CDSP*, Vol. XXI, No. 13, April 16, 1969, pp. 3–5.

14. *Pravda,* April 12, 1969, in *CDSP,* Vol. XXI, No. 15, April 30, 1969, p. 18.

15. *The Asian Student* (San Francisco), April 12, 1969, p. 2.

16. *The New York Times,* May 4, 1969, p. 12; and May 11, 1969, p. 6 (E).

17. *Peking Review,* May 16, 1969, p. 3.

18. *Ibid.,* May 30, 1969, pp. 3–9.

19. *Ibid.*

20. *Ibid.*

21. Hsinhua News Agency dispatch, June 7, 1969.

22. Moscow Radio, June 13, 1969, in *The Washington Post,* June 14, 1969, p. 14.

23. *Ibid.*

24. See *The New York Times,* June 12, 1969, p. 2; *Peking Review,* June 13, 1969, pp. 3–5; July 11, 1969, p. 6; Aug. 15, 1969, p. 3; Aug. 22, 1969, pp. 4–5; *Pravda,* July 9, 1969, in *CDSP,* Vol. XXI, No. 28, Aug. 6, 1969, p. 34; *Pravda,* Aug. 14, 1969, in *CDSP,* Vol. XXI, No. 33, Sept. 10, 1969, p. 3; and Tass International Service, Sept. 10, 1969, in *The New York Times,* Sept. 11, 1969, p. 9.

25. *Peking Review,* June 13, 1969, pp. 4–5.

26. *Ibid.,* Aug. 22, 1969, pp. 4–5.

27. *Ibid.*

28. Tass International Service, Sept. 10, 1969, in *The New York Times,* Sept. 11, 1969, p. 9.

29. *Ibid.*

30. For this agreement, see *Pravda,* Aug. 9, 1969, in *CDSP,* Vol. XXI, No. 32, Sept. 3, 1969, p. 16.

31. *Peking Review,* Aug. 15, 1969, p. 3; and Hsinhua News Agency dispatch, Aug. 13, 1969.

32. *Pravda,* Aug. 28, 1969, in *CDSP,* Vol. XXI, No. 35, Sept. 24, 1969, pp. 3–5.

33. *Ibid.,* p. 3.

34. *Ibid.,* p. 5.

35. *Ibid.*

36. Cited in *The Washington Post,* Oct. 9, 1969, p. 27.

37. See *The New York Times,* Aug. 29, 1969, p. 5; Sept. 13, 1969, p. 5; and *The Washington Post,* Aug. 17, 1969, p. 7; Aug. 28, 1969, p. 7; and Sept. 7, 1969, p. 12.

38. *The New York Times,* Sept. 18, 1969, p. 5.

39. *Ibid.*

40. *Ibid.*

41. See Introduction of this book.

42. Mao Tse-tung, *Selected Works* (London, 1954–), Vol. II, p. 206.

43. Audrey Topping's dispatch from Peking, *The New York Times,* May 21, 1971, p. 10.

44. *Peking Review,* Oct. 10, 1969, pp. 3–4; and Edgar Snow, "Talks with Chou En-lai: The Open Door," *The New Republic,* March 29, 1971, p. 23.

45. *Peking Review,* Oct. 10, 1969, pp. 3–4.

46. *Ibid.,* p. 4.

47. *Ibid.*

48. *Ibid.*

49. *Ibid.*

50. *Ibid.*

51. Huang Yung-sheng was purged in September 1971.

52. See Tai Sung An, *Mao Tse-tung's Cultural Revolution* (Pegasus, a Division of the Bobbs-Merrill Co., Inc., 1971), pp. 1–132.

53. This fact was clearly revealed in early October 1969, when Peking issued two radically different documents related to the Sino-Soviet boundary dispute. Peking's October 7, 1969, statement announcing agreement in principle on the border talks dropped several preconditions that had been spelled out in its earlier May 24, 1969, statement. It was milder than usual and omitted the personal attacks on Soviet leaders that had become a habitual form in Communist China's polemic against Moscow. But the next day, October 8, the Mao regime issued another "Document of the Ministry of Foreign Affairs" which was emotional and belligerent on the border issue, berated the Soviets, and thus returned to Maoist rigidity on Sino-Soviet differences. In short, Peking's negotiating strategy toward border discussions with Moscow in the fall of 1969 was hatched by a compromise between the moderates and the ideologues in the Chinese capital. As Peter J. Kumpa astutely observes, Peking's moderates "got their talks and set forth their position in a business-like statement" of October 7, 1969. The next day the Maoist ideologues were given their chance to assert their

dogmatic view again. See *Peking Review,* May 30, 1969, pp. 3–9; and Oct. 10, 1969, pp. 3–4; and *The Sun* (Baltimore), Oct. 12, 1969, p. 4.

54. For the full text of Ho Chi Minh's final statement, see *Peking Review,* Sept. 19, 1969, pp. 21–22.

55. *The New York Times,* April 20, 1969, p. 12.

56. *Ibid.,* Sept. 12, 1969, p. 2.

57. *Peking Review,* Oct. 10, 1969, p. 3.

58. *Ibid.*

59. *Kommunist,* No. 15, Oct. 1969, in *CDSP,* Vol. XXI, No. 43, Nov. 19, 1969, pp. 3–7.

60. *Pravda,* July 11, 1970, in *CDSP,* Vol. XXII, No. 28, Aug. 11, 1970, p. 15; *The New York Times,* Dec. 21, 1970; p. 11; and Hsinhua News Agency dispatch, Dec. 24, 1970.

61. Snow, *op. cit.,* p. 23; and *The New York Times,* June 11, 1970, p. 1.

62. *Ta Kung Pao* (Hong Kong), Nov. 5, 1969.

63. The discussion of Peking's bargaining position at the current top-level Sino-Soviet border negotiations in Peking is based on the following three documents: (1) the Statement of the Government of the People's Republic of China, May 24, 1969, in *Peking Review,* May 30, 1969, pp. 3–9; (2) the Statement of the Government of the People's Republic of China, October 7, 1969, in *ibid.,* Oct. 10, 1969, pp. 3–4; and (3) the Document of the Ministry of Foreign Affairs of the People's Republic of China, October 8, 1969, in *ibid.,* Oct. 10, 1969, pp. 8–15.

64. See also *The New York Times,* March 1, 1970, p. 27; and March 20, 1970, p. 3.

65. International Boundary Study No. 64, *China-USSR Boundary,* pp. 13–14; and the Note of the U.S.S.R. Ministry of Foreign Affairs to the C.P.R. Ministry of Foreign Affairs, *Pravda,* June 12, 1969, in *CDSP,* Vol. XXI, No. 24, July 9, 1969, p. 11.

66. See Chapter 1 of this book.

67. Jackson, *op. cit.,* p. 118.

68. See note 62 of this chapter.

69. *The New York Times,* March 1, 1970, p. 27.

70. See Introduction of this book.

71. *Pravda*, June 12, 1969, in *CDSP*, Vol. XXI, No. 24, July 9, 1969, p. 12.

72. *The Sun* (Baltimore), April 16, 1970, p. 1.

73. *Pravda*, June 12, 1969, in *CDSP*, Vol. XXI, No. 24, July 9, 1969, p. 11.

74. *Ibid.*

75. *Ibid.*

76. *Sovietskaya Rossia*, Aug. 2, 1970, cited in *The Washington Post*, Aug. 3, 1970, p. 1.

77. In the fall of 1970, for example, Moscow and Peking agreed to fill the vacant ambassadorial posts in both capitals after having lacked them for nearly five years. V. S. Tolstikov, former Leningrad party boss, took his post as Moscow's ambassador on October 10, 1970, and Liu Hsien-chuan left Peking for Moscow on November 22, 1970.

78. For the full text of the German-Soviet friendship treaty of August 12, 1970, see *The New York Times*, Aug. 12, 1970, p. 2.

79. *The New York Times*, Oct. 26, 1969, p. 2 (Section IV).

80. See Introduction of this book.

Chapter 4. SINO-SOVIET WAR IN THE 1970's?

1. Salisbury, *op. cit.*, pp. 193–211.

2. Lin Piao's remark at the Ninth Party Congress, April 1, 1969, in *Peking Review*, Special Issue, April 28, 1969, p. 26.

3. For Sun Tzu's military doctrine, see Sun Tzu, *The Art of War*, tr. and with an introduction by Samuel B. Griffith (Oxford University Press, 1963).

4. See Mao Tse-tung, *Lun-chi'ih-chiu-chan* ("On the Protracted War") (Yenan: Chieh-fang-she, 1939); and Mao Tse-tung, *Selected Works* (London, 1954–   ), Vol. III, p. 199.

5. Mao Tse-tung, *Imperialism and All Reactionaries Are Paper Tigers* (Peking: Foreign Languages Press, 1958), p. 27; and *JMJP*, Dec. 15, 1962.

6. See Hsinhua News Agency dispatch, Oct. 4, 1969; and *Peking Review*, April 30, 1970, pp. 4–5.

7. An, *op. cit.*

8. See Chapter 3 of this book.

9. See, for example, Edmund Clubb, *loc. cit.*, pp. 28–40; Clark W. Tinch, "Quasi-War Between Japan and the Soviet Union, 1937–1939," *World Politics,* Jan. 1951; and David Dallin, *Soviet Russia and the Far East* (Yale University Press, 1948), pp. 22–25.

10. See Chapter 3 of this book.

11. See Charles Murphy, "Mainland China's Evolving Nuclear Deterrent," *Bulletin of the Atomic Scientists,* Jan. 1972, p. 29.

12. *The Washington Post,* Sept. 18, 1970, pp. 1, 8.

13. *Ibid.*

14. See *The Military Balance 1971–72* (London: The International Institute for Strategic Studies, 1971), p. 40; and *The New York Times,* Nov. 23, 1970, p. 4.

15. A. Doak Barnett, "A Nuclear China and U.S. Arms Policy," *Foreign Affairs,* April 1970, p. 428; *The Washington Post,* July 6, 1970, p. 19; Sept. 18, 1970, p. 8; and *The New York Times,* April 26, 1970, p. 2. Peking's missile program was largely insulated from the upheavals of the wild Cultural Revolution, but the deployment of medium-range missiles has apparently slowed down. *The Economist* (London), Sept. 20, 1969, p. 36. The State Council's Seventh Ministry of Machine Building is in charge of developing aircraft, rockets, missiles and other accessory electronic parts. It is believed that the Peking regime spends roughly $1 billion a year—10 to 12 percent of Communist China's gross national product—on scientific research and development. *The Washington Post* (Sunday Outlook Section), May 3, 1970, p. 4.

16. *Peking Review,* April 30, 1970, pp. 4–13; and March 19, 1971, p. 17.

17. *The Washington Post,* April 26, 1970, p. 1. See also Alice Langley Hsieh, "China's Nuclear-Missile Programme: Regional or Intercontinental?" *The China Quarterly,* Jan.–Mar. 1971, pp. 85–99.

18. Barnett, *loc. cit.*, p. 428; and Murphy, *loc. cit.*, p. 32.

19. For a comprehensive analysis of Soviet military doctrine in the 1960's, see Thomas W. Wolfe, *Soviet Strategy at the Crossroads* (Harvard University Press, 1964); and William R. Kintner and Harriet F. Scott (eds. and trs.), *The Nuclear Revo-*

lution in Soviet Military Affairs (University of Oklahoma Press, 1968).

20. Sources: *The Military Balance 1971–72*; *U.S. News and World Report,* June 22, 1970, p. 53; and *The New York Times,* April 8, 1971, p. 1.

21. For Soviet views on the importance of nuclear weapons in the initial period of war and on the need to occupy enemy country with conventional weapons and troops in order to achieve final victory, see Raymond L. Garthoff, *The Soviet Image of Future War* (Public Affairs Press, 1959); Herbert S. Dinerstein, *War and the Soviet Union: Nuclear Weapons and the Revolution in Soviet Military and Political Thinking* (Frederick A. Praeger, Inc., 1959); Raymond L. Garthoff, *Soviet Strategy in the Nuclear Age,* rev. ed. (Frederick A. Praeger, Inc., Publishers, 1962); and Vasilii D. Sokolovskii (ed.), *Soviet Military Strategy,* tr. and with an analytical introduction, annotations, and supplementary material by Herbert S. Dinerstein *et al.* (Frederick A. Praeger, Inc., Publishers, 1963).

22. It must be noted that Vladivostok is the base of the Soviet Pacific Fleet, which is estimated to have 80 conventional submarines, 25 nuclear submarines, 86 major surface ships, backed up by about 250 naval shore-based aircraft, some of them armed with air-to-surface missiles. See *The New York Times,* Nov. 13, 1970, p. 35; and J. Malcolm Mackintosh, "The Soviet Generals' View of China in the 1960's," in Garthoff (ed.), *Sino-Soviet Military Relations,* p. 187.

23. *The New York Times,* July 22, 1970, p. 5.

24. Siberia constitutes half of the territory of the Soviet Union, but it contains only 11 percent of the Soviet population. About one half of its people are of Asiatic origin and may not be entirely politically reliable to the Moscow regime. The northern two thirds of Siberia is uninhabited for climatic reasons. Most of the Siberian population are settled mainly along the Trans-Siberian Railroad and in the industrial centers in southern Siberia. About three million people inhabit the Soviet Maritime Province.

25. According to Raymond L. Garthoff, it took about four months for the Soviet high command to move 27 divisions and 3 division-sized armored corps to the Manchurian frontier in

1945 to take part in the invasion of Manchuria against the Japanese. See Garthoff, *loc. cit.,* pp. 57–81.

26. After the Bolsheviks came to power in 1917, the Trans-Siberian Railroad was turned into a two-track system and supplemented by a motor highway.

27. See Introduction of this book.

28. Sinkiang is linked to China Proper only by two long, thin, puppet strings of road and a single-track railroad.

29. See Chapter 2 of this book.

30. Sinkiang contains most of China's uranium supplies, and the mines reportedly have one of the highest ore concentrations in the world. It also produces over half of China's output of crude oil.

31. Khalkin-gol is a river in the eastern tip of Mongolia. In May 1939, in an undeclared war, the Japanese army invaded Mongolia. Their objective was to knife through to Soviet territory, cut the Trans-Siberian Railroad, and isolate the Soviet Far East from Soviet Europe. The war involved at least 100,000 troops on each side plus a considerable number of aircraft. The Soviet forces were led by Marshal Georgi Zhukov, who subsequently, in the Second World War, was to defeat Hitler's armies in the European theater. Zhukov and his troops trounced the Japanese in Eastern Mongolia at Khalkin-gol during ten days between August 20 and 30, 1939. After that, although the Soviets were later to be attacked massively on the European front by Hitler's armies, the Japanese army refused to attack the Soviet Union in the Second World War.

32. See note 25 of this chapter.

33. See, for example, *Izvestia,* Aug. 22, 1969, in *CDSP,* Vol. XXI, No. 34, Sept. 17, 1969, p. 3; *Pravda,* Aug. 19, 1969, in *CDSP,* Vol. XXI, No. 34, p. 3; and Sept. 2, 1969, in *CDSP,* Vol. XXI, No. 35, Sept. 24, 1969, pp. 5–6.

34. Cited in *The Washington Post,* Sept. 29, 1969, p. 24.

35. *Ibid.*

36. See Chapter 3 of this book.

37. Tibetan guerrillas have been fighting against the Chinese Communists in Tibet in recent years. See *The Times of India* (New Delhi), Dec. 23, 1970; *The Times* (London), Dec. 23, 1970; and *Free China Weekly* (Taipei), Jan. 3, 1971, p. 3.

38. Mao Tse-tung, "On the Protracted War," in Mao Tse-tung, *Selected Works* (London, 1954–), Vol. II, pp. 157–243.

39. *Ibid.*

40. It must be emphasized that *only some portions* of the entire officer corps of the Chinese Communist army belong to this modernizing professional officer group. This group includes both veteran guerrilla officers and young junior officers who have graduated from military academies of various kinds since 1949.

41. Alice Langley Hsieh, "China's Nuclear Missile Programme: Regional or Intercontinental?" *The China Quarterly,* Jan.–March 1971, p. 85.

42. Mao Tse-tung, *Selected Works* (London, 1954–), Vol. I, p. 75; and Vol. II, p. 272.

43. See *Chieh-fang Chün-pao,* Aug. 16, 1967; and *Kung-tso T'ung-hsuan* ("Military Correspondence," Peking), No. 3, Jan. 7, 1961, p. 3; and No. 24, June 18, 1961, p. 1. See also David A. Charles, "The Dismissal of Marshal P'eng Teh-huai," *The China Quarterly,* Oct.–Dec. 1961, pp. 63–76.

44. *Ibid.* After this event, Lin Piao became Defense Minister. Lo Jui-ch'ing, who had been secret police chief of Communist China between 1949 and 1959, was appointed chief of the general staff of the Chinese People's Liberation Army.

45. The new system of military ranks and badges was introduced in Communist China in September 1955. But Peking announced in 1965 that as of June 1, 1965, the system of ranks and all badges and titles of office were to be eliminated from its armed forces. Hsinhua News Agency dispatch, May 25, 1965. This policy was designed to curb professionalism in the military and also to eradicate a status-conscious, professional officer corps.

46. *Peking Review,* May 14, 1965, pp. 7–15; Aug. 6, 1965, p. 5; and Sept. 3, 1965, pp. 38–39; *JMJP,* April 19, 1967; and Donald S. Zagoria, *Vietnam Triangle: Moscow, Peking, Hanoi* (Pegasus, a Division of Western Publishing Co., 1967), pp. 63–98.

47. *Ibid.* See also *Chieh-fang Chün-pao,* Aug. 1, 1966; *Peking Review,* Aug. 5, 1966, pp. 1–10; and *JMJP,* Nov. 3, 1967.

48. Lin Piao, "Long Live the Victory of the People's War!" *Hung Ch'i,* Sept. 3, 1965.

49. See "Document Concerning the Lin Piao Incident," *Issues and Studies* (Taipei), May 1972, pp. 77–83; *The New York Times*, July 23, 1972, pp. 1, 16; July 28, 1972, pp. 1, 6; and July 29, 1972, p. 7.

50. *JMJP*, April 9, 1967, and Aug. 28, 1967; Hsinhua News Agency dispatch, Aug. 25, 1967; and *Chieh-fang Chün-pao*, May 16, 1968.

51. See note 45 of this chapter.

52. See, for example, *Peking Review*, Jan. 9, 1970, pp. 15–17; Jan. 16, 1970, pp. 13–16; and Feb. 6, 1970, pp. 7–9.

53. See, for example, *Peking Review*, Jan. 9, 1970, p. 15.

54. Alice Langley Hsieh, *Communist China's Strategy in the Nuclear Era* (Prentice-Hall, Inc., 1962); and Alice Langley Hsieh, "China's Secret Military Papers: Military Doctrine and Strategy," *The China Quarterly*, April–June 1964, pp. 79–99.

55. Mao Tse-tung, *Selected Works* (London, 1954–   ), Vol. II, p. 272.

56. Hsinhua News Agency dispatch, August 30, 1967; and *Peking Review*, Jan. 3, 1968, p. 42.

57. It must be stressed that Communist China's military professionals are critical of the Maoist strategy of a "people's war," principally as it applies to the United States and the Soviet Union offensively and defensively. They are not critical of its offensive aspect of insurrectionary revolutionary warfare in non-Communist underdeveloped countries of the world.

58. *Kung-tso T'ung-hsun*, No. 12, March 10, 1961; Hsinhua News Agency dispatch, Dec. 18, 1967; and *Peking Review*, Jan. 3, 1968, p. 41.

59. *Chieh-fang Chün-pao*, Aug. 1, 1965.

60. The overwhelming majority of Chinese army officers are Party members.

61. *JMJP*, Feb. 7, 1967.

62. Hsinhua News Agency dispatch, Aug. 30, 1967; and *JMJP*, Aug. 28, 1967.

63. *Peking Review*, Nov. 24, 1967, p. 14; and Hsinhua News Agency dispatch, Sept. 16, 1967.

64. See note 45 of this chapter.

65. *Chieh-fang Chün-pao*, Aug. 1, 1965.

66. *Kung-tso T'ung-hsun*, No. 3, Jan. 7, 1961; No. 26, July

13, 1961; and No. 20, Aug. 1, 1961. See also *Peking Review,* Aug. 6, 1965, p. 5; and *JMJP,* Sept. 3, 1966.

67. Mao Tse-tung, *Selected Military Writings* (Peking: Foreign Languages Press, 1963), pp. 217–218; *Peking Review,* Sept. 25, 1964, pp. 17–18; and *Chieh-fang Chün-pao,* Sept. 2, 1966.

68. *Peking Review,* Nov. 24, 1967, p. 13.

69. Mao Tse-tung, *Selected Works of Mao Tse-tung* (Peking: Foreign Languages Press, 1961), Vol. IV, pp. 98–101; *Chieh-fang Chün-pao,* May 25, 1965; June 10, 1965; and Oct. 13, 1965.

70. Hsinhua News Agency dispatch, Aug. 29, 1967; and *Peking Review,* Dec. 3, 1965, p. 4; and Jan. 3, 1968, pp. 33–37.

71. See Henry A. Kissinger, *Nuclear Weapons and Foreign Policy* (Harper & Brothers, 1957), pp. 362–372.

72. *Chieh-fang Chün-pao,* Nov. 25, 1965, and Aug. 23, 1966.

73. *JMJP, Hung Ch'i,* and *Chieh-fang Chün-pao,* Oct. 1, 1969.

74. *Peking Review,* Feb. 5, 1965, p. 20; and *JMJP,* Sept. 7, 1967.

75. *JMJP,* May 14, 1965; *Chieh-fang Chün-pao,* Sept. 17, 1966; and *Peking Review,* May 14, 1965, pp. 15–22; and Sept. 23, 1966, pp. 29–30.

76. "Leninism or Social Imperialism?" a joint editorial of *JMJP, Hung Ch'i,* and *Chieh-fang Chün-pao,* April 22, 1970. Ironically and interestingly enough, the following apocalyptic view of the downfall of the Soviet Union held by Mao is shared by a young dissident Soviet writer named Andrei Amalrik. See Andrei Amalrik, *Will the Soviet Union Survive Until 1984?* (Harper & Row, Publishers, 1970), pp. 1–112.

77. The term "the Chinese federation" was used by Mao Tse-tung in 1936 when he had a long interview with the American correspondent Edgar Snow. See Edgar Snow, *op. cit.,* p. 96.

78. Hsinhua News Agency dispatch, April 27, 1960.

79. *Hung Ch'i,* Nov. 21, 1964; and *JMJP,* May 9, 1965.

80. *Chieh-fang Chün-pao,* Dec. 15, 1965; and *JMJP,* Aug. 1, 1966.

81. *Chieh-fang Chün-pao,* Aug. 1, 1965.

82. See, for example, Maury Lisann, "Moscow and the Chinese Power Struggle," *Problems of Communism,* Nov.–Dec. 1969, p. 40.

83. See, for example, *The Washington Post,* May 16, 1970, p. 20.

CONCLUSION

1. Cited in *The Washington Post,* April 30, 1969, p. 15.
2. *Pravda,* June 8, 1969, in *CDSP,* Vol. XXI, No. 23, July 21, 1969, pp. 3–17.
3. *Pravda,* July 11, 1969, in *CDSP,* Vol. XXI, No. 28, Aug. 6, 1969, p. 9.
4. See Chapter 2 of this book.
5. On July 23, 1969, *Izvestia* reaffirmed that Brezhnev's call for a new Asian "collective security system" would be open to all Asian countries—including the Soviet Union.
6. *The Christian Science Monitor,* March 3, 1972, p. 6; and *The New York Times,* March 6, 1972, p. 3; and March 3, 1972, p. 10.
7. *The New York Times,* March 19, 1972, pp. 1, 9.
8. *The Los Angeles Times,* March 13, 1970, p. 19; and *The New York Times,* Sept. 7, 1969, p. 1; Sept. 24, 1969, p. 8.
9. *The Washington Post,* June 30, 1969, p. 21; Jan. 12, 1970, p. 19; and March 18, 1972, p. 16.
10. For details, see *The Washington Post,* Dec. 3, 1968, p. 19; Feb. 17, 1969, p. 23; March 23, 1969, p. 10; April 19, 1969, p. 20; April 20, 1969, p. 20; June 7, 1969, p. 3; June 8, 1969, p. 7; Jan. 12, 1970, p. 2; *The Evening Bulletin* (Philadelphia), April 19, 1969, p. 20; *Peking Review,* March 14, 1969, p. 13; and Hsinhua News Agency dispatch, March 6, 1969; March 26, 1972.
11. *The New York Times,* June 22, 1963, p. 3 (Section 4); *The Christian Science Monitor,* Feb. 10, 1972, p. 4; *The Washington Post,* Feb. 25, 1972, p. 20; and *The Sun* (Baltimore), Feb. 25, 1972, p. 2.
12. *The Christian Science Monitor,* Feb. 25, 1972, p. 20.
13. Hsinhua News Agency dispatch, June 28, 1969.
14. See *Congressional Quarterly Service. Weekly Report,* March 12, 1971, p. 5; and *The New York Times,* July 22, 1969, p. 1; Dec. 20, 1969, pp. 1, 4; Feb. 26, 1971, pp. 12–13; July 30, 1971, p. 7.
15. See Chapter 3 of this book.

Index

DATE DUE

MAY 8 '74			
OC 3 1 '77			
MR 20'80			
AP 2 '80			
AP 18'80			
AP 6 '81			
AP 21'81			
AP 5 '82			
FE 28'84			
GAYLORD			PRINTED IN U.S.A.